ALTERNATIVE SOCIOLOGIES OF RELIGION

Alternative Sociologies of Religion

Through Non-Western Eyes

James V. Spickard

NEW YORK UNIVERSITY PRESS

New York

NEW YORK UNIVERSITY PRESS
New York
www.nyupress.org

References to Internet websites (URLs) were accurate at the time of writing.

Neither the author nor New York University Press is responsible for URLs that may have expired or changed since the manuscript was prepared.

Library of Congress Cataloging-in-Publication Data
Names: Spickard, James V., author.
Title: Alternative sociologies of religion : through non-Western eyes / James V. Spickard.
Description: New York : New York University Press, [2016] | Includes bibliographical references and index.
Identifiers: LCCN 2016041814| ISBN 9781479826636 (cl : alk. paper) | ISBN 9781479866311 (pb : alk. paper)
Subjects: LCSH: Religion and sociology. | Religions.
Classification: LCC BL60 .S6625 2016 | DDC 306.6—dc23
LC record available at https://lccn.loc.gov/2016041814

New York University Press books are printed on acid-free paper, and their binding materials are chosen for strength and durability. We strive to use environmentally responsible suppliers and materials to the greatest extent possible in publishing our books.

Manufactured in the United States of America

10 9 8 7 6 5 4 3 2 1

Also available as an ebook

In memory of

Mary Alice Adkins Spickard (1920–1981)

Donald Elliot Spickard (1920–2003)

We should not be ashamed to acknowledge the truth from whatever source it comes to us, even if it is brought to us by former generations and foreign peoples.

Yaʾqub ibn Ishaq al-Kindi (ca. 801–866; translated by Richard Walzer, *Greek into Arabic*)

CONTENTS

ACKNOWLEDGMENTS

This book has been incubating for a long time. I owe thanks to a special set of colleagues and friends, who have encouraged my work through thick and thin. I especially wish to thank Meredith McGuire, Mary Jo Neitz, Roberto Blancarte, Ole Riis, the late Ivan Varga, the late Otto Maduro, Peter Beyer, Afe Adogame, Adam Possamai, and my brother Paul Spickard. My many long conversations with them helped me work out my ideas. Paul Spickard, Titus Hjelm, Tekle Woldemikael, and Blaine Pope also read parts of the manuscript and gave me helpful ideas. Mia Lövheim, Vanja Mosbach, and Jörgen Staarup made insightful remarks on a presentation that helped me reshape the final chapters. Margit Warburg sponsored an event where I could present some of these ideas, as did Lene Kühle. Farid Alatas encouraged me at two key points. William Swatos encouraged me at two others. Other colleagues too numerous to name asked questions at conferences, joined conversations in the halls, and otherwise inspired me. I thank them all. I appreciate how they have stimulated and strengthened my thinking.

I owe special thanks to the University of Redlands for the 2014–2015 sabbatical during which I finished the manuscript and for supporting my presentations of these ideas at many conferences. I particularly want to thank former Vice Presidents for Academic Affairs Phil Glotzbach and Nancy Carrick for allowing me to structure my job so that I have more time for scholarship than is typical at our teaching-heavy university. The staff of Redlands' Armacost Library provided me with several crucial resources. The Society for the Scientific Study of Religion gave me a couple of small grants that helped fund my interviews with religious social activists. The Redlands Faculty Review Committee also funded research that has found its way into this book. I wish to thank the members of the Los Angeles Catholic Worker for their hospitality during the years that I visited them. That experience helped to shape my argument in Chapter Eight, and also my life.

Many thanks to Jennifer Hammer and the staff at NYU Press for helping make this book a reality. I also owe thanks to various journal and book editors for seeing value in the dozen or so articles that I have published on this topic. I thank their publishers for permitting me to use passages from these works for which I no longer own the copyright, though none of that material appears here without major reshaping. I have listed these at the end of the book.

TYPOGRAPHIC NOTE

Where possible, I have used diacritical marks in the display of Chinese, Arabic, and Navajo words. I speak none of these languages, so I have relied on the best authorities I can find. I distinguish between two types of quote marks. Double quotes indicate that I am quoting someone directly. Single quotes are shudder-quotes; they indicate a term from which it is helpful to maintain a bit of intellectual distance.

ALTERNATIVE SOCIOLOGIES OF RELIGION

Community Church. Photograph by Steven Pavlov, 2009 (Creative Commons BY-SA 3.0).

Introduction

A Sociologist Thinks about Religion

I was not raised to be religious. Though some of my childhood play-mates came from families that believed in God, prayed before meals, and went to church on Sunday, I did not. At least not most of the time. Every so often, my grandmother would go on the warpath about how I was being raised 'heathen', and my parents would send me down the street to the local Episcopal parish. Though young, I knew that they did this to keep her off their backs. At this time, they had no sense of religious duty.

My father sometimes went with me. He once told me how he, as a child in similar circumstances, had imagined a banner proclaiming "Allah is the All-God" descending over the altar of his own grandparents' Methodist church. My memory is now vague, but I think he was trying to help.

Like most churches in that era, mine recognized children's limited attention spans, so my age-mates and I trooped off to Sunday School classes, where we learned what we were supposed to believe to be good Christians. These were Episcopalians, so we did not get lakes of fire to burn the wicked or a glorious Rapture to transport the saved. We mostly got Bible stories. But I still got into trouble by asking who Cain married, whether the Hebrews were right to slaughter the Canaanites, why the Kingdom of God did not arrive as soon as Jesus had said it would, and why a good God would allow six million Jews to be murdered in the war. As my mother put it, I was a bit of a pill.

In my child's view, religion was something that happened in churches, mosques, or synagogues, that involved believing improbable things about unseen beings, and that was set about by 'shoulds' or rules. I was not alone. This image has a long pedigree in Euro-American culture, and I now know that it does considerable disservice both to religion and to religious people. Whatever I may have thought as a child, I now see that religion is more than just a set of beliefs and rules, plus an organization that encourages people to believe and obey them. To use the Latin, religion is more than *ecclesia, doctrina,* and *moralis.* Among other things, it involves community, ritual, a sense of the sacred, the cultivation of hope in the midst of despair, and a host of other matters. In many cases, it concerns one's attitude toward life as much as it does any particular set of supernatural and moral views.

As I child, I knew none of this. I specifically did not know that religion could happen outside of church buildings, that not all religion involves clergy, and that some people consider themselves very religious who have given churches, synagogues, etc. a wide berth. Though people 'do religion' in official places, they also do it on mountaintops, in schools and businesses, and in the privacy of their homes. I do not mean just that they pray there as an adjunct to church life. Some people refuse to center their religious lives in the ways that religious organizations want them to. In short, religion and church are just about as connected as are peas and carrots in Midwestern American cooking: they go together well, but they can also go separately.

This notion of 'churchless religion' is still controversial. Not only do many preachers decry it; even people who practice it sometimes favor other terms. For example, I have heard many Americans say, "I am very spiritual but not at all religious"—meaning, among other things, that they are very interested in having a connection with 'higher powers', the meaning of life, and so on, but they do not patronize any religious establishment to do so. Furthermore, they do not think that they are missing anything worthwhile. They have various reasons for this stance, from bad personal experiences to some religions' bad public reputations. In many cases, they just do not want religious leaders to tell them what to think or do.

Such people typically see 'spirituality' as personal, set against 'organized religion' as an impersonal institution. They honor the former while suspecting the latter. This may be cultural, for Americans have long proudly questioned authorities and have emphasized their own individuality. Yet the 'spiritual but not religious' trend also tells us that many people now think that religious organizations have no monopoly on the connection with 'higher powers', the meaning of life, and so on, that have typically been their *raison d'être*. If church leaders act as if they own the word 'religion' for such connections, then dissidents will just use another term.

Even people who participate regularly in official religious life do things that their leaders shun. Most Christian religious elites, for example, look down on home altars, petitions to St. Jude, May Fests, the use of the Bible for divination, and the purchase and display of Christian-themed trinkets such as Precious Moments figurines (often derisively called 'Christian kitsch'). They treat these as perhaps suitable for un-educated folk but certainly not as 'real' religion. Such practices, though, are central to many people's religious lives.[1] Leaders bemoan them as tangential, but an increasing number of ordinary church members reply: "What do those leaders know? Why should religious leaders get to tell us what to do?"

The survey data about this dismissal are stunning. For example, only 43% of adult Americans think that one needs to attend church or syna-gogue regularly to be a "good Christian or Jew." Fifty-five percent of those who identify themselves as strongly religious say that it is impor-tant or very important to follow one's conscience, even if it means going against church authorities. Just 30% of these "strongly religious" people have "a great deal" of confidence in organized religion. In 2000, nearly half of American Catholics reported that they would be just as happy in another church than their own. This was before the clergy sex scandals, which by 2002 had cut by a third (to 19%) the percentage of Catholics who say they have "a great deal of confidence" in church leadership. (This number has since rebounded to about 25%.) Interestingly, the per-centage of conservative Protestants claiming "a great deal of confidence" in their own leaders declined by one third (to 22%) during the same pe-riod. Disaffection in the pews seems to be rather common in American religious life.[2]

The same is true in other parts of the world. Polling data from West-ern Europe show that only 18% of people who identify themselves as religious have a great deal of confidence in their churches and that 35% of religious people have little or no confidence in them. That low/no confidence figure drops to 27% in Latin America, though this varies from country to country. For example, 45% of Argentines have little or no confidence in their churches, as opposed to 'just' 30% in Mexico.

That counts the whole population, however, not only those who are religiously oriented. The figures for the latter are respectively 27% and 23%. That's pretty close, overall.[3]

My point is: even religious people do not have perfect faith in their leaders and do not follow their dictates—at least not in any simple way. I am not thus alone in thinking that religion involves more than church life and more than whatever supernatural beliefs those churches preach about the ultimate nature of the universe. My child's image of religion was mistaken. Official religious organizations—churches, synagogues, mosques, temples, gurdwaras, and so on—no longer monopolize religious life. As a result, I now see religion as far more interesting than I did when I was younger.

The precise story of how I moved from my childhood rejection of religion to my adult appreciation of it is not relevant to this book. It involves, among other things, work with religiously based anti-war protesters, a stint teaching at a Catholic college run by some very perceptive nuns, study (as a self-described "lapsed atheist") at an interdenominational seminary, several years spent doing research among odd, interstitial religious groups, and a long and varied encounter with Quakers.

My parents, too, ultimately outgrew their identification of religion with unresponsive churches, odd beliefs, and top-down morality. Religious sensitivity became, for each of them, an emotional solace and a healing. I have dedicated this book to their memory.

Two Stories from the Field

Every book has an intellectual inspiration and this one is no different. I am a professional sociologist, and my decision to write it began with my observation that the sociology of religion has been scarred by a too-limited sense of its subject matter. Just as my childhood experience led me to identify religion with churches, beliefs, and rules, so the central role that Christianity has played in Western history has led most sociologists to emphasize organizations, ideas, and morality as the universal core of religious life. Too many sociologists seem unaware that these elements do not dominate many non-Western religions; nor do they dominate Judaism, Western Christianity's much-abused cousin. Church organization and doctrinal purity have not even been central through major stretches of Christian history. They achieved their current stature during a specific institutional crisis: the struggle between elites and laity over the essence of Christian life that took place during the period that historians now call the "long reformations" (1350–1750).[4] That struggle deeply shaped the West. Intellectually, it created many of the lenses through which we now see the world.

Sociology as an intellectual discipline was not born during those reformations, however. It arose in 19th-century France. As we shall see, sociology had to justify its claim to scientific relevance, and it did so in part by distinguishing itself from a particular kind of backward-looking religion. In France, this involved opposing a reactionary, anti-Republican Catholicism. In the Protestant parts of Europe and in the United States, the enemy was a form of Christian revelation that emphasized personal sin as the source of social ills. The well-known fight between science and Fundamentalism played a part, with sociology coming down on the scientific side.

Scholars are no less likely than other people to base their thinking on their own culture and history, so it is no wonder that sociologists' default view sees church, belief, and morality as central to the religious enterprise. To use a slightly broader, and still recognizably Christian, language, we sociologists focus too many of our studies on creed, canon, cult, and cathedral—the centerpieces of post-reformations Protestantism and particularly of the 19th-century religions against which the early sociologists struggled. This renders invisible great swathes of the religious landscape.

I did not know this when I began my sociological career. My views have changed from listening to religious people as part of my field work. They have also changed as I read and interacted with two generations of sociological colleagues who have also questioned our discipline's default view of religion. I shall present some of their work in Chapter One, where I describe that default view in greater detail.

First, though, I want to tell two stories from my field work on American religions. Each pushes the limits of what sociologists used to look for in religious venues. If pictures are sometimes better than words, stories can convey the sense of an intellectual argument more clearly than philosophical prose. By telling them, I hope to give readers a trial run, so to speak, at this book's central message. I also hope to encourage readers to recall similar tales from their own experiences.

My first story takes place in an Episcopal parish, where I was hired to explore the sources of that parish's spiritual vitality. I shall call the site Redemption Parish (a pseudonym), and note, first, that the study was a nationwide study of "spiritually vital parishes," and, second, that neither the sponsors nor the leaders of the study knew at the outset what the term "spiritually vital" meant. They hired a team of researchers to learn what went on at various parishes that had been described as "vital" by their respective bishops. I suppose that the sponsors hoped to replicate such vitality, though the study was never published. In fact, the study leader recently told me that our research sites had little in common. Some 'spiritually vital' Episcopal parishes were quasi-Pentecostal, others emphasized social service, others favored meditation. My parish emphasized study programs in various spiritual traditions. This was part of its vitality, but not the central part, as I was to learn.

Let's start, though, with belief—that supposedly core element of religion. Episcopal services certainly seem to highlight Christian belief, and those at Redemption Parish were no exception. Its services followed *The Book of Common Prayer* (*BCP*), which specifies exactly what is to be said at each moment of the ritual, and by whom. The priest and congregation read along, reciting specific creeds, prayers, and intentions. Core Christian beliefs are prominently displayed; indeed, on a verbal level the service resembles a public catechism. There are choices, of course; the prayer book contains two versions of the ritual. "Rite I" was the order of service common in my childhood, dating, I believe, from 1928. "Rite II" was composed about fifty years later. Different parishes emphasize one or the other of these, sometimes even using them at alternate services to make sure that everyone feels at home. Episcopal services also vary through the liturgical year, all of which is specified in the *BCP*. As much as possible, the prayer book covers all occasions.[5]

Even the "prayers of the faithful" go by rote: "we pray for our country's leaders," "we pray for our pastors and bishops," "we pray for the poor," etc. Then comes a six-second pause[6] during which individuals can pray (silently) for specific people whom they think need special care. Only the sermon and the announcements are not predetermined.

This sounds more rigid than it is in practice, at least at Redemption Parish. Though the services that I attended followed the *BCP* exactly, they never felt forced. They proceeded smoothly, with both grace and style. What struck me, though—and was my first clue that belief was not at the center of what was going on—was the fact that both priest and parishioners always read the order of service from their prayer books, even though they already knew it by heart. This seemed to me both strange and useless. Though it had been over thirty years since I had last attended an Episcopal service, I remembered Rite I rather well. It did not take me more than a couple of services to pick up Rite II. Why read along, when one knew exactly what one was supposed to say?

I asked Redemption's head priest why he and the parishioners always read from the book rather than memorizing the relatively easy lines. His answer told me quite a bit about the parish. The reason for reading along, he said, was so that the congregation could be sure of his orthodoxy. "The great Episcopal compromise was on wording," he said, "not belief. We've got a big tent: everyone from Anglo-Catholics to Anglo-Baptists. You can believe anything you want, but you all have to say the same words. It's the words and the ritual that keep us together. Individuals can mean quite different things by those words. We don't want those beliefs to divide us."

Though this was probably a jest,[7] it matched what I had already learned about Redemption Parish's spiritual vitality. As I have noted, the parish offered study programs in various spiritual traditions. Among these were a popular Celtic Spirituality course, a course on Desert Fathers and Mothers, another on Women's Spiritualities, Bible studies from various points of view, and a theology reading group. The parish also regularly sponsored *Cursillo* retreats, a healing ministry, and a contemplative *Taizé* service.[8] During my fieldwork, one parish group set up a labyrinth and taught labyrinth-walking as a form of contemplative prayer. Another group explored Jewish traditions, opening the pulpit to local rabbis. "I've just discovered that I am a Jew," one parishioner told me after one of these guest sermons. He meant this spiritually, for what he had learned about Judaism taught him something about himself and about his own inner life. For him, as for many of Redemption's congregants, the purpose of religion is to develop a deep personal spirituality. He saw no conflict in learning from many religious traditions. Indeed, he welcomed it. The more open one is to other people's paths, he said, the more likely one is to discover one's own.

A story I heard about the head priest illustrates this openness. A Presbyterian had apparently come to him seeking advice about the Nicene Creed. The visitor had underlined passages in various colored inks, depending on whether he agreed or disagreed with them. How could he be a good Christian, he said, if he disagreed with so much? The priest's response was to note that the key matter was whether he believed in the God whom Jesus had followed, and whether he was willing to follow that God too. Beside this, said the priest, church doctrines and creeds only get in the way.

For this priest, as for his congregation, belief was not central to religious life. Any study that limited itself to belief would have missed most of what was going on in this parish. Almost uniformly, my informants spoke of the importance to the parish of each individual's spiritual life and of building a setting in which that inner life flourishes. For them, spirituality does not operate at the level of ideas. The church certainly does not exist for the sake of religious purity. Instead, they believed that spiritual vitality operates at the level of the individual, nurtured by the organization. Though parishioners appreciated Redemption's study programs, and spoke of how such programs facilitated their personal growth, they saw them as merely tools. The same was true of the parish's culture of tolerance. Yes, it was good that Redemption Parish encouraged people to be themselves, and it was good that it encouraged wide spiritual diversity, but these, though they can help sustain an inner life, do not create one. What made Redemption Parish spiritually vital, for its members, was its ability to let its parishioners create their own inner lives—and its willingness to support them as they did so.

In keeping with this approach, most of my informants defined the spiritual life as a personal quest, as a response to what they called "God's redemptive call." Most members used idioms of "growth" and "journey" to describe their spiritual paths. Many used Twelve-Step language; others used the languages of various mystics, often rationalized by such psychological metaphors as James Fowler's "stages of faith."[9] In this understanding, spiritual growth is a process of coming to terms with life as a manifestation of God, of learning to see and to seek God through the midst of life's externals. One's personal problems are one's opportunities; firmly grasped, they are God's helping hands.

Though perhaps unusual, Redemption Parish is a recognizable part of the American religious scene. The question that we shall pursue in the following chapters is whether the sociology of religion's received concepts help or hinder our understanding of such cases. To the degree that we see beliefs, rules, and church structures as the center of the religious life, they miss much of what goes on at Redemption. Are there other concepts, still sociological, that might do better?

At least Redemption Parish had walls and a roof. We cannot capture its religious life by asking its members about their beliefs, quizzing them about their social connections, nor asking about their church attendance, but at least the parish provided a place, a container, for religion. At least it is a clearly religious organization. My next story breaks even this bound.

Over the last twenty-something years, I have interviewed scores of religious social activists. I talk to them about their work, their sense of calling, their religious lives, their personal histories—whatever will help me understand how people can devote years of service to others. I am especially interested in those who work for social change. These activists seek to transform society's way of treating people, and are willing to interrupt their careers, risk public hostility, and even go to jail to carry out what they see as God's call.

All of these activists identify themselves as religious, and all identify themselves with one or another religious tradition. Yet they do not typically accept the institutionally generated identities that most scholars assume accompany these traditions. For example, one woman, working full-time in a Catholic women's peace and justice center, described her religious identity as follows:

> I have to say that, in a public sense as well as a private sense—I grouse a lot about it, but I'd say—yes, I'm a Roman Catholic, comma, damn it! And worse yet, I'm a Roman Catholic woman. And so I think that will be for me what I will continue to identify myself as being—for all the good of it, for all the bad of it, and all the stuff in between. . . . I think it would be easier to change the color of my eyes or to get a new genetic code than it would be to stop being a Roman Catholic.

She is not, however, willing to let the Catholic hierarchy define for her what a 'good Catholic' should do. In fact, she thinks that the priests, bishops, archbishops, cardinals, and even the Pope have lost sight of the Catholic mission. She agreed with one of her co-workers, a nun, whom I asked why she remained in a church with which she is so often at odds:

> I see many cases in which the Roman Catholic Church is no longer faithful to the tradition . . . [yet] I believe that culturally and to the very core of my being, I'm Catholic, and I do believe that there are members of the Catholic Church beyond the hierarchy who are capable of being even more faithful than they [the hierarchy] are. And so, [the hierarchy] is going to have to leave me, because I'm not going anyplace. [laughter]

What does 'being a Roman Catholic' mean to these women? It certainly does not involve regular Mass attendance, especially so long as the official Mass has to be conducted by a male. As the first of these interviewees described her evolving religious life, she said:

> So I really set aside exclusive Roman Catholicism. . . . I remained a religious woman and I have never stopped thinking of myself as a religious woman, ever, not for a moment. But I began to weave in understandings of a variety of different religious and . . . spiritual traditions, and . . . ways of behaving in the world—concrete actions. So the traditions that I looked most closely at were Native [American] traditions, the Jewish tradition—and I (because of intermarrying in my family) have a number of men and women who came out of a Jewish faith tradition—and Zen Buddhism and Tibetan Buddhism.

In actual fact, her ritual life takes place among her co-workers. She describes combining elements from various traditions into a rich woman-centered spirituality, which she practices with them:

> What we do when we pray together is the same model that we do [for] everything else. We pray together collaboratively. We have experience, we reflect on it socially, . . . and on most days we are given to do an action around that.

I haven't been to Mass in a long time. There's a longing in me . . . the memory of how good it felt to have the sensuousness of church. But then I get very angered because I immediately remember what the priest sounded like, and these damn, excuse me, male homilies that had absolutely nothing to do with experience. . . . [So] I choose to pray with women. And I choose to pray collaboratively. I choose to pray toward action. That's how my community's set up.

Like many of my interviewees, she and her co-workers have taken control of their religious self-definition. They allow no Church hierarchy to tell them how to live their Catholicism. Instead, they fashion it as they feel the spirit leads.

I often get an interesting response from people whom I tell about my social activist research—one that reinforces the common image of religion as a matter of belief. Many folks, including scholars, have what I have come to call a "What heroes!" reaction to my project. They say that they wish that they could be like the people I am interviewing. They take me aside or drop their voices, admitting to me in confidence that they have long been fascinated by religious social activism and admire such activists greatly. Of course, they tend to admire those activists with whom they agree: leftists admire those working for peace and justice; the right wing admires anti-abortion groups like Operation Rescue. But in both cases their admiration is palpable and deep.

In my observation, such folk think of these activists as heroes on two counts. First, they are heroes for their willingness to 'put themselves on the line', non-violently, for social causes. Second, they are heroes for their imagined firmness of belief. My interlocutors—especially quasi-secular left-liberals—appear to project onto those activists the religious certainties that they, themselves, think they lack. They say (in paraphrase), "Wouldn't it be wonderful, to be so sure of my beliefs that I could go to jail for them? Wouldn't it be good to stand up for things about which I'm certain?"

Like default sociology, the "What heroes!" response puts belief at the center of religious life. It imagines that religious social activists accept their creeds to a depth impossible for ordinary people. It imagines that their activism grows out of a root intellectual certainty. It thinks them to be so steeped in religious conviction that they will suffer for their beliefs, knowing that they are doing God's work.

The fact is, however, that the activists I interview are, on the whole, no more certain of religious truth than is anyone else. Quite the contrary: one of their distinguishing marks is that they do not have answers. Over and over in my interviews, it became clear that they are making their lives up as they go along. They start from a sense of what is right, but they constantly test that sense, to see if it is true. Sometimes, even often, they find they have been wrong. When they do, they modify their beliefs, saying that they now understand their faith more deeply. Their 'religiousness' consists precisely in their taking seriously the idea that God demands something of them, clues to which can be found in their religious traditions. Clues, but not answers! Indeed, most of the activists, especially Catholics, are so alienated from their churches that they leave almost nothing unquestioned. They even question God, to put a traditional label on whatever it is that they hear calling them. Instead, their spiritual lives are a constantly evolving mix of alienation, devotion, action, and passion. These inner lives are turbulent but fulfilling. The only constant is that these activists insist that their lives be meaningful.

Challenging the Default View

Both of these stories challenge the standard depiction of religion in much of the sociological literature. Neither the members of Redemption parish nor my social activist interviewees placed 'belief' at the center of their religious lives. Instead, "personal transformation" and "community" played larger roles. Only Redemption members located themselves in a formal religious organization, though they did not see it as controlling their lives. Most of the activists struggled against the religious organizations with which they were supposedly identified. Rather than defining themselves out of Catholicism, for example, the Catholic activists tended to define themselves as the true Catholics and the hierarchy as having fallen away. Textbook sociology of religion cannot illuminate either group very well.

Besides questioning the centrality of 'belief' and 'church', these two stories similarly draw into question the ways in which sociologists have treated people's religious identities. With few exceptions, the pattern is supposed to be as follows.

First, one is born into a family, which either is or is not a member of a religious group. One's earliest religious identity comes from that family. One learns how to be a Catholic, for example, or a Presbyterian or a Quaker—or even an atheist—from one's family, growing up thinking that their beliefs, practices, and so on are normal. I would agree with this: having rebelled from her Baptist upbringing, my mother raised me not to believe in a child's image of an angry Baptist God. It worked, and I do not, but it did not inoculate me against religion of every kind.

The second step, however, is more problematic. Sociologists trace another form of religious socialization, one that involves formal institutional training, usually in childhood, that is supposed to result in a dedicated church member. Sunday School, confirmation classes, First Communion, and the like provide formal religious socialization that is supposed to generate a solid religious identity. Once established, this institutionally generated self is supposed to produce religiously appropriate behavior, religiously motivated actions, and commitment to the religious group in which one was raised.[10]

Mainstream sociology typically presumes that religious identity forms around church-defined patterns of religiosity, morality, and role-behavior. It sees such elements as central parts of how religious people understand themselves and of how they organize their individual lives. It allows, at the edges, some diversity in individual ways of being religious. A Catholic, for example, might choose praying the Psalms over praying the Rosary, or might participate or not participate in Wednesday night devotionals. Sociologists typically assume, however, that the options open to the individual come from a socially recognizable set, accepted if not encouraged by official religious institutions.

This is clearly not what is happening to the activists I interviewed, nor to the members of Redemption Parish.

The plot gets thicker. In the default sociological view, one measures both religiosity and religious identification organizationally. Survey research, in particular, takes such items as the frequency of church attendance, one's agreement or disagreement with established church doctrines, and the like as indications of one's religious commitment. One problem is that such research would count these activists as irreligious, when just the opposite is the case. A greater problem is that such measures do not necessarily capture even churchgoing people's sense of religious life.

What is central to contemporary religious life? Though there are several answers to this, at least one stream of sociological thinking sees religious individualism as a growing trend. Meredith McGuire wrote about the various ways that religious people now define their faith for themselves. Clark Roof charted a growing religious individualism in America, especially among Baby Boomers; Tom Beaudoin tracked this among "Gen Xers." Robert Bellah and his colleagues noted the rise of what they call "Sheilaism"—individualized religions made up of personal preferences. Nancy Ammerman suggested that the effort to craft a spiritually meaningful personal life may be a central aspect of postmodern individualism.[11]

Among earlier scholars, Thomas Luckmann argued that worldviews used to be mediated by official religions, which could articulate coherent, relatively stable, socially supported systems of ultimate meaning for their members. In his view, many social-structural changes have undermined, perhaps eliminated, the ability of any official religion to direct the construction of individual identity. Growing pluralism—the tolerated co-existence of competing worldviews within the same society—meant that no worldview could present itself as the final arbiter for each individual's system of ultimate meaning. Luckmann suggested that the marginalization of official religious organizations and the concomitant privatization of several spheres of life (among them religion, family, leisure activities) have reduced both religion and personal identity to a private affair. As such, each individual is now free to construct an utterly personal identity and an individual system of ultimate significance.[12]

Though this does not describe all religious people, it clearly matches both the religious activists and the members of Redemption Parish. Sociology's default view of religion captures only parts of their religious lives. Yet religion is a core constituent of their self-identity. Any sociology of religion that ignores this kind of religiosity, or (worse) treats it as irreligion, needs repair.

My full treatment of these religious social activists will have to wait for another book, and the data from the Spiritually Vital Episcopal Parish Project are likely to remain forever in the archives of the agency that commissioned it. Both stories, however, tell us that religion-as-practiced is a whole lot more complex than the mere combination of supernatural beliefs plus organizational structures on which sociologists of religion typically focus.

What Lies Ahead

I have written this book to explore some alternative ways of seeing religion—ways that remain sociologically fruitful while emphasizing the parts of contemporary religions that default sociology generally misses. The first two chapters outline what I am calling sociology's "default view": the idea that religion is largely constituted by formal organizations, is focused on beliefs, and promulgates moral rules.

Chapter One looks at the present. It shows how sociology textbooks and the two dominant sociological theories of religion typically take this default view for granted. It also notes some current alternatives, including the just-mentioned focus on religious individualism, a push to examine religion in non-religious places, and an attempt to develop an 'agent-oriented' sociology that treats organizations and beliefs as less important than personal religious action. These efforts have shaken the default view but they have not replaced it. Though worthy, these approaches have not wrestled with the default view's historical-cultural roots nor traced that view to the particular historical-cultural circumstances of sociology's emergence as an intellectual discipline. I do this in Chapter Two. I chart the historical and cultural forces that let the default view became dominant in sociology. Once dominant, it became the place from which sociologists had to start. It became 'natural' and thus largely unquestioned. That, I argue, is an important reason why it is so hard to overcome.

If Euro-American sociology of religion developed its core concepts out of a particular culture and history, what happens if we set that history aside? What if sociology had arisen in another civilization, with a different religion and culture? What could we see about religion, if we set sociology's default view of religion aside? Chapters Three through Eight explore three alternate approaches to religion, arising from three non-Western civilizations. They form the core of this book's effort to construct conceptual alternatives.

Chapters Three and Four take us to China. In Chapter Three, I focus on the early Confucian notion of the relational self and on the role of ritual propriety (*lǐ* 禮) in generating personal and communal virtue (*dé* 德). Confucian thinkers located the sacred in the activities that maintain proper human relationships. Their understanding of the sacred would produce a profoundly different sociology of religion than we find in the West. Chapter Four explores what that sociology might look like. To show my cards just a little, it would pay a great deal more attention to women's work in church life: such things as church suppers, guilds, Sunday Schools, visitations, and so on—all of which focus on the creation of community. It would also pay more attention to non-church-based religion, although in a less individualistic mode than is common among those Western sociologists who are already studying religions outside formal religious organizations. As we will see, these under-studied parts of religious life are more central to religious life than Western sociology would have us believe.

Chapters Five and Six take us to Muslim North Africa. Chapter Five explores the writings of the great 14th-century Muslim jurist Walī al-Dīn Abū Zayd 'Abd ar-Raḥmān Ibn Muḥammad Ibn Khaldūn al-Tūnisī al-Haḍramī—known to posterity as Ibn Khaldūn. His central concept, *al 'aṣabiyyah*—generally translated as "group-feeling"—highlights a form of social solidarity that is oriented toward centers, not toward borders. Much current sociology focuses on the divisions between groups, showing how those divisions drive social conflicts. Reading Ibn Khaldūn encourages us to examine what draws people together, and he shows us how religion can do so, overcoming other social divisions. Unlike default sociology, which uses one set of concepts to understand 'race' or 'ethnicity' and another set to understand 'religion', Ibn Khaldūn used *al 'aṣabiyyah* to understand both ethnic and religious solidarities. The resulting sociology is potentially as useful for the contemporary world as it was for the multi-religious, multi-ethnic North Africa of his time. Chapter Six applies this sociology to two recent cases of multi-religious and multi-ethnic conflict. The first is the events surrounding the 'miracles' at Medjugorje—the early 1980s apparitions of the Virgin Mary in a Bosnian-Croatian village surrounded by Bosnian Muslims. The second is the rise and attractiveness of the current Islamic State in Iraq and Syria (ISIS). How might our understanding of these two cases change were we to see them with Khaldūnian eyes?

Chapters Seven and Eight take us to the American Southwest. Chapter Seven explores traditional Navajo religion, particularly focusing on its healing rituals. Navajo religion does not center on church buildings, nor on congregations, nor on beliefs and creeds. Instead, its five- to nine-day ceremonies seek to maintain or restore *hózhǫ* (beauty, harmony, goodness) and counteract *hóchxǫ* (evil, disorder, ugliness). In Navajo theology, the world was created in harmony, but that harmony is often destroyed. Ritual renews this harmony, which brings physical health to individuals and social health to communities. It does so not just symbolically, but in the moment-to-moment experiences of its participants. Chapter Eight explores the potential of this approach to religion by applying Navajo concepts to the house Masses celebrated by the members of a radical Catholic commune. We will see how these rituals restore members' hope in their mission to create social justice. The chapter develops this into a theory of ritual that puts experience at the heart of the ritual process. This gives ritual a much different role in religion than does sociology's default view.

These three themes—the creation of sacred community, the relationships between religion and ethnicity, and the role of ritual experience in generating community healing—are the focus of this book's central chapters.

The book's last chapter locates these cross-cultural explorations in our contemporary historical-cultural situation. Ours is a global world, but an unequal one. Politically, economically, militarily, and intellectually, it is still shaped by three centuries of Western colonialism. Though the former colonies are now technically free, the power relationships that bound them to their European and American masters have not disappeared. Our world revolves around New York, Paris, London, and Berlin far more than it revolves around Dakar, Colombo, and Santiago. To think otherwise is to be hopelessly naïve about the world in which we live.

Edward Said famously pointed out the perils of "Orientalism"—the intellectual move by which scholars from the colonizing powers dominated (and misunderstood) the colonies, devaluing their indigenous knowledge.[13] On one level, this book attempts the opposite. It shows the limits of Western sociology's default view of religion and proposes that other civilizations' ways of seeing can highlight things that we have missed. Said and I both show the limits of an unconscious Western view.

On another level, however, this book risks being one more colonial imposition. To express this in personal terms, is it not rather colonialist for a White, male, American scholar to pluck Confucian, Muslim, and Navajo ideas out of their indigenous contexts and bring them home for his own society's intellectual enjoyment? Chapter Nine draws the parallel between this effort and Lord Elgin's early-19th-century theft of the Parthenon Frieze. Who gets to appropriate whose ideas in a world where some people rule and others must submit? To put the matter more neutrally, if the intellectual consequences of the sociology of religion's unconscious reliance on Western history for its core concepts limits our vision, what does the unconscious appropriation of other civilizations' insights do? Chapter Nine explores this matter, with examples.

Chapter Nine also responds to this challenge. Said based his work on the close connection between intellectual attitudes and colonial power relations in the 19th and early 20th centuries. That era was much more intellectually unipolar than our own. Specifically, we have much more international communication than was then possible. We have much more access to other voices. Those voices, indeed, are increasingly skilled at producing their own messages. Where the Orientalists could (in Said's presentation) interpret the East quite freely, now the Empire talks back.[14] Post-colonial theorists contest Euro-American intellectual hegemony,[15] 'indigenous theorists' tout the superiority of native worldviews,[16] and deconstructive methodologists expose the colonial underpinnings of Western scholarly techniques.[17] While acknowledging continuities, has not the situation changed?

I think it has. Rather than looking backward to an era that has partially passed, what happens if we look forward to an era that is partially emerging? What kind of sociology can we now create, to match a world in which cross-civilizational contact is a daily affair? Perhaps more importantly, how would we have to position ourselves, intellectually, to take ideas from other traditions as seriously as we take our own?

For that is what this book is trying to do. I am, essentially, engaged in an act of imagination. What parts of religion would we understand more clearly, were we to stop privileging the ideas about religion that stem from Western civilization's Christian heritage? We cannot know until we try. I have written this book in a spirit of exploration.

Kim Robinson's wonderful novel *The Years of Rice and Salt* imagines a world history without a Europe.[18] My task is similar, but on a different intellectual level. What would the sociology of religion emphasize, had it developed in other civilizations than our own? My goal is not to replace Western sociological insights; they have, after all, been very useful. My goal is to expand our disciplinary toolkit—to supplement established ways of thinking with other ideas drawn from other histories, eras, and cultures. A global era demands nothing less.

Wordle by J. Spickard.

1

Sociology's Default View of Religion

I teach a course called Saints, Sects, and Society at a small liberal arts college in California. I used to call it Sociology of Religion, but the name intimidated students. California is part of the great unchurched belt that runs along the west coast of North America from Alaska to Mexico. Fewer people belong to religious organizations there, per capita, than anywhere else on the continent, and fewer people attend religious services. Over a third of my students have never been inside a religious building. To many of them, the word "religion" means 'old', 'boring', and 'stale'. Enrollments have doubled since I came up with the new name.

I ask students to define 'religion' on the first day of class. They write down their definitions, then get in small groups to compare notes. The results are telling. For most students, religion is about belief—specifically about beliefs in unseen, powerful beings. They think that religions are about God, angels, Jesus, Allah, saints, guardian spirits, etc., taking care of the universe, punishing the wicked, and responding to prayers. Most students find this implausible. Still, "That's religion!" they say: implausible beliefs about unseen beings.

They also say that religion is about rules. Some people get to tell other people what they're supposed to do, and those others are supposed to do it. The Pope, someone always says, tells women not to get abortions and not to use birth control. Everyone laughs, thinking of the bowls of condoms in their dorm lobbies, part of my university's ongoing anti-AIDS campaign. Even the few students who are religious do not think much of celibate elders giving them sexual advice.

They also think that religion happens only in certain times and places. It happens on Sunday mornings in churches and cathedrals. It happens on Saturday mornings in synagogues and Fridays at mosques. The best students know that Jews celebrate Shabbos at home on Friday night, that Muslims pray five times a day wherever they are, and that

Evangelical Protestants attend services on Wednesday nights as well as on Sunday mornings. Except most of them do not know what the word "Protestant" means, even if they were raised in a historically Protestant congregation. Evangelical Protestants in the U.S. now typically call themselves just "Christians" and my students do not know enough history to make the connection. Why should they? The world has changed since the 1950s heyday of Mainline Protestantism, when 40% (or more) of Americans attended religious services and Will Herberg could write a best-selling book titled *Protestant, Catholic, and Jew.* Now a bit over half that percentage attend weekly services and people claiming to have "no particular religion" are the fastest growing segment of the U.S. population.[1]

Many scholars have charted this religious decline, focusing particularly on shrinking participation in formal religious organizations.[2] My course sends students to visit such organizations and to interview religious people. These interactions show them that religion consists of more than just beliefs, moral rules, and churches, synagogues, mosques, gurdwaras, and so on. Like any teacher, I try to expand my students' conceptual universe and help them see things in new ways. I do not ask students to throw out their old ideas; I merely want them to realize that religion is a lot more complex than they ever imagined.

The Textbook View

I periodically wonder what students would learn if I did not send them out exploring. If I ran a 'normal' classroom, would they move beyond their beginning ideas? Not if they learned about religion from American sociology textbooks! With a few exceptions, those books describe religions as congeries of beliefs, moral teachings, and organizations—exactly the notions with which my students start.

Most people know that textbooks dominate American university teaching, giving students—and thus us—a snapshot of any discipline's intellectual approach to the world. Though few texts contain cutting-edge material and none describe what professionals in any discipline actually do, all of them provide a standard model of their fields.[3] Introductory sociology texts tell students what matters in sociology, at least as that discipline's gatekeepers present it to the world at large. These texts tell us a lot about sociology's default approach to religion.

In fact, American introductory sociology textbooks are all pretty much the same. Whether they come as 750-page comprehensive hardbacks, 500-page paperback 'essentials,'[4] or 250-page 'brief introductions', they all have the same structure. With some variation, they all begin with a chapter that defines sociology as a discipline, typically by showing how sociology can help them better understand their daily lives. Then comes a chapter about sociological theory (often titled "Thinking Sociologically"), followed by a chapter about sociological research methods. Chapters on culture and socialization almost always come next, followed either by chapters on social stratification (by class, race, and gender) or by chapters on major social institutions. Religion is presented as one of these institutions and is treated as a separate institutional sphere. It sits alongside chapters on the family, education, politics, criminal justice, work, and perhaps some others. Many texts, though not all, end with a chapter on social change.[5]

The 'religion chapter' typically takes up about 3–4% of the book.[6] It always begins by defining religion, focusing on the claim that religious beliefs give meaning to people's lives. It further highlights belief by distinguishing 'the believer's' view of religion from the sociological approach. A section on religious organizations distinguishes churches, sects, denominations, and cults as competing organizational types.[7] As of this writing, three of the market-leading comprehensive texts contain maps showing U.S. denominational distributions. A fourth has a list of denominational membership figures and a fifth has a chart comparing the numbers of Christians, Muslims, Jews, Hindus, and so on worldwide. Such materials encourage the reader to see 'belonging' as a key part of religious life and again highlight the importance of formal religious organizations.

Most texts then discuss secularization: the supposed decline in religion's role in contemporary society. They present this either as a process of religious disenchantment—a loss of belief—or as the result of institutional differentiation: the increasing assignment of education, charity work, counseling, etc. to secular professionals rather than to the religious sphere. Both of these diminish religion's social role. Some texts question whether secularization is really occurring, typically with polling data that show that the majority of Americans still believe in God. Some note the growth rates of self-styled 'conservative' religious groups, both in the U.S. and worldwide.

There are other elements. Rituals frequently appear in pictures, which tend toward the exotic; this emphasizes religion's separateness from the ordinary world.[8] Several include short essays on women's roles in religions or on religion and race. Most mention televangelism and the continuing role of religion in politics. Several discuss Islamic fundamentalism. Though all texts cite research in the field, they are not so much sociology as slow journalism. They use sociological evidence to reinforce a common, unquestioned view of the religious world.

The most significant pattern in these texts is their strict segregation of religion into the religion chapter and their focus in that chapter on religious beliefs and organizations. Though the family, education, and other institutions have their chapters as well, only religion is so limited to one small set of pages. The few references to religion outside this chapter occur only in passing: Calvinism is usually (but not universally) mentioned in the theory chapter in connection with Weber's "Protestant ethic" thesis about the origins of capitalism. Some texts follow Comte in arguing that religious authority was stronger before the modern era than it is now. For the most part, however, religion is missing from the chapters on other topics. One text even ignores religion in its treatment of the Israeli-Palestinian conflict! These texts portray religion as separated from the rest of life.

In short, introductory sociology textbooks portray religion as a separate institutional sphere, embodied in particular organizations that are defined by their beliefs and to which religious individuals belong.[9]

As we should expect, the specialty textbooks in the sociology of religion provide much more detailed information about religion, though most of them still emphasize beliefs, organizations, and moral teachings. These are designed for third- and fourth-year sociology majors, though they find a market among beginning graduate students as well. Five such texts dominate the American market. Three of have been prominent since the mid-1980s, through several editions; one of the newer texts is quite similar to these, while the other is written for undergraduates and non-sociologists, not for the discipline *per se*. Two European texts round out the mix. These two are aimed exclusively at graduate students and so emphasize theory and research methods more than do their American counterparts.[10]

In some ways, each of the American texts is a 'religion chapter' writ large. Each begins with a definition of religion and some discussion of the sociological point of view. Each summarizes early efforts in the field, especially the work of Émile Durkheim and Max Weber. Most have chapters entitled something like 'Religious Groups and Organizations' or 'Religion as Social Organization', though one text takes a more interpersonal, dynamic view. All cover the church-sect-denomination-cult typology. Most have a series of 'Religion and . . .' chapters: 'Religion and Race', 'Religion and Gender', 'Religion and Social Change', etc. These emphasize religion's separation from other parts of social life. All touch on secularization and rational-choice theories, the two frameworks that have dominated American scholarship for the last few decades. All discuss the connections between religion and social inequality, religion and social conflict, how people become religious, and so on.

There are, of course, differences between them. Some treat churches as the primary religious units, and devote chapters to American denominational history, including ecumenism. One is more concerned with social processes than with institutions; another devotes considerable attention to religion's role in popular culture. The European texts focus on European themes: secularization, the nature of the contemporary era, and the increasing number of migrants from Muslim countries.

In all cases, though, religion is treated as a matter of belief that is primarily embodied in religious organizations. That is the standard. Individual religion, religion beyond church walls, the religious aspects of public discourse, and other 'unusual' aspects of religious life are at the margins, not the center. If we looked at the texts alone, we would never know that these are some of the more creative areas in which sociologists have been working throughout the last decade. In textbooks, the default view holds sway.

As a sociologist who has studied religion for a long time, I find this depressing. There is too much about religion that the textbook view does not see. Most of my own fieldwork has concentrated on aspects of religion that barely receive mention here. So has much of my colleagues' most admirable work. We will see some of their work later in this chapter, because it runs parallel to mine. It has raised the same questions that my studies of Redemption Parish and of religious social activists posed. Why does the sociology of religion continue to treat religion as a matter of beliefs embodied in formal organizations? What other options are there? What does it take to get the sociology of religion to expand its vision?

This book will present some answers. Chapter Two will trace sociology's default view of religion to the 19th-century historical-cultural milieu that gave birth to our discipline. That milieu shaped sociology's root ideas. It directed our attention toward certain aspects of religious life and away from others. The textbook presentations of religion are a natural result.

We can do better, and this book will do so by exploring three other historical-cultural milieux, so see what alternate sociological view of religion they might have produced, had our discipline been born in one of them. Chapters Three, Five, and Seven present, respectively, sociologies of religion based on classical Confucianism, on the social philosophy of the 14th-century Arab jurist Ibn Khaldūn, and on traditional Navajo religion, which centers on healing rituals. Chapters Four, Six, and Eight, respectively, apply these, to see what these alternate views show us about religion that we typically miss.

In short, time and place matter to intellectual life. Intellectual disciplines emerge from particular contexts and can only with difficulty recognize the blinders that those contexts impose. The default view has proved to be very strong in the sociology of religion. I am hoping that exposing it to different views will weaken its grip.

I recognize, of course, that a discipline's textbooks do not describe that discipline completely. They do, however, capture a discipline's first-order presumptions. The issue is not (just) that American sociology textbooks misapprehend religion. It is that they display a particular image of religion that, at this point in intellectual history, needs to be overcome.

Two Major Theories

Before engaging in that endeavor, we need to make this argument more concrete. The default view is presumed not just by textbooks but by some of the major theories in the field. We can see this by examining the two dominant theories in the sociology of religion of the last few decades. One, the secularization thesis, has been around a long time. The other, the market model of religion, was invented in the 1980s, argued strongly in the 1990s and early 2000s, and is beginning to fade. Both take what I am calling "the default view" as given: that religions are primarily about beliefs and are embodied in religious organizations. They are thus good ways to show what this default view fails to see.

We will start with the market model of religion, developed by Rodney Stark, Roger Finke, Laurence Iannaccone, and their associates. This model is admirable in its clarity and its argumentation. It focuses on religious organizations, arguing that these organizations compete for members in a "religious marketplace." Like businesses, "religious firms" have to provide what their "customers" want. Failure to do so results in religious decline; success produces church growth.[11]

In their various writings, Stark and his associates have treated this market language as more than just a metaphor. They have argued that standard economic concepts help us understand a lot of things about religions that other theories do not. For one thing, they have opposed theories that traced religious decline to a changed desire for religion in the contemporary world. Following the supply-side economists who were influential in the 1980s, they argued that the demand for "religious goods" is pretty much the same in all times and places. What changes is the shape of the religious market and the supply of goods that religious "firms" make available.

Religious markets come in several varieties. Open religious markets consist of hundreds of competing churches each working hard to attract members. They offer many different flavors of religion and can thus satisfy many people's religious demands. Closed markets, on the other hand, consist of one or a few large churches that hold a religious monopoly. They do not have to work so hard for members, because religious people have nowhere else to go. They also satisfy fewer people, so religion as a whole declines. Demand does not have to change; religions thrive when they meet more people's needs and shrink when they need fewer of them. In this sense, religion is just another good for people to consume.

To market theorists, Europe is the perfect case of a closed religious market. There, state churches dominate the religious landscape. Some are still state-supported, as is the case of the Danish Lutheran Church and until recently was the case for the Church of England, the Church of Sweden, and several others. Others are culturally dominant, as is the Catholic Church in much of southern Europe. In all cases, religion has declined considerably. Market theorists say this is because the lack of competition makes religion unattractive to all but a few. Religious "monopolies" also encourage organizational laziness. Secure elites do not work hard to meet their followers' religious needs. Europe's low rates of attendance at state church services are *prima facie* evidence for this, in the market theorists' view.[12]

The United States, on the other hand, has an open religious market, as do West Africa and parts of Latin America. The U.S. free market stems directly from the U.S. Constitution, which says that the government has to treat all religions equally. This produces lively competition between religious groups seeking growth. This keeps religious organizations on their toes and attunes them to the needs of their members. Many people find religions that meet their needs, so religion in general prospers.

The most prominent historical application of this method is Roger Finke and Rodney Stark's *The Churching of America*. Creatively using church membership statistics, the authors traced the rise and fall of several Protestant denominations since America's founding. They charted the growth and relative decline of Congregationalists, Methodists, Baptists, and various sectarians—the market share of each rising as it exploited promising market niches and falling as it liberalized its theology and accommodated to the world. Their version of the supply-side story was relatively simple: "successful" (i.e., growing) churches are otherworldly and conservative; churches decline as they move up-market by appealing to the liberal elite rather than to the conservative masses. Religious monopolies reduce religious participation, as clergy do not depend for their livelihood on "selling" their "product." Religious competition increases total religious activity, though particular "firms" may lose members. According to this story, early sociology's prediction that religion would disappear from the modern world is simply not true.[13]

What, then, do the market theorists recommend to religious leaders who wish their churches to remain strong? First, they should deregulate the religious marketplace. Increased religious competition will increase the total number of church members and attenders, as a higher proportion of the population finds churches that cater to their specific needs. Not everyone wants a metaphysical religion, for example, but some people do; they will stay away from church unless a deregulated market gives them access to their kind of worship. The same is true for biblical literalists, mystics, Wiccans, and the ritualistic: a religious free-market increases the total supply of religious goods, increasing the consumption of religion overall.

Second, wrote Finke and Stark, religious leaders should emphasize the supernatural. They claimed that most people want a supernaturalistic "old-time religion"—one that provides firm beliefs, promises salvation, and gives people certainty in an uncertain world. The market theorists' analysis of church membership trends claims to show a cross-cultural preference for supernaturalism that offer such a vision. The growth of contemporary Evangelical, Fundamentalist, and Pentecostal denominations (including the various charismatic renewals) and the membership declines of American Mainline Protestantism fit this pattern well.[14]

This is not the place for me to criticize this theory in detail. I have done so in a couple of other venues and others have done so much more thoroughly than I.[15] For present purposes, however, three things are worth noting. First, market theory is a theory of religious organizations. It simply assumes that religion is always organized and that religious organizations ("firms") are in the business of meeting people's religious needs. It considers individualized religion to be religion in decline. Stark even wrote about the European Middle Ages' "lack of religiosity"—a clear contrast to the picture that historians have painted of the period, which we will encounter in the next chapter. Religion, to the market theorists, means church religion; they measure it by church attendance, by affirmations of belief, even (for the era before survey research) by the rate of installation of church pews. This matches the culturally standard definition of religion that my American students espouse.

Second, this model fits American Protestantism rather well. American Protestant churches do live in a religious marketplace, they do compete with one another for members, and they do rise or fall depending on their ability to attract the contributions those members bring. California's famous Crystal Cathedral is a perfect example of this. Begun in

1955 by a Dutch Reformed pastor who preached the power of positive thinking, by 1980 this early megachurch had thousands of members, a world-spanning television ministry (*Hour of Power*), and a stunningly designed church building. It hosted scores of self-help groups and ran seminars for other church leaders about how to grow their ministries. Unfortunately, it spent money too freely, so when attendance declined after the founding pastor's retirement, the church got into financial trouble. It recently declared bankruptcy and sold its building to the local Catholic diocese. Market theory's economic terminology is here quite apt. For American Protestantism, the religious field is not just *like* a marketplace; it *is* a marketplace. Failing to attract customers causes churches to die.

Yet there is a particularly bloodless aspect to this way of thinking. Like most economic theories, the market model treats people as genderless, cultureless beings whose personal choices determine whether a particular religion succeeds or fails. Yes, individual choice does matter; no doubt about it. But market theory can only predict what people will choose retrospectively. It does so by seeing what they did in fact choose. Choosing Mormonism over Calvary Chapel or vice versa is thus a bit like choosing Pepsi over Coke: a matter of personal taste. The theory presumes that people's choices meet their needs, without ever being able to specify beforehand what those needs are. Market theory says nothing about religious demand.

Furthermore, the theory has a very shallow notion of organizational failure. 'Failure' is a matter of failing to attract members. It is not, to take an alternative possibility, the failure to live up to its espoused ideals. Was the pro-Nazi German Evangelical Church of the 1930s more successful than the anti-regime Confessing Church, whose leaders lived its Christian witness—and sometimes died for doing so? Yes, in terms of numbers. Yet numbers are not everything and individual choices are not made without culture and context. For most of Western history, for example, Jews have been unable to choose their religion, no matter how little organized Judaism met their needs.

Perhaps this is why the market approach seems so applicable to U.S. Evangelical Protestants and perhaps Mormons, but less applicable to others. For these groups, 'doing religion' involves belonging to religious organizations and affirming core beliefs, which are matters for individuals. The market model explains other religions and their notions of the religious life less well.

I am not saying, here, that the market model is useless. Far from it. Fenggang Yang's reinterpretation of the model to fit contemporary China, for example, illuminated aspects of the Chinese religious situation that had long been unexplained. My point is that market theory highlights some aspects of religions while ignoring others. Like my students and like much sociology, it focuses attention on religious organizations and religious beliefs. It simply does not see other things that are going on.[16]

Other sociological approaches have similar blinders. Secularization theory (market theory's *bête noir*) famously argued that religion is passing from the contemporary scene. In this view, religion is connected to traditional life, not to modernity, and in two ways. First, the theory argues that medieval and early modern religions were among their societies' core social institutions, with their fingers seemingly in every pie. Churches provided not just religion but education, health care, charity, social work, and the like; they were even involved in politics to a degree unimaginable today. This is no longer the case. Churches have ceded these activities to other institutions and have retained just their religious function. Second, religions formerly provided societies with a unified worldview, one to which most people gave assent. They no longer do so: worldviews have become multiple, and conceptual pluralism reigns. In both areas, religious organizations have suffered a reduced sphere of influence. That, say the secularization theorists, is why they have gone into decline. In Bryan Wilson's words, secularization

> relates to a process of transfer of property, power, activities, and both manifest and latent functions, from institutions with a supernaturalist frame of reference to (often new) institutions operating according to empirical, rational, pragmatic criteria. That process can be demonstrated as having occurred extensively, if unevenly, over a long historical period, and to have done so notwithstanding the spasmodic countervailing occurrence of resacralization in certain areas and instances of cultural revitalization exemplified in the emergence of charismatic leaders and prophets.[17]

R. Stephen Warner traced two main branches of this theory among American sociologists of religion. One, following Talcott Parsons, predicted that if religion tries to stay in the public sphere, it will become increasingly generalized and indistinguishable from secular worldviews. The other, following Peter Berger's early work, said that if religion maintains a specifically supernatural content, it will retreat into itself and leave a secularized world behind. Both expected a public world cleansed of gods. Secularization theory celebrates (or mourns) what the early sociologist Max Weber called "the disenchantment of the world."[18]

Whether or not secularization theory is accurate is not my concern here; Warner argued that it fits the European experience but not the American. European religion is declining, he said, while American religion is vibrant. Be that as it may, I am struck by the degree to which secularization theory, like the market approach, defines religion in a Western way, making it less able to comprehend religious currents in other cultural settings.[19]

Like the market model, secularization theory equates religion with beliefs and doctrines, which it thinks are less and less relevant to contemporary people. It also focuses on religions' organizational structures, which it thinks have lost much of their influence in the late modern world. To take the first point: secularization theory casts its main predictions in terms of a decline in the plausibility of religious beliefs. It opposes the 'supernatural' to the 'scientific'; it measures religiosity by adherence to creeds; it treats religions as primarily symbol-systems or worldviews. Though these notions are not unique to the approach, secularization theory is unimaginable without them.

I have already noted that this is a peculiarly Western religious view. It is also empirically questionable. Anthropologist Mary Douglas, for example, showed that doctrine is not terribly important to some tribal religions, as well as to some moderns. In a later chapter, we shall explore the role of structured experience in Navajo religion, to which belief takes a clear back seat. Secularization theory's focus on beliefs makes some sense for Christianity, from the 4th-century Christian battles between the *homoiousians* and the *homoousians* to the Inquisition, the various Catholic and Protestant catechisms, and the transformation of Reformation 'salvation by faith' into American Fundamentalist 'salvation by belief'. Doctrine has traditionally mattered for elite Christians, which made it matter for secularization theory. The scholarly insistence—not limited to secularization theorists—that the status of Buddhism and Confucianism as religions depends on their belief in supernatural beings is part of the same picture.[20]

Second, secularization theory also focuses on formal religious organizations. The question of religion's importance becomes a question of the relative strength of a society's churches and synagogues vis-à-vis its other institutions. Not only are religious worldviews claimed to disappear from the public sphere in the current era; they are seen resurfacing in special times and places where people gather to reinforce their 'private' beliefs and to gain strength for their secular roles. Secularization theorists study these events and their interactions with the outside world. They focus on institutional hierarchies, on clergy-laity relations, on religious movements and mobilizations, on denominational growth and decline. They are not the only sociologists of religion to do so; at times it seems that few sociologists can conceive of religion without some kind of organizational imprimatur. But the influence of Christianity, for which formal church structure has long been a central focus, seems hard to miss.

Indeed secularization theory typically accounts for other forms of religion by absorbing them into its organization-dominated approach. What about Navajo religion, which conducts days-long 'sings' but has no abiding organizational structure? It is 'primitive', the secularists say, a holdover from a time when religious notions pervaded society and had not yet taken institutional form. What about modern privatized faiths—the "Sheilaism" to which Robert Bellah and his associates referred? This is not primitive, they say, but is a sign of modernity's dark side; the many modern Sheilas show how secular the world has become. Throughout, church religion is still the norm to which other forms are compared.[21]

Some feminists have challenged this approach, noting that the supposed 'privatization' of women's faiths is as much a result of church politics as it is of modernity. The medieval Catholic Church neglected women's religious experiences, but it was certainly not modern. Neither secularization theory nor the historic Christian churches have made much room for women's lives (though the Mainline Protestant churches have made recent progress here). Where both secularization theorists and church officials worry about the degree to which religious organizations have 'lost control' of their members, feminists see women channeling their spirituality in a different mode. Focused on official religion, secularization theory misses this development.[22]

There are other problems with secularization theory than these, but all have a similar origin. By taking Western Christianity as normative and projecting a particular interpretation of the past, the secularization approach hides non-doctrinal and non-organizational ways of viewing religious life. It plays down ritual, privatizes religious experience, and discounts intellectual diversity. It types popular religion as 'syncretic' and neglects informal religious groups. It fails to see much of what goes on in religious spaces, largely as a result of its ethnocentric point of view.[23]

We will revisit this approach in the next chapter, as we try to understand why the default view has been so influential in sociology for so long. For now, the point is that both of the sociology of religion's major approaches to religion focus their attention on only a few aspects of religious life. This is why beliefs, organizations, and moral teachings loom so large in sociologists' accounts.

Current Alternatives

I am not the only sociologist of religion to have noticed that our discipline's key intellectual tools give us a limited vision of religious life, much less the only scholar to do so. Several others have explored how our dominant ideas about religion were shaped by Western culture generally and by Western Christianity in particular. Among them, Talal Asad, David Chidester, and Tomoko Masuzawa have offered extended critiques of Western definitions of 'religion', attempting to show that the term itself is a Western construct. Peter Beyer has responded with a nuanced account of how the current concept of religion was co-constructed by Europeans and others in the process of colonial and transnational encounter. Addressing one of our two just-presented theories, Manuel Vásquez has argued that the secularization thesis was built into sociology from its birth, along with a bias that identified religion with the past and sociology with the future. (We will revisit his argument in the next chapter.)

Addressing the other, John Simpson long ago noted how closely Rodney Stark's market theory of religion reflects U.S. cultural values. These scholars all advocate a broader view of our subject matter, precisely to avoid the culturally biased standpoints from which the sociology of religion typically begins.[24]

There have, however, been positive efforts to provide new views. For example, Larry Greil and David Bromley devoted a volume in the series Religion and the Social Order to expanding the definition of religion so it could encompass more than just Western Christian insights. I contributed to that volume, as did several others; each of us, in our own ways, explored alternate paths forward.[25]

Younger scholars are also trying new approaches. Courtney Bender has stepped beyond examining religious organizations to exploring the ways that language shapes our images of religion, as well as the ways by which religious language appears in supposedly non-religious places. Peggy Levitt has explored religion as a transnational phenomenon, not limited to single countries or single religious organizations. Afe Adogame has traced the African Christian colonization of Europe, a phenomenon that calls for rethinking the old Euro-American concepts of how religion works. In short, there seems to be a wave building. As yet, however, it has not altered the fundamentally Euro-American conceptual tools with which sociologists of religion do their work.[26]

Let me present a few recent attempts to shift the discipline, without, however, trying to be thorough. This will help locate the present volume as one of several compatible and (I hope) promising efforts. It would be silly to claim that its approach is the best of these. I do, however, bring certain things to the table that my co-conspirators do not. This makes the book you are reading worthwhile.

We can start with a recent volume: *Religion on the Edge*, edited by Bender and Levitt, along with Wendy Cadge and David Smilde. The book's subtitle—"De-Centering and Re-Centering the Sociology of Religion"—says a lot about the editors' concerns. They argue that the sociology of religion has suffered from four distinct sets of blinders.[27]

First, they say, the sociology of religion focuses too much on the United States. They note that between 1980 and 2010, over 70% of the articles on religion in the major U.S. sociology journals—plus the specialty journals in the sociology of religion—have focused on the United States. This is not just an empirical problem. It affects research methods and theory as well. For example, the American identification of church membership and attendance with religious commitment

> is embedded in surveys of religion around the globe. Little attention is paid to other kinds of formal and informal religious participation and identification, or to the widely varying relationships between religion, economics, law, and politics.[28]

Treating American religion as a universal norm prevents us from seeing how religion operates in other places.

Second, they see an implicit Christo-centrism in the sociology of religion's root definitions of its subject matter. For most sociologists, religion

> is above all a moral order, [and is seen as] a framework that guides action and consistently influences behavior. . . . Religion emerges as a category that is primarily about belief, identity, and worldview . . . that are always oriented toward otherworldly desires or ends.[29]

This is more than just any old Christo-centrism; it replicates American Protestant theology, to the detriment of other religious forms. This is especially true of the market model of religion, for which "beliefs and practices spread through individual conversion; the religious actor with the greatest agency is the entrepreneurial evangelizer."[30]

Third, they say, the sociology of religion has been too focused on congregations as the sole place where religion is practiced. This is particularly true in the United States, but the trend also infects European sociology.

> Given that the American congregational form is primarily and historically a Protestant form that emphasizes voluntary participation and identification, a sociological focus on religion as produced and experienced in congregations further sediments the Christo- and U.S.-centricness of perspectives in the discipline.[31]

Finally, Bender and her co-editors find most sociology of religion to be excessively pro-religious. They reject both mainstream sociology's treatment of religion as a holdover from the past and the contrasting scholarship that focuses on religions' benefits, both for society and for individuals. They cite Smilde and May's article count, which showed that "by the beginning of the twenty-first century, [religion] was five times more likely to be described in positive terms than negative terms" in sociology journals. Negative coverage has returned since 9/11, but it lacks nuance; I have argued elsewhere that the negative treatment of resurgent conservative religion undercuts all religions' ability to critique the neo-liberal world order. Bender and her co-editors argue that sociologists should "critically engage religion, the way it functions, what it does for people, what people do with it, and its social impacts, be they positive or negative."[32] They do not provide viable solutions, but they do at least identify the problem.[33]

Bender and her co-editors are reacting to the same problems with the default view as I am.

Fortunately, there are other approaches on the table. One of these involves the exploration of "lived religion"—the ways in which people actually practice their religions in everyday life. Meredith McGuire's 2008 book of that title is one representative of the trend. Nancy Ammerman's recent *Sacred Stories, Spiritual Tribes* is another. Along with similar works by David Hall and Robert Orsi, these books demonstrate that religion is a far more complex factor in people's lives than we suppose.[34]

McGuire, for example, draws a series of contrasts between what individuals regard as religious or spiritual and "the tidy, consistent, and theologically correct packages [that] official religions promote." From 'Peter', an ordained Presbyterian minister who finds his religious center in work for the poor and homeless, to 'Hannah', a devout Jew whose life is focused on her women's circle and on contemplative dance, to 'Laura', a Latina Catholic who prays daily in front of her home altar but never attends official Mass, we encounter people who do not fit the institutional boxes that their religious organizations have built for them. McGuire argues that mainstream sociology has misunderstood contemporary religion because it has assumed that religious elites define religion for others. If this was once true, she writes, it is no longer. She argues that the organizational hegemony built during the 16th-to-18th-century "long reformations" has crumbled in the contemporary world.[35]

Ammerman similarly focuses on individuals—though she chooses individuals who are embedded in local religious communities. Based on interviews, spiritual diaries, and other material drawn from some ninety-five Americans from across the religious spectrum, *Sacred Stories* shows how ordinary Americans live their religions. Most are what she calls "Golden Rule" Christians (with a few "Golden Rule" Jews): they tell her that their religions give them the tools they need to be 'good people'. Beliefs matter less than conduct, morality is a matter of inner personal choice. Though these people find their religious communities to be important, their religious lives are not just confined to certain buildings at certain times of the week. In short, their lived religions are far different from sociology's (and my students') standard view.

McGuire and Ammerman exemplify two of six recent trends in the sociology of religion, none of which I can explore in depth here.[36] McGuire focuses on religious individualism—a narrative that describes the ways in which individuals are taking control of their own religious lives, particularly claiming the right to determine what is and is not important to them. Ammerman's work, both past and present, emphasizes the ways that religious people interact with each other in local communities. Her interviewees talk about their own spiritual lives but the majority see those lives as intertwined with others. For her, religion is still collective, though at the local level and not at the cost of individual growth.

These two narratives—one that says religion is becoming increasingly a matter of individual taste and another that focuses on the role of local communities in people's religious lives—go beyond the standard sociological approaches to religion with which I began this chapter. They still, however, fail to venture far outside the Euro-American box. Individualism is, after all, a long-standing Western concern. The relationship between local communities and society-wide institutions is likewise a recurrent sociological concern. Ferdinand Tönnies and Alexis de Tocqueville gave these themes masterful treatment in the 19th century. Though welcome, just examining religions as they are actually lived does not take us out of the Euro-American sphere.[37]

How about a feminist sociology of religion? Mary Jo Neitz has produced a series of pathbreaking articles on women, gender, and religion that call much received wisdom into question. Ethnographically grounded and theoretically subtle, Neitz's work steps beyond the boundaries of standard sociology. It certainly steps beyond the trio of concepts that define religion to my students: beliefs and moral rules embedded in formal religious organizations.[38]

Neitz's most interesting work is on feminist Wicca. Sometimes called "contemporary witchcraft", sometimes "neo-paganism", Wicca is an amorphous socio-religious movement that reinvents earth rituals, affirms religious individuality, and institutionalizes improvisation in the search for spiritual power. It is, in many ways, the opposite of the standard model of religion. Beliefs matter or they do not matter, depending on individual choice and temperament. There are rules or no rules, depending on how Wiccans interact with one another. There is no membership, there are no standing organizations. Instead, Wiccans gather in festivals or they work as isolates. Their participation is flexible and not ruled by status. True, there is social status among Wiccans, as there is in all human endeavors; it is just not fixed, formal, or beyond question. Above all, Wiccans are boundary breakers. They are very different from the religions that sociology usually takes as its subject matter.

That, in fact, is why Neitz studies them. Early in her research, she told me that they were a perfect foil for understanding contemporary life. We live, she said, in a world in which individuals find themselves subject to mass institutions. Religions and families (and a few other groupings) connect people with each other, giving them a sense of 'home'. We have normative models of both: church-on-Sunday for religions and mother-father-2.5-kids-plus-dog-and-babysitter for families. These were the white-bread 1950s standards. We now know there are other kinds of families and other kinds of religions but most sociologists still treat these other models as exceptional. Wiccans force us to rethink our position. They are clearly making up their religion as they go along: despite occasional pretense, their rituals change to suit time, temperament, season, and much else.[39] They also create new family structures: gay, lesbian, bisexual, ambi-sexual, multiple, and so on; pretty much anything but patriarchy is okay. As Neitz pointed out in her 2000 Furfey Lecture,

Wiccans overturn the standard sociological claim that gender is a social construct while sexuality is biologically fixed. Wiccans vary both and celebrate doing so. They are thus an ideal religion to force us to rethink our accustomed ways of seeing.[40]

We need not go into details here; for that, you can read Neitz's work. Her methodological reflections, however, relate directly to this book's project. Commenting on the work of the feminist sociologist Dorothy Smith, she remarks:

> Feminist theorists asked what would happen to the theories themselves, if we were to put women at the center of the analysis? Would that process suggest new categories and relations? Would there be a change in the ways that we understand the world?[41]

Neitz recounts her own theoretical movement, while studying Wicca, from what she calls "a gender frame" to "a queer frame." She began by asking how a woman-centered spirituality affected gender roles; taking her informants seriously forced her to rethink her sociological and feminist theories as well as her own life. The result expands the sociology of religion's ability to understand *all* religions, not just 'marginal' exotica. Her point is not just to describe Wiccans. It is to help us question the way we study religions of all kinds.[42]

This is precisely what this book will accomplish. By taking an imaginative leap, by taking seriously other cultural and civilizational contexts, I want to see how the sociology of religion might change. And I want to do it in detail. Chapters Three through Eight are not about the joys of being traditional Chinese, about the genius of Ibn Khaldūn, or about Navajo wisdom. They are concrete attempts to show what the sociology of religion can learn about all religions from these examples—particularly things that our Euro-American blinders keep us from seeing.

Before I start, however, I need to mention one more author. Raewyn Connell is not a sociologist of religion. She is, however, a vigorous advocate of what she calls "Southern theory": social theories that originate in the global South but provide useful insights about social phenomena worldwide. Her project intersects mine, though our aims are different. A few words of description will help you see both our complementarity and our differing intents.

Connell's *Southern Theory* is one of a number of recent post-colonial works that challenge dominant Euro-American philosophies. Unlike works by Dipesh Chakrabarty, Gayatri Spivak, and a few others, Connell is not content to criticize Northern dominance. She seeks out alternate voices and examines what they have to say about the contemporary world. She shows their insights for understanding the world socio-economic-political system. She also shows their inadequacies. That is to say, she treats Southern voices as real social theory. She hopes they will help us better understand our contemporary world.[43]

Connell criticizes several major current sociological theories of world society, most clearly the efforts of James Coleman, Anthony Giddens, and Pierre Bourdieu. (They are mere examples, on whom she spends more time than others.) She objects to their claimed universalism; to their belief that Euro-American patterns can be found everywhere; and most of all to the fact that they ignore the power differentials that shape our world. She then presents the contributions of writers from five 'southern' regions: West Africa, Iran, South America, India, and aboriginal Australia. She examines each of these writers for her or his ability to explain world inequalities. She also applauds their theoretic creativity. She does not claim that only Southern theory has value, but she does claim that it has been ignored. The social-scientific establishment, it seems, cannot see its own role in the colonial enterprise. One needs views from the margins to capture the whole picture.

Contrast this to the various sociologists of religion we have just listed. Unlike Bender and her associates, and unlike McGuire and Ammerman, Connell actively seeks the insights of people from other societies and cultures; she asks what peoples on the margins can contribute to understanding the entire world. These sociologists are not necessarily opposed to such insights; they just do not seek them out. Like Neitz, Connell thinks that putting marginal peoples at the center generates insight, and she does not just want to use those insights to understand those people's lives; she also seeks new ways to understand the overall inequalities of the world's socio-economy. Put otherwise, she has an agenda. The touchstone of any theory, for her, is whether it can comprehend the global political, economic, and social imbalances that typify our world. That is a good agenda, but it is, to put it bluntly, a Western agenda. It not the heart of Neitz's work, nor is it of mine.

In fact, all of these approaches are worthwhile. Connell is right that we need Southern theories, the better to understand our unequal world. Bender, Levitt, Cadge, and their associates are right to seek new ways to understand religion's role in that world, and they might take a leaf from Connell's book in their attempts to do so. McGuire and Ammerman are right to look closely at how religion is actually lived. And Neitz is certainly right that putting women at the center of our theorizing expands our theoretic toolkit in hugely productive ways. We need many such efforts.

This book takes a somewhat different tack than these. Like Bender et al., McGuire, and Ammerman, I recognize the limitations of the sociology of religion's traditional way of thinking about our subject matter. Like Neitz, I want to learn what we can see when we begin from a different social standpoint—here, different from the Western Christianity that has for so long shaped the field. Like Connell, I turn to marginal and unaccustomed sources for inspiration. I am not exactly following any of these scholars; we are, however, fellow travelers, engaged in compatible efforts to change the way that sociology sees the world.

The next chapter outlines in detail the historical-cultural origins of sociology's default view of religion, showing how and why our field is rooted in a culturally particular view of the world. Then we will travel to China, to imagine the sociology of religion we would have, were we to base our thinking on traditional Chinese principles. What would we notice about American congregational religion that we currently do not? What would we notice about non-church religion that scholars have otherwise missed in their efforts to understand that (non-default) phenomenon?

Next, we will apply insights from the work of the 14th-century Arab jurist Ibn Khaldūn to two recent cases in which religion and ethnic conflict are entwined. One is the 1980s and 1990s Marian apparitions at Medjugorje, Bosnia; the other is the very recent growth of ISIS: the "Islamic State in Iraq and Syria" (though the group goes by other names[44]). What does Ibn Khaldūn help us see about those events that our standard approaches miss?

Finally, we will explore the traditional Navajo approach to ritual. What does the Navajo understanding of ritual help us see in the rituals of contemporary American religious groups that we might otherwise have missed? How might it help us produce a better theory of ritual than the ones that we now have?

In each case, I seek to expand our awareness. In each case, I hope to show what a world-conscious sociology of religion might accomplish.

Liberty Leading the People, painting by Eugène Delacroix. Photograph by Dennis Jarvis (Creative Commons BY-SA 2.0).

2

The Default View's Historical-Cultural Origins

Where did sociology's default view of religion come from? All ideas start somewhere, and this one has not been around forever.

The ancient Greeks, for example, certainly did not think that religion only happened in temples. Temples housed priests and ritual sacrifices, which were important for civic life, but religion also happened in other places. Religious festivals happened in streets and along village roads, not in buildings. Dionysian *thiasoi* wandered mountain slopes seeking ecstatic union with the divine. The mysteries of Eleusis attracted pilgrims who sought enlightenment and security in the afterlife, but who went home afterward and might never return. Religious belief was not central. People could believe what they liked, so long as they practiced the rituals and did not deny the gods. None of this resembles sociology's default view of religion as located in religious organizations and focused on beliefs and moral rules.[1]

Europeans of the late medieval period also did not think of religion in modern terms. Yes, there was an authoritative church, but popular religion was more important to people's everyday lives than was formal church participation, at least beyond the yearly confession and communion expected in the Easter season. Late medieval religion differed from modern Western Christianity in two distinct ways.[2]

First, it was focused on practices rather than on beliefs. Certain acts were seen as central to Christianity: baptism, basic prayers, ritual gestures of blessing, yearly confession and communion, and so on. Doing these was what mattered. Except for monks and nuns, interior life was not so important. Here, for example, is an Italian peasant, speaking as a character witness for an Inquisition suspect. That suspect, he says, "performs all the duties of a good Christian":

> When he is not tending the herds and is at home in winter or when it rains . . . he always goes to Mass; he always makes the sign of the cross

when the Ave Maria tolls; he recites the Ave Maria, crossing himself first . . . ; blesses the bread and offers thanks to God after he has eaten; . . . in church he is respectful and recites the rosary.[3]

Note that this witness does not mention beliefs, though he does mention church attendance. We do not know what the suspect thought about anything, we just know what he did. This peasant clearly thought that religion was a matter of doing, not believing. This is different from the default view.

Second, religious practices before the Protestant and Catholic reformations were quite diverse. Individuals were free to choose from a large number of possible actions, shaping their religious lives to their personal needs. Here is how Meredith McGuire described the pattern:

> One woman's everyday devotional practices might include seeking help from a saint known for protecting and healing children, devotions at a nearby holy well known for promoting fertility, involvement in rituals for the patron saint of her valley, and such routine women's religious responsibilities as the daily blessing of the hearth on rekindling the fire. An older neighbor . . . might say similar blessings on the hearth and the kitchen, seek a different holy well (perhaps one for the health and fertility of her barnyard animals) . . . , [and follow] those saints who help persons with aches and pains, failing memories, and sore throats.[4]

The men in these households would have had their own personal rituals, oriented toward their own needs and daily tasks.

To moderns, this sounds like 'magic' or 'superstition', but that is an anachronism. Late-19th-century scholars such as Sir James Frazer and Émile Durkheim claimed there was an innate dividing line between 'magic' and 'religion', but such lines are matters of cultural definition.[5] Pre-reformations Europeans thought they were doing religion by engaging in such individualistic daily rituals.

McGuire analyzed this matter in depth. Based on the work of historians Robert Scribner and Keith Luria, she argued that calling such practices 'magic' or 'superstition' was an attempt on the part of religious elites to disvalue them.[6] It was part of the process, she wrote, by which those elites tried to monopolize sacred power during the period that these historians called the "long reformations" (1350–1750).

> The reformation movements—both Protestant and Catholic—attacked the popular idea of sacred power. Reformers tried to distinguish "true" religion from "mere" magic, and by the end of the Long Reformation, most religious organizations severely sanctioned unapproved persons' exercise of sacred power. . . . For instance, if a "wise woman" healer successfully healed a sick person, the churches' interpretation was that she did so with the aid of the devil and must be punished severely. . . . Various Protestant reformation movements tried to eliminate magic from religion altogether. . . . The Catholic Church still allowed some devotions and use of sacramentals to which many members attached magical meanings. Church authorities decried magic, however, and tried to centralize the mediation of divine power in church-approved rituals performed by priests who were under stricter control of the hierarchy.[7]

Here, we find the second and third elements of my students' definition combined. Religions, they saw, involve rules laid down by authorities, who use formal organizations to enforce them. The "long reformations" were efforts on the part of elites to control their subject populations. They did so by enforcing organizational control over religious beliefs and practices, suppressing anything that remained outside. Religion as belief, rules, and organizations is now the norm. Even without knowing the history, my students clearly see what is at stake.

McGuire posed a further wrinkle. She pointed out that we can see this trend now because we are entering an era in which the established definition of religion is breaking down. Many people no longer defer to religious authorities, they no longer see religion as just a matter of beliefs, and they are no longer willing to limit their religious lives to what formal religious organizations have to offer. McGuire described a good number of such people in her analysis of contemporary popular religion. She is one of the first sociologists to track elements of contemporary religious life that escape organizational purview.[8]

Frazer and Durkheim, however, absorbed the churches' post-reformations view. They saw religion as organized where magic was individual; Frazer, at least, thought that religion centered on belief in gods where magic centered on practices. Though later anthropologists knew better, their work never seems to have penetrated mainstream sociological thinking. The textbook treatments I summarized in the previous chapter certainly reflect the disciplinary norm.

Sociology's French Birth

The early modern religious elites' struggle for power is, however, just part of the story. Sociology was not forced to take up these definitions whole hog. Like all intellectuals, the early sociologists clearly began with the concepts current in their intellectual milieu. Yet they were able to reformulate most of the ideas they inherited about social life. They proposed new ways of thinking about society, about culture, and about the core elements of the human condition. Why did they not create a new, more nuanced understanding of religion than the one current in their day?

Manuel Vásquez has recently analyzed sociology's early-19th-century origins and has proposed an answer to this question. He pointed out that sociology was an epistemological child of the Enlightenment: like the Enlightenment thinkers, early sociologists saw rationality and empirical observation as the ultimate sources of knowledge. Specifically, the Enlightenment opposed knowledge based only on faith and revelation. As Vásquez put it, "Modernity defined itself . . . in opposition to the irrationality of the Dark Ages." From Descartes through Locke, Hume, Kant, and the 18th-century *philosophes*, early modern intellectuals developed "the notion of an autonomous, rational, and self-transparent subject capable of grasping and eventually mastering the laws of society." Sociologists took this idea and set it at the heart of their new discipline.[9]

This, wrote Vásquez, involved sociology in a critique of theology from its very beginnings. Auguste Comte (sociology's putative founder) famously distinguished theology, metaphysics, and science as the three stages of human intellectual development. Only the last of these grasps the underlying laws that rule the cosmos. Comte's "social physics" (later called "positive sociology") sought to do for social life what physics and chemistry were doing for the world of nature. It promised to uncover the natural laws that govern how people live.[10]

Vásquez's point is simple: any intellectual discipline must distinguish itself from other ways of thinking. Sociology had to show that society could not be reduced to biology, which treated (and sometimes still treats) human action as the result of bio-chemical processes. It also had to differentiate itself from psychology, by showing that social life is not merely the sum of individual behaviors. Émile Durkheim argued the former by showing that socially shared ideas cannot be reduced to neural conditions; he argued the latter by showing how "collective ways of acting and thinking have a reality outside the individuals who, at any moment in time, conform to it."[11] Vásquez argued that theology was sociology's third opponent, an especially important one at the time and place of its intellectual birth. In his summary,

> Sociology had to adopt a thoroughly humanistic perspective that wrestled agency away from the clutches of supernatural beings and forces and focused on the historical praxis of men and women. In other words, sociology had to differentiate itself from theology. It is thus not surprising that sociology took up the critical thrust of the Enlightenment, which sought to make "man the measure of all things" and to critique forms of authority not grounded in human reason, such as dogma and revelation. With sociology, a humanistic universalism replaced theological absolutism.[12]

Thus Comte's opposition between theology and science was not just rhetoric; it was central to early sociology's self-identity. By defining their field as the rational transcendence of faith-based theology, early sociologists read back their own self-understanding on religion, but in negative terms. Religion was cast as sociology's 'Other'. Sociology was designed to value reason; thus sociologists portrayed religion as valuing irrational belief. Sociology values free inquiry; thus religion must value authority and repression; sociology seeks the free development of individuals; thus religion creates organizations that seek to maintain their social monopoly on the sacred. By this process, sociology constructed "religion" as the imagined antithesis to its hopeful self-image. Is it any wonder that it saw belief, authority, and church organization as the defining elements of its chosen intellectual adversary?

Vásquez further pointed out that sociology's treatment of religion as its intellectual 'Other' biased the new discipline toward the belief that religion is passing from the world scene. If sociology is part of a scientific future, then religion must be the dying past. Secularization theory, Vásquez claimed, is thus built into sociology's very foundation. No wonder it has had such staying power in the discipline.

There are two additional historical factors that fed the sociology's sense that religion amounts to supernatural beliefs embedded in authoritarian organizations. The first is the political role that the Roman Catholic Church played in 19th-century France in opposing the Republic. This shaped the discipline particularly strongly, because France was where sociology was born. The second is the late-19th-century conflict between religion and science surrounding Darwin's theory of evolution. This shaped both American and European images of science and thus shaped scientific sociology's view of religion in both places.

First, religion and politics. Sociology developed as a separate intellectual discipline in France, where it was heavily influenced by 18th- and 19th-century French political history. Despite its flaws, Republican France carried the Enlightenment's hopes for human freedom. The Roman Catholic Church was one of its main opponents because the Church had had tremendous power under the *ancien régime*. Clergy had formed the first of the three Estates (clergy, nobility, and wealthy commoners). The Church had been the largest landowner, collecting massive rents as well as tithes. It had controlled the schools, had registered marriages, births, and death, and had run most hospitals. Its influence had been huge—enough so that France was often called the "elder daughter of the Church." Except for a few radical priests, the Catholic Church staunchly supported the monarchy.

The French Revolution confronted the Church directly. To break its power—and also to pay its own bills—the revolutionary government voted in 1789 to confiscate church property and to eliminate the Church's privileges and its authority to tax. The next year's Civil Constitution of the Clergy made priests state employees and required priests and bishops to swear allegiance to secular authorities. Some priests pledged, but in April, 1791 the Pope denounced the Constitution and a year later hundreds of "nonjuring" priests were executed or murdered (the "September massacres"). In 1793, public worship was banned and the Republicans installed the "Goddess of Reason" in Notre Dame Cathedral. Tensions relaxed somewhat after Robespierre's fall (1794), but it was not until 1801 that overt conflict ended. In that year, Napoleon signed an agreement with the Vatican, the Concordat, that recognized the Catholic Church as just one among four religions to be subsidized by the French state, while affirming that it was "the religion of the great majority." Thus Catholicism was no longer the only state church. The Pope could dismiss bishops but he could not appoint them without state permission. The Church did not regain its lost property and could not interfere in political affairs. With some wiggling, this remained official policy for the rest of the century.[13]

Unofficially, however, the Catholic Church remained a major intellectual and organizational supporter of anti-Republican reaction throughout the 19th century. The 1815 Restoration under Louis XVIII was relatively liberal and retained freedom of religion, but the government of his successor Charles was dominated by Ultramontanists— Catholics who supported the right of the Pope to influence national affairs. The Royalist parliament immediately passed a law against sacrilege, which implicitly gave the Catholic Church special protection: the prohibited 'sacrilegious acts' offended only Catholics, not Protestants or Jews. This law generated much opposition and was repealed after the 1830 July Revolution, which brought Louis-Philippe, Duke of Orleans, to power.[14]

However, Ultramontanists continued working to restore the Church's special place in public life, and not just in France. The First Vatican Council (1869–1870) was their major victory. It proclaimed papal infallibility in matters of doctrine and papal supremacy in matters of Church government. These were designed to centralize Church power, so that the Papacy could more effectively combat the growing strength of European nation-states. The irony, of course, was that the Council ended abruptly when Germany overran France in the 1870 Franco-Prussian War. The Kingdom of Italy no longer had to fear French interference, so it annexed Rome. Napoleon III's supposedly 'secular' Second French Empire had protected the Catholic Church—if only beyond French borders.

The French Third Republic (1870–1940) was not expected to last long. However, the inability of the French monarchists to unite around one royal family (Bourbon or Orleans) cost the Church the support it needed to regain political influence. The political crisis of 16 May 1877 ("Crise du seize mai") crushed the monarchists and established parliament's rule. The Republicans removed the Church's authority over education in 1880 and 1882 and gradually constructed the system now known as *laïcité*. This is more than just freedom of religion, in the way that Americans understand the term. It is rather freedom of the state *from* religion. People can be religious in their private lives, but not in the public sphere.[15]

Laïcité was solidified in a 1905 law that ended the 1801 Concordat and provided for strict church/state separation. Religious officials could not participate in politics or serve on charitable boards. Religious schools were closed and religious instruction was prohibited in the school system. Church land was confiscated. The state ceased paying priests' salaries and monastic orders were ended. The only positive feature for the Church was that the state no longer appointed bishops. Politics and religion in France finally went their separate ways.[16]

For the Republican French, this history encouraged their image of religion as a reactionary force in society. They long struggled against a powerful religious organization bent on exercising authority over the minds and morals of the French citizenry. They won, but the battle was hard fought. It is no wonder that French sociology, which saw itself as a progressive science, would see in this political history confirmation of its sense that religion is a holdover from an unenlightened past. The Dreyfus Affair (1894–1906), though not openly about Catholicism, certainly cemented the notion that religious intolerance was a negative social force. It is worth noting that Émile Durkheim—like Alfred Dreyfus, of Alsatian Jewish descent—signed the January 1898 petition calling for Dreyfus to be retried in the light of new evidence against his supposed treason. Like other progressives, Durkheim called for setting his 1894 conviction aside.

We will return to Durkheim later in this chapter, as his sociological work was crucial for the story we are following. First, however, please note that the French Republic's battle with religion encouraged the view that religions are authoritarian organizations. Though perhaps implicit, the Republic did not focus on religions as matters of belief. For that element, we need to look at the 19th-century conflict between religion and science—a fight that continues in the United States today.

Religious Past, Scientific Future

Most people know enough about the conflict between religion and science that there is no need to recount much here. We can merely recall two episodes. Each of these reinforced the sense that belief matters a lot to religion as it had come to be understood in the late-19th- and early-20th-century world—the period of sociology's intellectual birth.

The first is the controversy surrounding Charles Darwin's *Origin of Species* (1859).[17] This book presented no challenge to religious organizations; it was at most a challenge to the Christian belief that Genesis was literal history, even though that was a minority view in Darwin's day. Most mid-19th-century Christian theologians did not think that world had been created in an actual seven days. They did, however, think that it had been created and that God guided its development. Their "natural theology" also taught that species existed just as God had created them, except for some that had been destroyed in previous disasters and others that humans had altered for domestic purposes. Darwin famously drew a parallel between the way that humans bred pigeons (artificial selection) and the way that competition (natural selection) bred differently shaped birds. The former required an intelligent designer but the latter did not. Natural selection only required that some varieties of plants and animals be better able to survive the rigors of particular environments. Darwin argued that species arose through such natural processes; for many, this undercut the need for God.

Some Christians were outraged but others were not bothered. Many clerics were perfectly happy to learn of new ways that God managed His creation. Others saw a slippery slope to atheism. Asa Gray, the devout Christian botanist who published *Origin* for Darwin in America, wrote an influential article entitled "Natural Selection Not Inconsistent with

Natural Theology." This liberalism required, though, that humans be excluded from the evolutionary process. Even though Darwin scarcely mentioned humans in *Origin*, the book was soon read as supporting human descent from apes. Writing in 1874, Charles Hodge used this argument to equate natural selection with atheism. This charge appeared more frequently in coming decades, as the conflict between Evangelical Protestantism and science grew.[18]

It is commonly thought that Darwin delayed publishing his theory because he was worried that it would ignite religious controversy. The story, publicized by Stephen Jay Gould and others, was that he did not want to offend his deeply religious wife, Emma, and perhaps also his mentor, the *Beagle's* Captain Robert Fitzroy. It was not until he received Alfred Russell Wallace's manuscript on the topic that he knew he had to put his ideas into print. Historian John van Wyhe has recently argued that Darwin did not delay at all. Instead, wrote van Wyhe, he was simply working on other projects: first his reports of the *Beagle* expedition, then his treatises on barnacles. Only when these were finished did he turn to his work on species. Van Wyhe points out that Emma Darwin certainly knew of his evolutionary theories, as did many others.[19]

The issue here is whether Darwin himself thought belief was central to religion. Gould certainly thought so a century later, though he also thought that religion and science would not be in conflict, were each to stay in its own sphere. If van Wyhe is correct, Darwin did not worry about this problem when he published *Origin*. His later *Descent of Man*, however, was another story. There he wrote, "I am aware that the conclusions arrived at in this work will be denounced by some as highly irreligious."[20] He was right about this, for it was the application of evolution to human beings that religious people most strongly opposed. Christians could accept the natural origin of the earth and other species far more easily than they could accept the evolution of their own kind. It was not until 1996, with Pope John Paul II's encyclical "Truth Cannot Contradict Truth," that the Roman Catholic Church officially accepted evolution as a factual description of human history. Many sectarian Protestants have yet to do so.

This leads us to our second episode, the birth of Protestant Fundamentalism.

The Fundamentals: A Testimony to the Truth consisted of ninety essays published in twelve volumes between 1909 and 1915 by the Bible Institute of Los Angeles. These were not tracts by uneducated yahoos. They were reasoned essays by serious Christians (mostly men) who attempted to restate what they saw as Protestant orthodoxy in new times. Authors included ministers, evangelists, professors, doctors, and missionaries. Almost uniformly, they rejected liberal theology, biblical source criticism, Catholicism, socialism, spiritualism, Mormonism, Christian Science, the social gospel, and a host of other 'modernist' movements. Their essays wrestled seriously with their opponents, finding them wanting. They are definitely worth reading—far more than their current negative reputation among liberals would suggest.[21]

Four of the essays are about evolution. Two of them are critical minor pieces, and one—by the geologist George Frederick Wright—embraces theistic evolution: Wright claimed that the evolutionary process is driven by God's hands. The best, however, is by James Orr; entitled "Science and Christian Faith," it is worth examining in a bit of detail.[22]

Orr began by noting the common claim that religion and science are incompatible. He quotes scientists who claim that Christianity is disproved by natural law, and he acknowledges that religious authorities have suppressed science where it threatened established religious views. These are both, he said, mistakes. In fact, science's "supposed disharmony with the truths of the Bible [is] an unreal one." The difficulty is one of worldview: scientists do not have to believe in a Creator but Christians do.

> The Bible is a record of revelation. Christianity is a supernatural system. Miracle, in the sense of a direct entrance of God in word and deed into human history for gracious ends, is of the essence of it. On the other hand, the advance of science has done much to deepen the impression of the universal reign of natural law. The effect has been to lead multitudes whose faith is not grounded in direct spiritual experience to look askance on the whole idea of the supernatural. God, it is assumed, has His own mode of working, and that is by means of secondary agencies operating in absolutely uniform ways; mira-

cles, therefore, cannot be admitted. And, since miracles are found in Scripture—since the entire Book rests on the idea of a supernatural economy of grace—the whole must be dismissed as in conflict with the modern mind

Orr argued, however, that miracles do not undercut a belief in natural law. There is no logical problem with a God who created natural law being able to set it aside on special occasions. That is what miracles are: the suspension of the ordinary state of affairs. "The real question at issue," he says, is theism:

> Miracle can only profitably be discussed on the basis of a theistic view of the universe. It is not disputed that there are views of the universe which exclude miracle. The atheist cannot admit miracle, for he has no God to work miracles. The pantheist cannot admit miracle, for to him God and nature are one. The deist cannot admit miracle, for he has separated God and the universe so far that he can never bring them together again. The question is not, Is miracle possible on an atheistic, a materialistic, a pantheistic, view of the world, but, Is it possible on a theistic view—on the view of God as at once immanent in His world, and in infinite ways transcending it?

The answer, of course, was yes. Science does not contradict Scripture, wrote Orr, because science cannot prove that miracles do not exist. Science merely opens up "new vistas in the contemplation of the Creator's power, wisdom, and majesty," by showing how the world works in its ordinary mode. When the Bible makes statements about the natural world, it

> clearly does not profess to anticipate the scientific discoveries of the nineteenth and twentieth centuries. Its design is very different; namely, to reveal God and His will and His purposes of grace to men, and, as involved in this, His general relation to the creative world, its dependence in all its parts on Him, and His orderly government of it in Providence for His wise and good ends. Natural things are taken as they are given, and spoken of in simple, popular language, as we ourselves every day speak

of them. . . . To this hour, with all the light of modern science around us, we speak of sun, moon and stars "rising" and "setting," and nobody misunderstands or affirms contradiction with science. The Bible, using the language of appearances, was no more committed to the literal moving of the sun round the earth than are our modern almanacs, which employ the same forms of speech.

Orr cited John Calvin's commentary on the first chapter of Genesis: "He who would learn astronomy and other recondite arts," he said, "let him go elsewhere." Considered rightly, science is clearly no threat to religion, in his view.[23]

Both of these episodes are telling. Like Darwin and the rest of his critics, Orr saw belief as central to the religious enterprise. Christianity presents a theistic interpretation of the world; atheist science denies theism. These are both matters of belief. The science versus religion controversy is thus between two ways of seeing the world.[24]

This was, however, a shift from an earlier sense of what religion was all about. Belief was not so important for the late-medieval Italian peasant we quoted some pages ago. For him, religious practice mattered. He did not even mention beliefs as evidence for the religiosity of his friend. The shift from practical religion to belief-centered religion began during the "long reformations" but was reaffirmed by the 19th-century conflict between religion and science. This conflict continues today.

A demonstration of this landed on my doorstep the very morning that I sat down to write these lines. I live in Texas, where the State Board of Education decides which books can be used in public schools. The past several years have seen considerable controversy over the science curriculum, in part because several creationists got themselves elected to the board and have been trying to add "creation science" as an equally valid approach to evolutionary biology. At yet another hearing, former board president Don McLeroy—who is not a scientist—urged the current board to adopt changes that would "strike the final blow to the teaching of evolution." Other speakers complained that this proposal would treat religious belief as science and would furthermore impose the beliefs of a single religion on everyone. Belief, again, seemed to be central to the religious agenda.[25]

What's the point? Darwin had nothing to do with sociology, nor did Orr, nor does Don McLeroy. Of what interest are these people for this book? Nothing in themselves, but everything for the cultural pattern that they represent. I claim that sociology has taken on board several unexamined assumptions about religion, based on the organizational and cultural peculiarities of Euro-American post-medieval religion. It has particularly taken on the image of religion in the era of its intellectual origin. That image has three parts.

As Manuel Vásquez noted, religion was a core part of the intellectual milieu from which sociology emerged and against which it struggled to define itself. Religion was its 'Other'; thus it saw religion as benighted and authoritarian—everything it imagined it was not. Eighteenth- and 19th-century French political struggles defined religion as authoritarian and backward looking and moreover emphasized its organizational character. The Roman Catholic Church, as an organization, became a model for sociology of how religions manifest themselves in the social world. Finally, the late-19th- and early-20th-century conflict between religion and science reinforced the notion that religions are all about beliefs.

These three things—beliefs, rules, and organizations—are precisely the cultural definitions of religion with which my students begin my class. They are sociology's default view.

I've already noted Vásquez's argument that sociology's 19th-century origins primed it to favor sociology's secularization thesis: the notion that religion is disappearing from the modern world. The work of early sociologists bears him out. Auguste Comte thought that religious ways of seeing the world were primitive; they had been surpassed by philosophy and were being surpassed by science. Émile Durkheim's doctoral dissertation and first book, *The Division of Labor in Society*, argued that increased "social density"—population size, economic differentiation, and information flow—undercut religion by triggering a shift from a form of social solidarity that depended on fixed beliefs and rules to a form that depended on a well-developed division of labor. Max Weber famously wrote about the "disenchantment of the world." These and other early sociologists put religion in the past. (We will return to Durkheim and Weber below.)[26]

If, as Vásquez claimed, sociology identified itself with a progressive scientific future set against a religious past, then religion must pass from the scene in order for science to triumph. He wrote:

> For the founding fathers, religion was important only because it revealed the origin of our conceptions, a mode of thought that, while foundational, had been overcome by a new humanistic, naturalistic, scientific thinking. Thus, they approached religion with great ambivalence, granting it the power to shape worldviews and ethos, but also theorizing it as an anachronism, as a phenomenon bound to disappear or, at a minimum, to be drastically transformed—privatized or rationalized—by the juggernaut of modernity.[27]

Vásquez noted sociology's "tendency to see religion in mythic terms, as a reality that existed in the past, a formidable force that defined everything at the dawn of humanity, but that is increasingly irrelevant in the present."[28] He connected this to sociology's foundational dualisms: mechanical versus organic solidarity, *Gemeinshaft* versus *Gesellschaft*, and, on the one hand, traditional and charismatic authority, arrayed against means-ends bureaucratic authority on the other. Taken together, these dualisms shaped a grand narrative:

> of inexorable social differentiation, rationalization, and disenchantment. . . . These grand narratives of religion's fall from Eden have made it difficult for sociology to study in specific historical and cultural contexts the multiple and changing relationships that religion and modernity sustain.[29]

Vásquez is not, of course, the only, or even the most prominent intellectual to note this trend. He cited both Talal Asad and Pierre Bourdieu, who made similar points. Bourdieu is quite direct:

> The social sciences, having been initially built up, often at the cost of indisputably scientistic distortions, against the religious view of the world, found themselves constituted as the central bastion on the side of the Enlightenment . . . in the political and religious struggle for the vision of "humanity" and its destiny.[30]

Asad made a similar, if wider, point. He wrote that the intellectual movements of the 18th and 19th centuries created

> religion as a new historical object: anchored in personal experience, expressible as belief-statements, dependent on private institutions, and practiced in one's spare time. This construction of religion ensures that it is part of what is *inessential* to our common politics, economy, science, and morality.[31]

In short, secularization theory was implicit in sociology's foundation. Its continuing strength derives, at least in part, from its birth.

Counter-Arguments

There are two potential problems with the picture I have been painting. One is a well-established myth: the oft-told story that sociology was born out of a conservative reaction to the French Revolution. In contrast, I have described early sociology as being intellectually and socially progressive, bent on distinguishing itself as a rational science from irrational revelation. If the myth is right, sociology and religion both opposed the Enlightenment's faith that society could be reorganized along rational lines. They both emphasized the irrational aspects of human social life and the importance of traditional community bonds. Which tale is true?

The second problem has to do with my claim that the sociology of religion's core concepts are based on Western Christianity. This may be true of second-tier sociologists, but what about the early giants of the field? Émile Durkheim and Max Weber both treated religion subtly and creatively. Their work embraced cross-national and cross-cultural comparison. Though incomplete, that work was surely not culturally limited. Or was it? Let us see how.

We will start with the myth. This is the view, developed by Robert Nisbet and others, that many of sociology's core concepts stem from an early-19th-century reaction to the excesses of 18th-century rationalism.[32] Arguing that Auguste Comte, the founder of French sociology, was heavily influenced by the work of conservative ideologues like de Maistre, Bonald, and Chateaubriand, Nisbet noted that both Saint-Simon and Comte were strong in their praise of what Comte called "the retrograde school" . . . [who], Comte tells us, . . . were the first in Europe to appreciate the true nature of the crisis that was overwhelming Western Society.[33]

That crisis, wrote Nisbet, was an outgrowth of the Enlightenment's emphasis on individualism. He cited Comte's early *Essays* and their aversion to the basic principles of

popular sovereignty, equality, individual liberty, and [opposition to] the whole negative view of family, religion, local community, and intermediate associations which had been so much a part of the writings of the philosophes and of the enactments of Revolutionary legislators.[34]

This view, he claimed, shaped Comte's later approach to social life. Where the Enlightenment highlighted individualism and rationality, Bonald and de Maistre praised community and custom. Comte planned sociology to be the science of just these factors; indeed, community and custom remain central sociological concepts to this day.

Nisbet admitted, however, that though the young Comte of the *Essays* was still Catholic and Royalist, the mature, sociological Comte had long ago left his childhood faith. Unlike those whom he still praised as his influences, Comte did not advocate a return to an imagined medieval order. "Comte, recognizing the identical crisis [as de Maistre, Bonald, etc.] advocates instead a new body of intellectual-spiritual principles— those of Positivism." He praised both Enlightenment and Revolution for clearing away (in Nisbet's words) "the moribund Catholic-feudal system." And Comte insisted

that the second of his two great divisions of sociology, "social dynamics" owes just as much to such Enlightenment minds as Turgot and Condorcet as "social statics" owes to the postrevolutionary conservatives such as Bonald.[35]

Nisbet argued, however, that on balance the conservative strand proved more substantial than liberalism in dictating sociology's future direction. He cited the work of Frederick Le Play, "one of the most neglected sociological minds of the nineteenth century." Le Play's 1855 study *European Workers*, wrote Nisbet, "is hardly more than a detailed, empirically broadened fulfillment of ideas contained in Bonald's" essays.[36] Nisbet even portrayed Alexis de Tocqueville as a conservative, for "his obsession with equality and its potentially destructive effect on liberty," for his distrust of the centralized state, and for his

> veneration for family, local community, regionalism, division of political power, religion as the necessary basis of society, complete autonomy of religion from the state, and, far from least, veneration for profuse, voluntary, intermediate associations.[37]

The obvious objection, of course, is that de Tocqueville was a political liberal and a defender of a moderate Republicanism. Indeed, he played a prominent liberal role on the 1848 Constitutional Commission. Nisbet noted this but claimed that sociology's root concern with individualism versus "the conservative recognition of the priority of authority, community, and hierarchy to any genuinely free society" puts de Tocqueville in the conservative camp.[38]

I think those charges are misplaced. Nisbet's portrayal may have seemed plausible in 1960s and 1970s America, where hippie individualism and the "Me Decade" pitted individualism and authority against each other. Yes, America's conservatives opposed the New Deal, the Great Society, and other programs to help the poor. They did so in part because these programs centralized state power, which those conservatives feared. But reading that concern back onto early-19th-century 'conservatism' is anachronistic. It mischaracterizes the debate out of which sociology grew.

In fact, the Bourbon monarchy was itself centralized. It had Church support, such that the state and religion were the twin pillars of hierarchy. Nineteenth-century French reactionaries did indeed want to return France to an earlier era, but that era was not the small-town, community-oriented, family-friendly utopia that American 20th-century conservatives revered. The French monarchists were not Burkians, for Edmund Burke opposed the French Revolution on liberal grounds.[39] Sociology's founders were not apologists for the *ancien régime*. They saw the problems that revolution had brought, but they did not produce a conser-

vative philosophy. Indeed, they produced a science of society—exactly
what the Enlightenment had hoped.

I am by no means alone in this interpretation. Raymond Aron's analysis of early sociology, in his essay "The Sociologists and the Revolution
of 1848," came to strikingly different conclusions than Nisbet about early
sociology's supposed 'conservatism'. He wrote:

> August Comte was an almost unqualified admirer of modern society,
> which he called industrial, because this society would be peaceful and
> Comtist or, if you prefer, posititivist. In the eyes of the political school
> [de Tocqueville], modern society is a democratic one . . . one society
> among others . . . [although] not the ultimate fulfillment of human
> destiny.[40]

This sounds much more Republican than conservative, at least when
'conservative' is read in 19th-century terms. Nisbet has, I think, misread
the 19th-century French 'conservatives' as akin to the American 'conservatives' of his own day. Perhaps he projected his own distaste for 1960s
expressive individualism onto sociology's founders.

A central issue here is how one is to treat intellectual influences when
evaluating a sociologist's theories. As Anthony Giddens argued in his
own critique of the 'conservative sociology' myth,

> We may, and ordinarily we must, distinguish between the intellectual an-
> tecedents of a man's thought, the traditions he draws upon in forming his
> views, and the intellectual content of his work, what he makes of the ideas
> he takes from the tradition.[41]

Giddens argued that all social thinkers draw from previous theories;
however, they reconfigure them. Comte certainly drew on Bonald, de
Maistre, and so on, but he crafted a far different view of the world than
they. Durkheim in turn drew on Comte but, in Giddens's view, he

> explicitly rejected the basic features of [Comte's] model; it was Comte's
> methodological writing, as manifest in the *Positive Philosophy*, which
> particularly influenced him (together with the more proximate influ-
> ence of Boutroux). In evaluating and rejecting what he saw as the

reactionary implications of the Comtean hierocratic model, Durkheim drew upon elements of the overlapping, yet distinctively different analysis of the emergent society of the future seen by Comte's erstwhile mentor, Saint-Simon (while seeking to effect a critique of the latter also).[42]

I think the myth of sociology's conservative origins should not distract us. None of the early sociologists, and certainly not Comte, de Tocqueville, and Durkheim, based their sociological work on Christian ideas. Quite the contrary. Comte clearly distinguished his scientific approach from religion, in precisely the way that Vásquez claimed. De Tocqueville recognized religion's social utility, particularly in America (which lacked a hegemonic church), but his sociology was similarly opposed to religious worldviews. Durkheim, too—but here we need to take a closer look.

Et Tu, Émile?

It is no exaggeration to say that Émile Durkheim's *The Elementary Forms of the Religious Life* retains considerable influence some hundred-plus years after its publication.[43] Not only is it a magisterial treatment of religion's origin, it put forth a distinct way of defining religions that still resonates with scholars, and it drew into a single theory religious practices from across history and around the world. Though based on what we now regard as outmoded fieldwork and hobbled by a social evolutionism that most scholars now reject, few volumes can match this one for brilliance and depth. How does *The Elementary Forms* stand up to my criticism?

On the one hand, it stands up rather well. Remember my students' rough-and-ready definition of religion—as focused on beliefs, as emphasizing moral rules, and as being controlled by formal religious organizations? Each of these, I argued, makes sense for the Western Christianity of the last few centuries, but not for religion in other times and places. What did Durkheim have to say about these matters?

Clearly, Durkheim thought that religious beliefs were part of the picture but he did not define religion by them. He criticized reducing religion to beliefs, particularly beliefs in supernatural beings, no matter how broadly defined. He pointed out that many religions lack formal deities; this was a direct challenge to Edward Tylor's claim that religion always involved a belief in spiritual beings. He argued at length that Buddhism does not bother itself with deities; instead, pure "Buddhism of the South" centers on the Four Noble Truths and on the individual's efforts to attain salvation.[44]

That's not all. Against Herbert Spencer's broader contention that religions "consist essentially in 'the belief in the omnipresence of something which is inscrutable,'" and Max Müller's parallel claim that religion is "a struggle to conceive the inconceivable, to utter the unutterable, a longing after the Infinite," Durkheim argued that the concern with mystery and the ineffable varies from religion to religion and from age to age; it is thus poor ground on which to raise a universal definition. Moreover, "it is certain that this idea does not appear until late in the history of religions." Beliefs, even in amorphous 'higher powers', were for him only part of the picture.[45]

Morality was more central to Durkheim's definition, but not in the way that my students imagine. For Americans, 'morality' has to do with rules about how one should and should not act. It focuses on individual choices of right and wrong. The French "la morale," on the other hand, is just as much about inculcating the proper spirit as it is about guiding proper actions. It combines the two English words "moral" and "morale" into one concept. It includes action and judgment, but it also includes aspects of worldview and the sense of purpose that undergirds a well-shaped human life.

"La morale" is moreover a communal term, not primarily an individual one. One speaks (in French) of "la communauté morale" (the moral community), which does not mean a community that tells people how they should behave. Instead, a communauté morale is a community that is held together by a shared culture. This includes shared ideas about proper behavior, shared ideas about the nature of the world, and shared practices that unite the community's daily lives. Religions are, for Durkheim, excellent examples of such moral communities. For him, that meant far more than my students' claim that religions are about rules.

About the importance of churches, on the other hand, there is no question: Durkheim saw social organizations as central to the religious process. These organizations could take various forms and did so depending on a given society's evolutionary level. Durkheim noted that modern society is divided into functionally differentiated institutions, of which religion is one. These institutions are embodied in formal organizations: schools for education, police departments, courts, and prisons for criminal justice, and churches for the sphere we are considering. 'Primitive' societies, on the other hand—and Durkheim did use this now almost tabooed term—carry out the various life-functions as a 'committee of the whole'. They do not create separate organizations, but do everything mixed together. *The Elementary Forms* was, first and foremost, a description of religion in one such society, the Arunta of central Australia. There, clans and the society as a whole carry the religious burden. But religion there is still a social, not an individual, matter.

This was, in fact, Durkheim's ground for distinguishing religion from magic. For him, unlike for Frazer and for Malinowski, the difference was not that magicians tried to manipulate the world while religious people beg the aid of higher powers. It was instead that religions always involve organized groups, while magic can be an individual matter. As he put it:

> There is no church of magic. Between the magician and the individuals who consult him [and] between these individuals themselves, there are no lasting bonds which make them members of the same moral community, comparable to that formed by the believers in the same god or the observers of the same cult. The magician has a clientele and not a Church.[46]

Durkheim thus agreed with my students: religions happen in particular, organized places.

Not all social organizations are religions, however. Religions are typified by a specific focus: on things that are 'sacred' as opposed to things that are 'profane'.

> The real characteristic of religious phenomena is that they always suppose a bipartite division of the whole universe, known and knowable, into two classes which embrace all that exists, but which radically exclude one another. Sacred things are those which [religious] interdictions protect and

isolate; profane things [are] those to which these interdictions are applied and which must remain at a distance from the first.[47]

Durkheim thus put taboo at the center of the religious enterprise. It separates sacred things from everything else and specifies how we are supposed to act toward each of them. Religious beliefs are secondary, in that they provide the images that allow people to express ideas about the sacred. Yet it is the sacred itself that makes religion possible. The same is true of religious rules: for Durkheim these "prescribe how a man should comport himself in the presence of these sacred objects."[48] They are not primarily codes for everyday behavior. The sacred/profane division is central to Durkheim's sociology of religion.

We need to be a bit careful about that word "profane" here. Durkheim did not mean profanity, in the current sense of nasty language. Nor did he think that "the profane" needed to be something bad. Instead, he used the word to indicate everyday things as distinguished from "sacred" things that were set apart. Eating an ordinary lunch is a profane event, no matter what the state of one's table manners. Eating a communion wafer in the context of a Mass is, for Catholics, sacred. The valence is on the sacred side, not on the other.

Religion for Durkheim thus always involves sacred things that are set apart from ordinary life. It involves a perception of duality at the heart of the world—one pole of that duality having to do with the sacred and the other having to do with everything else. And it involves a community that recognizes and maintains this division. Different communities will treat different things as sacred, and they will decry any perceived violation of that sacrality. To take a contemporary and somewhat shocking example, Andres Serrano's 1987 photograph *Piss Christ*, which depicted a crucifix floating in a pool of urine, violated many Christians' sense of the sacred. The extreme outbursts against it, however, violated other people's sense of the sacredness of art, free speech, and the like. These competing senses of the sacred were carried by different communities. Each regarded the others' thoughts and actions as a violation of ultimate values. Durkheim would not at all have been surprised.

So how did Durkheim define religion? Here is his definition in French, followed by Joseph Swann's English translation:

> *Une religion est un système solidaire de croyances et de pratiques relatives à des chose sacrées, c'est-à-dire séparés, interdites, croyances et pratiques qui unissent en une même communauté morale, appelée Église, tous ceax qui y adhèrent.*

> A religion is a unified system of beliefs and practices relative to sacred things, that is to say, things set apart and forbidden—beliefs and practices which unite into one single moral community called a Church all those who adhere to them.[49]

Durkheim thought that both parts of this definition were crucial: the distinction between sacred and profane and the presence of a moral community. The actual content of the religious beliefs and practices was irrelevant, as was the identity of the particular community that supported them. He thus defined religion by what it accomplishes: the separation of the sacred from the profane and the unification of the moral community for which it does so. Is not this definition broad enough to escape Euro-American cultural bounds?

Yes . . . but. The problem is that Durkheim set his analysis firmly within an evolutionary framework that ranked societies from 'primitive' to 'modern'. He wrote about Arunta totemism because he thought it was the earliest religion, from which all others descended. Tracing religion to the belief in spirits—'animism'—or to a sense of awe before nature—'naturism'—would not do, he wrote. The first reduces religion to a system of hallucinations and the second fails to explain how the sacred/profane distinction began. Totemism does explain that distinction, so it (or something like it) must have come first. All other religions, from then to the present, inherited its sense that some things are sacred or set apart. *In principio finis.* At least, that was his presumption.[50]

We need not review how Durkheim demonstrated that totemic religion made possible the sacred/profane divide, except to say that it was social, experiential, and just as much of a category mistake as the animism he criticized. In his portrayal, the Arunta feel a "collective effervescence"—the sense of excitement that special social gatherings produce. They mistakenly attribute it to the presence of their clan totem, which they carry much like a flag. They thus feel themselves to be in the presence of something special, something holy; here the idea of 'the sacred' is born.

Yet, wrote Durkheim, that mistake is actually no mistake at all. The flag-like totem *does* create the clan's experience of being in the presence of something special, because in fact they are. They are in the presence of *the group itself*. The collective feeling that comes from group ritual is experienced as something special, something set apart. It does not just change people's beliefs; it changes their lives.

Durkheim thought that modern rituals did the same. In his words:

> The cult [ritual] is not simply a system of signs by which the faith is outwardly translated; it is a collection of the means by which this is created and recreated periodically. Whether it consists in material acts or mental operations, it is always this which is efficacious.[51]

Put otherwise, religion accomplishes something for its members and it does so by shifting their experiences. We shall see in Chapter Seven an entirely different and more plausible way of arriving at this conclusion.

So what's the problem? By setting 'primitive' totemism at one end of human history, Durkheim set early-20th-century industrial Europe at the other. Though not a survival-of-the-fittest evolutionist like Herbert Spencer, he, too, arrayed human societies on a line of development. His ranking depended on the level to which they had developed their social division of labor. Simple societies like the Arunta had a low division of labor; complex societies like France had a high one. Durkheim did not think one was more valuable than the other. He did, however, think that they had different strengths and weaknesses. Their religions also differed. He was not saying that reactionary 19th-century Catholicism was 'primitive'. But he was saying that religion changes its form as society evolves, and that authoritarian Catholicism was appropriate to past societies, not to the present. The transition to a possibly religionless future was never far from his mind.[52]

We get hints of this in *The Elementary Forms*. Writing of his own time, he noted that "There still remain those contemporary aspirations towards a religion which would consist entirely in internal and subjective states, and which would be constructed freely by each of us."[53] This individualized religion violated his insistence that religions require groups; he thus explicitly left it out of his definition of religion. Yet he returned to it at book's end, writing:

> If we find a little difficulty today in imagining what these feasts and ceremonies of the future could consist in, it is because we are going through a stage of transition and moral mediocrity. The great things of the past which filled our fathers with enthusiasm do not excite the same ardor in us. . . . The old gods are growing old or already dead, and others are not yet born.[54]

He hoped for revival, but he did not predict it. For him, science cannot see the future. Throughout his career, Durkheim worried that contemporary society was losing the social and moral glue that had held together societies of the past.[55] No wonder that his work was so easily assimilated to the secularizationists' cause.

That, of course, is the point. For all his genius, Durkheim still thought that Europe was at the leading edge of world history. Studying other societies was important, but only as grist for a European intellectual mill. He looked to Arunta social processes so that he could better understand religion in all times and places. He did not look to the Arunta for insights, either about their religion or about the religions of his day.

Mary Douglas, with her typical brilliance, hit the nail squarely:

> [For Durkheim], primitive groups are organized by similarities; their members are committed to a common symbolic life. We by contrast are diversified individuals, united by exchange of specialised services. . . . [Primitives'] knowledge of the world [was] unanchored to any fixed material points, and [was] secured only by the stability of the social relations which generated it and which it legitimised. . . . [On the other side stands] objective scientific truth, itself the product of our own kind of society, with its scope for individual diversity of thought. . . . [For Durkheim] the social construction of reality applied fully to them, the primitives, and only partially to us.[56]

Durkheim ultimately thought that only the modern West could understand the rest of the world.

Weber versus the Traditional World

What about Max Weber, the other giant of classical sociology? Is his sociology of religion as Eurocentric as are the others? He was certainly important to the subdiscipline's development. His *Protestant Ethic and the Spirit of Capitalism* helped shape our approach to religions. His exploration of the religions of China, India, and ancient Judaism are still influential, though seldom read. His contribution to the theory of sectarian groups helped launch a sociological subfield. And his sense of the importance of religious worldviews for shaping human actions gave the sociology of religion some of its most seminal insights. Not bad, for someone who famously considered himself "unmusical religiously"!

Perhaps he was not so tone deaf. William Swatos and Peter Kivisto discovered that this phrase is almost always taken out of context. The full passage, from a 1909 letter from Weber to Ferdinand Tönnies, reads,

> It is true that I am absolutely unmusical religiously and have no need or ability to erect any psychic edifices of a religious character within. But a thorough self-examination has told me that I am neither antireligious nor irreligious.

Swatos and Kivisto usefully weigh the extent to which Weber can be seen as a Christian sociologist, as were some American sociologists of his period. They argue that some of his sociological concerns reflect his liberal Protestant upbringing. They show how his background affected his choice of topics, especially his emphasis on duty and vocation. They see him as being a semi-secularized Lutheran, overtly free of his tradition but still colored by it.[57]

This is not, however, the particular rabbit hole that we need to explore. For the purposes of this study, the issue is not whether Weber was or was not a Christian, even if a partially secularized one. Nor does his religious background matter to our argument. The question is, are Weber's core concepts so shaped by his Western milieu that they fail to see important parts of religious life? To make sure that we explore this cleanly, we need to set Weber's sociology of religion aside for a moment and take up another part of his *oeuvre*: his sociology of authority. Here one finds an unconscious Eurocentrism that prevented Weber from see-ing religions clearly. His presuppositions prevented him from seeing the nuances of not just other societies, but of his own.

Every sociologist is familiar with Weber's work on authority. He pro-posed three models of why people grant others decision-making power over their lives. Traditional, rational-legal, and charismatic authority, for him, represent distinct types of motives for following others. People can obey a leader because they have always done so. They can obey because Reason (or rational law) tells them to do so. Or they can obey because that leader's personal qualities attract their allegiance. Weber called these "ideal-types." They are 'ideal' because they exist nowhere in actual social life; real cases are always combinations. But they out-line the logical possibilities, so they make analyzing actual cases much easier.[58]

Ancient China, for example, was for Weber a "patrimonial" and "Cae-saropapist" state in which religious and secular traditions supported the emperor's charisma.[59] Modern Europe is dominated by rational-legal thinking, mixed with a certain amount of tradition. Other social settings have seen other combinations. For him, the job of the sociologist is to sort out the details of any particular situation, using the ideal types as analytic lenses that deepen our understanding.

These types serve two functions. First, each type is logically distinct from the others. An appeal to tradition is fundamentally different than an appeal to reason. Following someone because of her or his personal charisma can likewise not be reduced to the other two. If a sociologist knows what possibilities can be present, then she or he can determine which in fact are operating at any given time. Ideal-types are thus tools that make social analysis possible.[60]

Second, Weber argued that each of the types carries with it an inter-nal logic that pushes people in predictable directions. The problem of political succession, for example, forces charismatic authority to evolve into one of the other two forms. Charismatic authority has a fundamen-tal problem: charismatic leaders die and their successors seldom inherit their full personal magic. How can one maintain charismatic authority in the face of inevitable death? One way is to follow the charismatic lead-er's heir, on whom the leader bestows her or his charisma. This trans-fer of charisma, however, never works completely. It devolves, Weber said, into either the charisma of an office—for example, the charismatic mantle that a Pope assumes on his election. Or it devolves into tradition: people follow the son or daughter of the leader, then her or his son or daughter, etc. In former times, this produced hereditary kingship. People followed their rulers by tradition, no matter if those rulers were weak, corrupt, or even insane.

Weber was particularly interested in another path, however: the path by which traditional authority is replaced by rational-legal authority. He noted that modern countries pride themselves on following "the rule of law." To use a contemporary example, George W. Bush became the U.S. president in 2001 not because he was a great person or the son of a former president, but because the Supreme Court decided to stop the vote count in Florida. As his opponent Al Gore put it, that decision was the law, which everyone had to follow. Anything else would produce chaos. Weber saw an increasing reliance on rational-legal authority in the modern world. His analysis of what he called the "Protestant ethic" showed how rationality replaced tradition in economics. The growth of modern bureaucracies had different sources, but it was part of the same trend.[61]

The problem is that Weber did not develop all of his ideal-types equally well. Though his image of rational-legal authority is quite clear, he presented "traditional authority" as a form of social inertia. He based it on "traditional action," which in his words "is very often a matter of almost automatic reaction to habitual stimuli, which guide behavior on a course which has been repeatedly followed." For example, the Chinese literati were 'traditional' because as a class they based their lives on a knowledge of ancient texts and eschewed formally rational rule for a substantive justice modeled on the past. True, their traditionalism gained them a charisma in the eyes of the common people that contributed to their social position. Yet Weber thought that both the traditional and the charismatic aspects of their authority prevented China from developing a modern rational governing system. (He could not, of course, foresee the later Communist-led revolution and the ruthlessness with which the Communist regime attempted to push China into the modern world.)[62]

Yet is 'tradition' just inertia? The central thrust of Weber's sociology was to understand the emergence and shape of the society of his day. He asked what forms of subjective action distinguished the modern world from its predecessors. Clearly, he saw the West increasingly typified by disembodied, instrumental Reason, notably goal-oriented rationality. He traced this to Protestant spiritual individualism: for Weber, Puritan value-rationality (the pursuit of holiness by rationally monitoring one own actions) gradually transformed itself into secular goal-rationality (the pursuit of wealth for its own sake). That in turn shaped the rationalistic "iron cage" within which modern life finds itself imprisoned.[63] As he put it at the end of *The Protestant Ethic*,

> The Puritan wanted to work in a calling; we are forced to do so. For when asceticism was carried out of monastic cells into everyday life, and began to dominate worldly morality, it did its part in building the tremendous cosmos of the modern economic order. This order is now bound to the technical and economic conditions of machine production which today determine the lives of all the individuals who are born into this mechanism.[64]

Weber knew quite well that the traditional world was familiar with rational motives, oriented toward both goals and values. His distillation of 'tradition' as a type, however, required him to strip out those rational elements, reducing tradition to unthinking habit. Only thus could he isolate the goal-oriented rationality that he saw as the key driver of modern life. In short, he constructed his ideal-types by working backward. Real traditional societies demonstrate mixed motivations, but that is true of all societies. Creating an ideal-typical 'reason' required him to impoverish 'tradition'. Only thus could he show the historical shift from one to the other. Yes, his ideal-types make logical sense, but only if they are seen from a modern point of view.

Edward Shils noted this problem in 1981 book *Tradition*. Weber, he argued, presented tradition as a negative rather than a positive quality. It is an absence, not a presence. It is mere continuity, not positive action. In short, it supports a worldview that portrays the modern West as active, rational, and the leading edge of world history. This is ethnocentric to the core.[65]

Yet what if we do not construct our ideal-types from that standpoint? What if we treat all of our types as positive? Can we create logical distinctions that are not so ethnocentric? A short visit to the field of theoretical ethics brings us an answer.

H. Richard Niebuhr distinguished between three ideal-types of ethics, which correspond to three of the four types of subjective social action that were the foundation of Weber's action-schema. Two of these correspond to Weber's well-developed rational types. Utilitarian ethics are concerned with goal-rational action: action that is designed to bring about some desired end. Deontological or rule-based ethics are concerned with value-rational action: action designed to support some absolute rule or value.[66]

As Niebuhr noted in his critique of utilitarian and rule-based ethics, both goal-rational and value-rational action depend on similarly isolated images of the self. He called these the "man-as-maker" and "man-as-citizen." In his view, both the instrumentalist and the law-follower are essentially separate from the society around them. Niebuhr thought people did act like that, but he also thought there were other possibilities. He proposed a third picture that starts with a social notion of the self: "man-the-answerer" set in a web of social relations. Where the goal-oriented self thinks of personal ends and the value-oriented self thinks of personal values or rules, "man-the-answerer" starts with his or her relationships and responsibilities. He illustrated this with the Hebrew prophet Isaiah:

> when Isaiah counsels his people, he does not remind them of the law they are required to obey nor yet of the goal toward which they are directed but calls to their attention the intentions of God present in hiddenness in the actions of Israel's enemies.[67]

In the story, Isaiah acts from his sense of responsibility to God and to his people. He calls each to its Covenant with the other. His ethics are thus social: we are all in relationship with other beings, to whom we have ties and responsibilities. This relationship generates its own ethical motives. These cannot be reduced to either goal-rational or value-rational action. They are not, however, mere negative inertia. They are a positive ideal-type.

The contrast between Isaiah and the stories of two later Christian divines, Augustine and Luther, is striking. Augustine described in his

Confessions how he found God individually, alone in his garden, as he surrendered his personal will. Luther's defining moment was his resistance to his superiors, standing alone with his conscience because he could "do no other." In these two normative images, Christians encounter God alone and call each believer to personal salvation. Individualism thus becomes a theological imperative. The ideal Christian thus resists the world and the blandishments of friends, choosing the road less traveled.[68]

The story of Isaiah also presents an individual before God, but this individual is not alone. Isaiah spoke for and to a community on behalf of a communal relationship. Yes, his visions came to him alone. Yet through him they served his community. He was no isolated individual and his was not an individual path. His story is typical of the Hebrew prophets: they consistently called their people to account for their disobedience to God and their violation of their Covenant. Yet they also stood with the people and argued with God on their behalf, when the people were found wanting.

Weber's work is clearly filled with Augustinian and Lutheran themes, yet it misses Isaiah's connection to the Hebrew people. His *Ancient Judaism* correctly noted the lack of support Israel gave to its prophets, but in his concern to trace the possible emergence of ethical rationalism, he neglected both the content and the context of these prophets' message. They sought to reestablish the tie between God and the Hebrew people. They were supremely 'traditional', not because they followed accepted patterns but because they thought in terms of communal relationships. Not isolated selves, they were nested in a community even as they lambasted that community's failings.[69]

Seen positively rather than as a foil for modernity, tradition is thus much deeper than Weber's sense of it being "almost automatic." One follows traditional authorities, for example, not out of inertia but because one has an ongoing relationship with those authorities that one is not willing to break for either goal- or value-rational reasons. Likewise a traditional leader acts out of an established, ongoing relationship with followers, not because of mindless habit but because these social ties establish the very selves that relate with one another. This is the very "man-the-answerer" that Niebuhr presented as a third ethical form.

Seeing "traditional action" and "traditional authority" as relational rather than as just oriented to the past undercuts many applications of the Weberian authority scheme to religions. Thomas O'Dea's classic "dilemmas" of religious institutionalization are good examples. Each of O'Dea's dilemmas arises from the problem of moving from a "charismatic" to an "institutionalized" form of religion, in which the so-called problem is how to keep members connected once the charismatic leader is gone. The dilemma of "mixed motivation," for example, imagines that each individual is separate from others; the problem is how to coordinate a movement in which people no longer share the same ends. The "symbolic dilemma" sees a natural urge in people to objectify and rationalize meaning-systems and to manipulate group symbols for individual purposes.[70]

Yet were individuals enmeshed in a web of traditional relationships (in Niebuhr's, not Weber's terms), none of these dilemmas would prove biting. People's ties would hold a religion together, not the congruence of their desires nor the identity of their beliefs. Symbols might become objectified yet the religion could prosper, because community, not symbolism, is the core of their common faith. Were tradition central, sociality and belief would not be at odds with one another, and we would not doubt people's religiosity when they express it through their social ties rather than through their ideas.

Weber saw the self as rational and individualized. He began with a self for whom society and social relations are a problem, not something to be taken for granted. For him, social ties certainly did not create the self nor were they central to it. Such radical individualism typifies much Western philosophy and—as the examples of Augustine and Luther show—much Christianity. Despite his cross-cultural sophistication, Weber's approach is thus a Western view, not something culturally universal. By presuming social disconnectedness, his sociology of authority is tied to Western-style modernity. When sociologists of religion use it as a central explanatory device, they bias and limit their understanding.[71]

Was not Niebuhr also Western, and a Christian theologian besides? Yes, but that makes no difference. Individualized, rationalized, Western-style modernity is normative for Weber; for Niebuhr it is not. Ethnocentrism comes from one's intellectual blinders, not from one's genes.

* * *

Why do history and culture matter? What is the point of recounting sociology's origins as an intellectual discipline? The short answer is that a discipline's past shapes its present. This is not a matter of sociologists affirming Comte's "law of the three stages," Durkheim's claim that 'primitive' peoples' cosmologies reflect their social structures, or Weber's claim that Western music is more rational than are the musics of other civilizations.[72] Such empirical claims are easily falsified and discarded.

Sociology's origins, however, continue to shape its core concerns. Sociologists still try to understand social change, though today's changes are different from those of sociology's founding era. They still try to understand what holds societies together and what tears them apart. They still explore the ideologies that shape people's actions. Sociology has added new questions, but these old ones linger. They are part of our identity as a discipline. They are part of what distinguishes our discipline from others.

Sociology's struggle to create itself as the 'science of society' happened in a particular historical time and place. Religion mattered to that era, so sociologists had to deal with it. Indeed, a specific image of religion mattered then, and that was the image with which sociologists had to wrestle. This is what I have called sociology's default view.

Like all views, the default view focuses on some aspects of religions and fails to focus on others. It does a good job of understanding formal religious organizations. It does a poorer job of understanding religion that takes other forms. It does a good job of tracking people's religious beliefs. It does a poorer job of understanding people's religious practices. It recognizes the importance of religious symbols. It too often fails to recognize the importance of religious experiences. It typically treats religion as a separate institutional sphere, which prevents it from easily seeing religions' connections with other spheres: race, ethnicity, inequality, war, peace, and so on.

The point is not that the sociologists of religion do not investigate such topics. They do. The point is that the historical-cultural context of sociology's birth has made such investigations marginal to the discipline, just as sociology's traditional male-centeredness has prevented it from seeing the complexity of women's lives.

What does this marginalization keep us from understanding? What would we see, were we to take off the blinders that hide these topics from our view? What would sociology understand better about religion, had it emerged from a different historical-cultural context? The next six chapters will explore three such contexts, to show how each would create a sociology of religion that focuses on a different aspect of the religious world.

Adkins Family House God. Photograph by J. Spickard, 2016.

3

To China

A Confucian Alternative

I never knew my grandfather. He died in 1935, when my mother was sixteen. He was a presence in our house, though, both because she had adored him and because some of the things he left her were a prominent part of our decor. He had lived in China after the Boxer Rebellion, working as a medical missionary near Swatow on the coast northeast of Canton. His first wife and infant child died shortly after their arrival—my mother said "in a plague." His sister came to join him for the six years he remained in charge of the Jieyang hospital. He brought home with him a carved Chinese chest and a bunch of artifacts. I remember a brass lock, foot-binding shoes, a mandarin's silk cloak, and some brush paintings. There may have been more, but most are now scattered.[1]

There was also a carved figure that my mother called a "house god," six inches high (its photo opens this chapter). It stood on our mantel, surveying the household, holding its palms together in blessing. I knew as a young boy that it was more important than the other bits of memory. My mother said it was connected to 'ancestor worship', which the Chinese did and we did not. Yet the house god signified family, both to the Chinese and to us. For my mother, it was a memory of where she came from and of a father she had loved and lost. I heard more about his time in China than I did of her own childhood. I only later realized that our house god was her unconscious altar to him. Lynn Davidman has written movingly of the ways that we construct altars as memorials, sometimes without knowing that we are doing so. I have seen this in my own and my children's lives. It took me a long time to see it in my upbringing.[2]

What is this 'ancestor worship'? My missionary grandfather probably thought of it as superstition, as a heathen belief that our forebears become gods that need propitiation. For the Chinese, he might have said, ancestors watch over us. They set moral standards. They demand attention. Offended ancestors bring bad luck, so no good Chinese wants to anger them. He would have said that the six-inch house god was not itself sacred; it was a mere stand-in for one's lineage and for the innumerable progenitors from whom one sprang. He was not a minister, as were his father and grandfather; he thus would not have thought it his calling to convert Chinese from heathen darkness to reverence for the One True Lord. Yet he would have recognized that the Chinese attention to their ancestors had a sacred quality to it. This would have made it religion, in his eyes.

Note the conditional phrasing I have just used. I have no idea what my grandfather actually thought, as my mother did not pass his insights down to me.[3] Such ideas as these, however, were common among Americans of his generation when they thought of China and the Far East. In that era, China was no rising dragon. It was at best a doddering empire, soon (they imagined) to be swept away by the forces of progress. American Christians believed that everyone has some sort of religion, however misguided. Religion for them was a matter of belief and of relations with the supernatural, most often worship. Thus the six-inch stand-in for one's ancestors was a 'god'—or at least a god-image. Putting it on a pedestal, my mother said, symbolized the elevated position that ancestors held in the Chinese mind.

In this chapter, we will see a somewhat different way of understanding 'ancestor worship'. We can mark this by calling it 'ancestor veneration', to lose the connotations that the term 'worship' has in Western ears. Traditional Chinese attitudes toward the ancestors exhibit a relational approach to the sacred that is quite far from Western religious norms. Two other commonly noted sacred concepts, 'the mandate of Heaven' and 'ritual propriety', are similarly relational. So is the traditional Chinese notion of the self, which, though not sacred, is the point from which religious action emerges. Exploring the traditional Chinese understanding of these terms, as embodied in the *rú jiā* ('tradition of the scholars', i.e., Confucian philosophy[4]), lets us understand these concepts in a new way. Once understood, we can use them to ask what American religious life would look like to a sociologist steeped in this traditional Chinese way of thinking.

We can start our journey with the Confucian way of understanding the self.

The Self and the Ancestors

At some point in life, all people probably ask themselves "Who am I?" The modern West, however, has made this question a fetish. From teen angst and coming-of-age novels to midlife crises, self-help books, and seminars on choosing a good death, Euro-Americans seem to be absorbed by self-creation. We have made 'finding oneself' into a life-project. Our nursery schools teach children to choose their own activities, our elementary and secondary schools help children identify their natural learning styles, and Facebook hosts quizzes that tell us our best colors, how we like to interact, what city best fits our personality, and what is our ideal sport. "Everyone is different," we hear. "Every one of us is an individual." Our culture reinforces this belief in small and in large ways.[5]

Listen, for example, to how we introduce ourselves:[6]

Hi. My name is Jim Spickard. I am a professor of sociology at the University of Redlands and the current president of the International Sociological Association's Research Committee on the Sociology of Religion. I teach courses on social theory, the sociology of religion, social science research methods, homelessness, human rights, and world hunger. I've written or edited several books, most recently a collection of work by younger scholars on the transnational dynamics of several contemporary African religions. I was educated at Stanford, the New School for Social Research, and the Graduate Theological Union. I have done extended fieldwork with one of the seven hundred or so new religions founded in Japan in the 20th century and also with a radical Catholic activist commune. I've done shorter research projects with various religious and activist groups. I am an inveterate learner and traveler, having visited some fifty-two countries (a few of which no longer exist).

In other words: "I, I, I, I, I."

This is not just me. Americans may take individuality to an extreme, but Europeans also typically think of themselves as individuals, separate from other people. They, too, emphasize their persons and their personal accomplishments. As we saw in the previous chapter, this corresponds rather well to the Protestant emphasis on the individual relationship with God, though it is part of general Western Christian culture. Both Augustine and Luther encountered God alone, in their inner stillness. Christians call each believer to personal salvation. To this way of thinking, individualism is a theological imperative as well as a social one.

We even find our penchant for individualism in the Euro-American reverence for human rights. The 1948 United Nations Universal Declaration of Human Rights has gained worldwide acceptance, but its language reflects the political legacy of Locke, Hume, and Jefferson, not Confucius, Hsün Tzu, or Zhu Xi. It famously enumerates the rights due to individuals: "the right to life, liberty and security of person"; the rights "to freedom of thought, conscience and religion" and "to freedom of opinion and expression"; the rights "to social security," "to equal pay for equal work," and "to a standard of living adequate for the health and well-being of himself and of his family," among others. As the Chinese delegate to the U.N. Human Rights Commission, Peng-Chen Chang, noted at the time of its writing, this individualistic language is a Western legacy, not a universal one. (He still voted for the Declaration on pragmatic grounds.)[7]

Philosopher Henry Rosemont has argued that the Confucian view of the self is very different.[8] Confucianism, the most influential of China's many philosophical traditions, does not start with the individual, at least not as a separate entity. It sees the individual as nested in, even constituted by, a set of relationships. Following Rosemont, here is how I would introduce myself in a Confucian mode:

I am Jim Spickard, son of Donald Spickard and Mary Alice Adkins, grandson of Vernon and Mildred Spickard and of Russell and Mary Adkins. I am brother to Paul Spickard, husband to Meredith McGuire, father to Janaki and Dmitri Spickard-Keeler. My principle teachers were George Spindler, Trent Schroyer, Charles McCoy, and James McClendon.

My many students include Blaine Pope, Javier Espinoza, Whitney Washington, Maggie Smith, Aaron Olive, and Julia Pazzi.

I would go on to name my colleagues and my friends, my leaders and my followers, perhaps even those intellectuals whom I have never met but who clearly influence me: Marx, Kant, Arendt, Durkheim, Barrington Moore, Mary Douglas, and so on. I could note those whose lives have inspired me: Martin King, Howard Thurman, Dorothy Day, Jeff Dietrich. I would, in short, identify myself by my relationships. I would call out those people who have shaped me, who have made me who I am.[9]

Rosemont noted that the Confucian way of speaking does not erase my sense of self. It simply expresses it in an unaccustomed way. It points out that I am uniquely shaped by those around me. Having my particular parents made me different than I would otherwise have been. Raising children changed me. So did my first wife's death and also my subsequent remarriage; I am simply different as the result of such relationships than I would have been without them. My teachers and colleagues also shaped me, much as I shape my students (though sometimes I wish the latter happened a lot faster than it does).

Both introductions, in fact, display true things about us—specifically what each of these two cultures finds sacred. The individual is central to the modern West; thus we abhor violations of individual integrity and honor human rights. Classic Confucianism, on the other hand, saw the self as a nest of relationships and it sees those relationships as sacred themselves. One maintains them through *lǐ* 禮, the practice of ritual propriety. *Lǐ* is seen as the origin of *dé* 德, which is typically glossed as 'virtue'.[10] Maintaining the sacredness of relationships is a chief duty, not just for leaders, but for everyone.

Rosemont drew out the implications of the Confucian way of describing oneself, which is so different from the Western notion of individual autonomy:

> For the early Confucians there can be no me in isolation, to be considered abstractly: I am the totality of roles I live in relation to specific others. . . . Taken collectively, these roles weave, for each of us,

a unique pattern of personal identity, such that if some of my roles change, others will of necessity change also, literally making me a different person.

He noted that marriage made him a different person, as did becoming a father.

Again, the point is obvious, but the Confucian perspective requires us to state it in another tone of voice: my life as a teacher can only be made significant by my students, in order to *be* a friend, I must *have* a friend; my life as a husband is only made meaningful by my wife, my life as a scholar only by other scholars.[11]

Jianxiong Pan and William Lakos have separately argued that this attitude is not merely Confucian, but part of the general Chinese way of seeing things. That, however, does not undercut Rosemont's point.[12] Whether specifically Confucian or Chinese in general, the self is seen as a bundle of social relationships rather than as an isolated individual, standing separate from others. What are the implications of this kind of self for the religious life? How does a connected rather than an isolated self change religion's social side?

Let us start with 'ancestor veneration', which many scholars see as central to historic Chinese life. Kenneth Latourette stated it bluntly:

No attempt to understand the Chinese can be anything but imperfect without at least a brief description of the ritual practices concerning the departed kin, ancestor worship and ancestor veneration.[13]

The practice goes back a long way. David Keightly traced it to the earliest Chinese written records, noting that Shang dynasty (ca. 1600–1100 BCE) documents described rituals to propitiate deceased kings and their consorts. William Lakos argued that the practice goes back to the late Neolithic. No matter its origin, there seem to have been three separate sites for ordinary people's ancestor veneration throughout Chinese history: graveyards, home shrines, and the clan or lineage hall.[14]

Graveyards are easy to understand, as ritual visits to family graves are common in many cultures. *Dia de los Muertos* (November 1) in the southwestern United States, for example, is a time for Mexican Americans to hold picnics in their cemeteries and to commune with the relatives that have passed on. Lakos cited anthropologist Francis Hsu in writing that Chinese grave worship "included such actions as cleaning and repairing graves and tombs, showing reverence by doing prostrations, sharing meals with the ancestors, lighting incense, and burning paper money." Daniel Overmyer opened his survey text on Chinese religion with a vignette of the eldest son of the Liu family consulting a geomancer and an astrologer to pick the best place and time for his father's burial. Such practices have been routine throughout Chinese history.[15]

Clan or lineage halls are similarly understandable. Particularly common in southern China, where lineages were stronger than in the north, these were built to house a wooden tablet commemorating the clan founder, with dates of his birth and death. Other personal tablets were placed there to remember the founder's descendants. Most tablets celebrated the rich and the socially prominent, though they could include any ancestor more than five generations removed from the living. In Lakos's description:

> Here ceremonies and worship to the founding ancestor and all that he symbolically stood for could take place. [The hall] was the centre of rituals and often a place for political meetings, and was also used for other more worldly functions such as lineage meetings and events, schooling, and as temporary accommodation.[16]

The key practice, though, was daily veneration at the home shrine. Every house had one. Lakos described them as follows:

> Most commonly each ancestor is represented by a wooden tablet with their name and age inscribed upon it. Other information would include the time and date of the deceased person's birth as well as geomancy instructions for the burial site. Ancestor tablets are often decorated with coloured silk and arranged in a special order. Daily ritual sacrifices of food, incense, flowers and so on are placed in front of the tablets. The

tablets and other associated ritual paraphernalia constituted an altar, and "every house has an altar in its main hall" or it was "placed in such a position that it overlooked much of the life that went on there, a permanent presence watching over the doings of its descendants."[17]

Daily care of these shrines fell to women, and married women venerated their husband's ancestors, not their own. Rituals were simple. They often amounted to offering the ancestors a bit of the daily meal and a few short prayers. The ancestors were informed of special events, particularly births, deaths, and marriages. This was not temple worship, but it was more than pro forma. Indeed, until the early 20th century, the newlyweds' joint veneration at the man's family shrine was what made the marriage legal.[18]

This is, of course, a general picture; practices varied widely from place to place and from age to age. The whole complex, however, was remarkably resilient. Even Communist repression did not eradicate these folk practices. Both Lakos and Overmyer noted that ancestor veneration and traditional funerals have been revived since the Cultural Revolution (1966–1976). Overmyer suggested that East Asian nations' recent strong economic performance might have been aided by the fact that "each generation is taught to be grateful and loyal to the family tradition and to work hard to keep it going."[19]

Importantly, one's ancestors were not 'gods' in the Christian sense. Traditional Chinese religion had these, too, but the gods were neither progenitors nor did they serve just a single lineage. Ancestors were not even personal supernatural actors, set over against individual descendants. Instead they were a collective—'the ancestors'—who amounted to a compressed symbol for the family or lineage to which one belonged.[20] Rituals at the family altar reminded people that they belonged to a continuing group, with duties to each other that must be upheld. They reminded participants that they were anchored in the past and connected to the future. Venerating one's ancestors meant to remember who one was: the son or daughter of X, the grandson or granddaughter of Y, and so on. It was to house one in a nexus of related kin. Indeed, it was to give one character. One's family determined who one was, for good or for ill. Coming from a good family was supremely important, equaled only by carrying on the family honor.

The family-centered nature of character has long been a core aspect of Chinese society. Sociologist C. K. Yang told the story of a Chinese college boy accosted by a Baptist missionary and urged to repent of his sins. Yang wrote that the young man replied:

> I come of reputable ancestry, I have a good conscience, and I have always been strict about my moral responsibilities and conduct. How is it that I am full of sin?[21]

Note that he listed "reputable ancestry" first. Venerating one's ancestors brings to memory one's stream of relationships, going backward and forward in time It encourages one to live up to the full set of endowments that one has inherited from them.[22]

My brother and I understand this, though we have each had our periods of Western rebellion against family strictures. We now joke about inheriting the 'duty gene' from both our parents. Though we recognize the psychological truth of Christian warnings against temptation and we both value repentance, we are also rather resistant to the Christian notion that humans are innately sinful. Responsibility is a struggle, but it is one that our family trained us for rather well. That is, in the end, the central point of Chinese ancestor veneration. As Laktos wrote,

> In a world underpinned by the reverence towards ancestors the individual exists by virtue of his descendants, and his ancestors exist only through him. The importance of the reciprocity of kinship values may be seen very clearly in Chinese family relationships, and in the phenomena of these relationships writ-large in the politico-social realm. The sense of mutual responsibility between parents and son was central to the operation of the family as a continuing and strong unit, and conversely important for the operation of the state.[23]

The Mandate of Heaven

This brings us to our second traditional Chinese concept, the so-called 'mandate of Heaven' (*tiān ming* 天命). This idea was similarly relational, but on a political, not a familial level.

From the Shang period, China was ruled by kings whose authority depended on a traditional but evolving set of relationships with the *mín* 民: their laboring but non-slave subjects. The ruler was supposed to care for the *mín*, both because it is a virtuous thing to do and because Heaven (*tiān* 天) holds the common people in special regard. When the Zhou dynasty (1046–256 BCE)²⁴ replaced the Shang and instituted a more formal feudal system, they developed the idea that the 'mandate of Heaven' could pass from one ruler to another, depending on the ruler's virtue (*dé* 德). So long as the ruler treated the *mín* well, Heaven would smile on him. As the philosopher Hsün Tzu (Xun Zǐ or "Master Xun"; ca. 312–230 BCE) wrote during the Warring States period toward the end of Zhou rule:

> [A true king's] benevolence is the loftiest in the world, his righteousness is the loftiest in the world, his authority is the loftiest in the world. Since his benevolence is the loftiest in the world, there is no one in the world who does not draw close to him. Since his righteousness is the loftiest in the world, there is no one who does not respect him. Since his authority is the loftiest in the world, there is no one who dares to oppose him. He gains victory without battle and acquires territory without attack. The whole world is won over to him. This is the way of one who understands how to be a king.²⁵

Virtuous rulership is rewarded with success: the 'mandate of Heaven' falls on the ruler who maintains his righteousness.

According to Mencius (Mèng Zǐ or "Master Meng"; ca. 372–289 BCE) that mandate also falls *from* the ruler who does evil. Mencius famously developed what A. T. Nuyen has called the "liberal interpretation" of *tiān míng*.²⁶ Where both Confucius and Mencius taught that a legitimate ruler is someone who has Heaven's blessing and a deposed ruler is someone who has lost it, only Mencius explicitly argued for the people's right to revolt against an unrighteous superior. Passage 1B:8 in the *Book of Mencius* reads:

> King Hsüan of Ch'i asked, "Was it a fact that T'ang banished King Chieh and that King Wen punished King Chou?" Mencius replied, "Yes, according to records." The King said, "Is it [thus] all right for a minister to mur-

der his king?" Mencius said, "He who injures humanity is a bandit. He who injures righteousness is a destructive person. Such a person is a mere fellow. I have heard of killing a mere fellow Chou, but I have not heard of murdering [him as] the ruler."[27]

In this view, a ruler who abuses his rule has forfeited his kingship and should be overthrown.

The central concept here is *dé* 德. This is usually translated as 'virtue', and I shall mostly follow that practice, but its true meaning is much deeper than how Westerners use that term. Henry Rosemont wrote: "*Dé* approximates 'dharma' in denoting what we can do and be if we realize (i.e., make real) the full potential of our concrete physical, psychological, and cognitive endowments."[28] In other words, a person exhibits *dé* if she or he is living up to her or his full positive potential. This potential depends not just on the person's innate skills and not just on circumstances, but also on the relationships that the person has with others. *Dé* is as relational as is the Confucian notion of the self. We can call this 'virtue', but it is virtue of a particularly social kind.

A ruler must be virtuous and benevolent toward his people to maintain Heaven's favor. Whether one follows the 'liberal' interpretation, in which the people enforce this virtue, or the what Nuyen calls "the divine command theory," in which the people must wait for Heaven itself to right wrongs, exhibiting *dé* was a matter of treating one's subjects appropriately. There is no talk here of the people's rights sct against the ruler's power. Rulership requires reciprocity. The ruler and the ruled have obligations to one another, which they must each carry out. The ruler actualized *dé* by treating his subjects properly; the subjects then remained loyal to the ruler.

As Chung-ying Cheng put it: "*Dé* is not the will of God but the ability to hold on to rule by following the advice of one's ancestors." Cheng quoted the *Book of Zhou*, one of the ancient texts: "Heaven sees through the seeing of people, Heaven hears through the hearing of people."[29]

Just as 'ancestor worship' is not like Western worship, the early Chinese notion of 'Heaven' is not like the Christian 'God' and the 'mandate of Heaven' is not like the Western notion of "following the will of God." To Westerners, God is personal and active. Traditional Chinese Heaven is not active in the same way. Benjamin Schwartz described this difference as follows:

> The different aspects of Heaven [active and impersonal] were to serve the purpose of laying out an ethical goal, i.e. the gap between what is and what ought to be, to be implemented by the humans. Often, in religion, such as the Hebrew Bible, such a gap is illustrated as the gap between the divine legislator and humans, but in the Chinese case, it is presented as an order that ought to be rooted immanently in the sacred biological ties of the family. Although Heaven is the "emanator" rather than "legislator" of the normative order it must nevertheless be deeply concerned with the actualization of the order. Heaven throws its support to the party that seems likely to actualize that order in society in the form of a mandate.[30]

As a further point of contrast, the Judeo-Christian God is not always ethical: think, for example, of the genocides in the *Book of Judges*. The Chinese Heaven, on the other hand, is supremely ethical; *tiān míng* enforces *dé*, which involves the proper care of the community and is meaningless outside of that communal context. No Christian would say that God is meaningless outside of the community of believers, but for traditional Chinese, this anti-individualism is the normal state of affairs.

Also note the continuity in Chinese thought between the human and the divine. Rulers who possess Heaven's mandate succeed, those who do not, fail; in either case it is *human* success or failure that is at stake. In traditional Chinese thinking, virtue brings reward, so the ruler can, in theory, control his success by actualizing *dé* in his relations with his subjects. True, the Hebrew prophets also thought that following God's will would bring worldly political success, but in their image, God was far more inscrutable and unpredictable than was the Chinese Heaven. For the traditional Chinese, the ruler and Heaven were alike. Both were far above the people but were also responsible for them. Both addressed them collectively, not individually. Heaven was more powerful than the Emperor but less active in ordinary affairs.

One finds this same continuity in the veneration of one's ancestors. One venerates one's ancestors in the present, expecting to be venerated in turn after death. In both cases this continuity regularizes human-divine interaction. It also socializes these interactions by placing them in the same conceptual framework as human-human relationships. To each relationship there is a proper *lǐ* 禮, a proper ritualized reciprocal propriety. To each there is a proper *dé* 德: a proper virtue. For each there is a proper set of mutual responsibilities. In traditional Chinese thought, the ancestors were a part of human society, not of another realm.

In short, both 'ancestor veneration' and 'the mandate of Heaven' emphasize the relationships that stand at the center of social life. 'Ancestor veneration' emphasizes the connection between family and self; rituals at the graveyard and the home shrine acknowledge this, affirming that one is shaped by one's forebears and that one shapes one's descendants in turn. The 'mandate of Heaven' emphasizes the connection on a political scale. The ruler is connected to the people, must care for them, watch out for them, and ensure their well-being; only thus will he be able to continue his rule.

Neither of these ideas is compatible with Western individualism. Traditional Chinese society was not made up of individuals, but of descendant/ancestor and subject/ruler relationships. Ancestor veneration presumed that a person is nothing without a family. The mandate of Heaven presumed that the ruler is nothing without his good treatment of the *mín*. The mandate does not result in Western-style democracy, which is based on the individual rights of the ruled. Yet neither is it Western-style dictatorship. The ruler must act with *dé*, which means living up to his responsibilities to others. Those responsibilities are simultaneously part of his core self. Heaven smiled on the ruler who could manifest the benevolence and good leadership that his role required.

In short, traditional Chinese thought highlighted the interpersonal ties without which no society can exist. Those ties were an integral part of everyone's core selves.

Confucianism, Thick and Thin[31]

We need to pause to address a matter of history. I have been speaking of 'traditional Chinese thought', 'traditional China', and so on, as if these were monolithic. We know that was not the case. Chinese civilization has been complex in each of its historical epochs, and these epochs have been many. As with all civilizations, there have been both main trends and counter-movements. There still are. No Euro-American historian would dare reduce the 'Western tradition' to a single strand. We must similarly take care not to treat Chinese civilization simplistically.

Yet many scholars have noted a great continuity to China over the last two or three dozen centuries. Historian John K. Fairbank, for example, wrote that the "distinctive features of China today . . . come down directly from prehistoric times." In his 1976 presidential address to the Association of Asian Studies, Ping-ti Ho argued that the continuity extends back at least four millennia, far longer than is the case with the civilizations that began around the eastern Mediterranean.[32] Continuity does not mean stasis, but it does mean that we can make some generalizations. Still, we need to get a better sense of the landscape before we proceed.

The current scholarly consensus traces the first Chinese political groupings to the Yellow River valley in the 3rd millennium BCE. Their exact form of organization is still unclear, though archaeologists have found early signs of ancestor veneration. The first written records come from about fifteen hundred years later; these show the growth of a class system, of hereditary kingship, and of the treatment of ancestors as at least quasi-deities. In Lakos's telling:

> The picture of ancient China as was once understood, especially by the readings and interpretations of the Classics and ancient Chinese histories, is now considered incorrect. The three ancient dynasties of the Xia, Shang, and Zhou were not only centered in three different areas, but also appear to have co-existed. . . . During the Three Dynasties, a fluid and dynamic situation developed where prominent clans jostled with each other for influence over other clans and villages. . . . Another important socio-political feature of ancient China, from the family, clan, village to city and state, is that they became highly stratified along genealogical lines.[33]

Lakos argued that ancestor veneration grew out of this emphasis on genealogy. It was at first limited to the upper classes, but by the end of the Zhou dynasty (ca. 220 BCE) it had been taken up by other classes, too. The development was not linear but it grew steadily over the next thousand years.

Importantly, ancestor veneration began as religion but did not stay in a strictly religious mode. Ho wrote that Confucius (551–479 BCE)

> weakened ancestor worship as a religion. His skeptical and agnostic attitude toward the afterlife and spirits is summarized in the following terse statements. "He sacrificed [to the ancestors]," he said, "as if they were present." On another occasion, Confucius said: "To devote oneself earnestly to one's duty to humanity, and while respecting the spirits to keep away from them, may be called wisdom."[34]

On the other hand, Confucius emphasized the innate worth of maintaining a ritual respect for one's relationships. Everyone should do this, not just the rulers. In Confucius's view, anyone could attain virtue (*dé* 德) by acting correctly toward others (*lǐ* 禮). We will explore *lǐ* a few pages hence; here let us note that the concept is not just Confucian, but is part of Chinese tradition in general.[35]

Confucius lived toward the end of China's feudal period, as did his chief disciples. That period ended with the rise of the Ch'in dynasty (221–206 BCE), followed by the Han Empire (202 BCE–220 CE). These dynasties perfected the famous Chinese bureaucracy, which was staffed by *literati*, who won their positions by mastering the writings of Confucius and his early followers. This period solidified 'Confucian philosophy' as the core expression of Chinese wisdom. Not that the Chinese referred to it as "Confucianism"—i.e., as a religion founded by Confucius on a parallel with "Buddhism," "Mohammidanism," etc. The closest Chinese term for what we call 'Confucianism' is *rú jiā* 儒家, which means 'tradition of the scholars'.[36] In any event, Confucian teachings have been a central part of Chinese philosophical culture over the centuries. We thus need to know a bit about the various kinds of Confucian teachings that we can find in Chinese history.

When Rosemont referred a few pages back to "the Confucian perspective," he explicitly aligned himself with what he called "the early Confucians." It was they, he said, who developed the theory of the social self. These include Confucius himself, Mencius, who emphasized the optimistic and humanist side of Confucius's teaching, and Hsün Tzu, who emphasized humans' inability to act correctly without good training. Early Confucians codified what are called the *Shih Shu* (Four Books), which were collections of the sayings of Confucius and Mencius along with commentary by their followers. These include the *Lun Yü* (*Analects*), the *Ta Hsüeh* (*Great Learning*), the *Chung Yung* (*Doctrine of the Mean*), and the *Book of Mencius*. They emphasize the development of *dé* (personal virtue/positive potential) through attention to *lǐ* (right relationships). A realized *dé* is what marks a *chün-tzu* or perfect gentleman.[37]

These teachings are primarily ethical, not religious. Though Americans often conflate the two, and Confucius himself upheld the importance of formal rituals, his chief concern, to quote Xinzhong Yao, "was with humans and the fundamental principles of humanity." His four main principles aimed to solve human problems through right behavior. They were *dào* 道 ('the way'), *rén* 仁 ('humaneness'), *dé* 德 (virtue/potential), and *lǐ* 禮 (right relationships/ritual propriety). He emphasized education and self-cultivation; formal religion was present but secondary. He was quoted in *The Analects*: "If a person lacks humaneness (*rén* 仁) within, then what is the value of performing rituals?" Yao argues, however, that Confucius's teaching was not simply ethical, in the sense of dealing with merely moral issues:

> As morality is integrated with religion and politics [for Confucius], moral virtues become essential both for governing and for religious activities. As religion and metaphysics are part of morality, religious ritual and practice are a way of moral improvement.[38]

This moral improvement worked on four levels simultaneously: person, the family, the state, and society at large.[39] This was not—and this is Rosemont's point—just advice for individuals about how to develop good character. A close analysis of the classic texts shows an intimate connection between self and others. Right relationships (*lǐ*) produce virtue (*dé*) in individuals and in the social order simultaneously. (We will return to this matter below.)

Depending on how one counts, there are at least three, perhaps four other periods in which Confucian teachings took subtly different forms. The first was the establishment, under the Han dynasty, of an imperial bureaucracy with an examination system based on the Confucian classics. A Middle Han philosopher, Dong Zhong-shu (179–104 BCE), integrated metaphysical speculation into the classics' ethical focus, though some of what appears under his name was probably not his work. He did, however, emphasize the role of Heaven as a counterweight to the Emperor and the importance of sages in holding the Emperor to ethical account. He spent some time in jail for this and one of his later followers was executed for asking a profligate emperor to resign. The *rú jiā* remained the official state philosophy, however, until the fall of the Han dynasty in the 3rd century CE.[40]

A period of chaos then ensued, and Confucius's teachings went into decline. Daoism and Buddhism became much more prominent. Though the *rú jiā* returned to favor under the Tang dynasty (618–907), the tradition was revised considerably during the next dynasty, the Song (960–1279). Scholars generally call the teachings of this period 'neo-Confucianism', because the tradition absorbed elements of its Buddhist and Daoist rivals. Its most prominent figure was Zhou Dunyi (1017–1073), who used Daoist metaphysics as a basis for a Confucian cultivation of self. He heavily influenced Zhu Xi (1130–1200), who rationalized much Confucian philosophy. Zhu Xi is remembered for his book *Family Rituals*, which laid out the proper ways to honor ones relations and the ancestors.[41]

Neo-Confucianism remained a state-supporting cult for the next several centuries, though it split into two schools: a 'law' school that followed Zhu Xi and a 'mind' school that followed his opponent Wang Yang-ming. Their differences are not relevant here, except that they emphasized philosophy over religion, at least in the Western way of seeing things. In the late 19th century, however, there was an attempt to revive Confucianism as a specifically Chinese religion in order to restore China's vigor vis-à-vis Western invaders.

Peter Beyer described this last history in some detail. He showed how Chinese intellectuals ultimately rejected the idea of Confucianism as a religion, choosing to retain its standing as a philosophic tradition. Beyer noted that there is no indigenous word for 'religion' in Chinese, though the term *zongjiao* was invented to cover the European examples that the Chinese encountered. In Beyer's words, the literal meaning of this neologism "is close to 'group teaching' or 'sectarian teaching,' implying the perspective of a delimited subgroup of society and not something universal." He argued that refashioning Confucian teachings as a religion would not have accomplished the national strengthening that its advocates had sought. "Those who saw [Confucianism] as humanistic, this-worldly, and moral philosophy carried the day because this view asserted both Chinese uniqueness and superiority." The tradition's central focus on ethics held.[42]

This brings us to a final group of Confucians, those of the present day. I do not mean ordinary Chinese; Anna Sun reported that just 12 out of 7,021 respondents to a 2007 survey of rural and urban Chinese households claimed "Confucian" as their religion.[43] I focus instead on a group of Chinese and Western philosophers, including Henry Rosemont, who look to Confucius's teachings for intellectual inspiration.

I do not read Chinese, so I cannot comment on the Chinese parties to this philosophical conversation. I have met and conversed with Tu Weiming, Henry Rosemont, the late David Hall, and Roger Ames, each of whom has done much to enhance contemporary interest in a Confucian worldview. They all advocate what they call 'comparative philosophy': the effort to identify both the commonalities and differences across various civilizations' philosophic traditions. They have each retranslated core ancient texts and written commentaries on the philosophical issues that these texts raise.

Tu has written extensively on Confucian humanism and has contributed to discussions of so-called 'Asian values'. He has rather successfully brought intellectual depth to what has at times been a deeply political conversation. Until his untimely death, Hall produced detailed formal philosophical analyses of Confucian terms and often connected Confucian philosophy with the American Pragmatist tradition. Together with Ames, he wrote a series of three volumes that explored in detail the implications of Confucian philosophy for Western culture. Ames has produced several studies of his own and has edited a book series that has greatly expanded academic attention to Confucian thinking. He, too, supports the Confucian dialog with Pragmatism and advocates attention to the philosophical, as opposed to religious, aspects of Confucian writings. Rosemont has mainly concerned himself with issues of interpretation. He is well known for demonstrating the ways that cultural presuppositions prevent us from understanding other societies' points of view.[44]

Each of these scholars emphasizes the inadequacy of trying to subsume traditional Chinese concepts into Western philosophical categories. Rosemont, for example, began the essay that I cited a few pages ago with a cogent critique of the Western presumption that human beings are at root "autonomous, freely choosing, rights-bearing individuals"; his contrast between Western and Confucian ways of self-description was a concrete example of how Confucian principles produce a different way of looking at the world.[45] In that world, the self is connected, not autonomous. Choice is constrained by context, not because individuals are forced to go along with the group but because individuals are constituted by their context and so must take it into account as a part of themselves. 'Rights' are not central to social justice; instead, the key category is 'dignity' or 'respect'. In a Confucian world, people must take into account the relationships in which they are enmeshed. Respect for and care for others are central to virtue (*dé*). Rosemont argued that Confucian philosophy arrives at social justice by another route than does the West.

Rather than discuss these writers broadly, let us examine a parallel approach to Rosemont's presentation of the Confucian social self: Hall and Ames's description of the self as a 'focus-field'.[46] Their discussion connects the two Chinese religious concepts that we have already examined—'ancestor veneration' and the 'mandate of Heaven'—to the third: 'ritual propriety'. Their approach shows how all three are relational, on an even deeper level than I presented before.

Hall and Ames began by noting two ways of thinking about the individual person. One can think of an individual as *distinct*: i.e., as "single, unitary, separate, and indivisible," an autonomous member of a class of equivalent separate beings. Alternately, one can think of an individual as *unique*—as a particular constellation of attributes, relationships, and so on that can be compared with others but not separated from them. Here, the individual is not reducible to a featureless monad. She or he is not distinct because s/he is not isolated from others. Instead, each individual is unique precisely because she or he carries a different combination of personal attributes and relationships—the latter of which connect her/him to others who are similarly complexly related to their social surroundings.

Hall and Ames argued that in Confucian philosophy, the self is unique but not distinct. In their words,

> the Confucian model [of] the self is contextual, it is a shared consciousness of one's roles and relationships. . . . The uniqueness of the Chinese person is immanent and embedded within a ceaseless process of social, cultural, and natural changes.

This is not just a matter of people realizing the importance of their social connections. Hall and Ames are making a philosophical point about the conceptual universe implicit in the very language of the Confucian texts. They write that unlike Western philosophies,

> Confucian distinctions such as "self/other" [*jǐ* 己/*rén* 人] are mutually entailing and interdependent correlatives. *Yīn* 陰 is always becoming *yáng* 陽 and *yáng* is always becoming *yīn*, as "day" is a "becoming night" and "night" is a "becoming day." For the *jǐ/rén* distinction, "oneself" is always "becoming other" and an "other" is always "becoming oneself."[47]

In short, the self and the other are intimately connected; neither can be conceived of without the other term. No Confucian would start philosophizing from a Hobbesian—or even Rousseauian—'state of nature', in which individuals exist separate from society. Nor is any individual just a replaceable cog. Instead each individual is the center of a web of relationships, each of which shapes that individual into a unique person.

Hall and Ames called this a field phenomenon. In their view, any set of interacting persons form a field, in which they mutually influence each other. They do not use this example, but we can think of this field as similar to the force field that surrounds several magnets. The magnets do not exist by themselves—at least not as magnets, though they can exist singly as lumps of iron. The magnetic field that they generate involves multiple lines of influence; the field structure at any point depends on each magnet's position vis-à-vis the others, the relative strength of its magnetism, and so on. We cannot describe that field by taking each magnet separately. We have to describe the field as a whole, noting the ways in which the web of connections surrounding each magnet creates a focus-point or node that cannot be separated from the field itself. The field shapes each focus-point and is shaped by that focus-point in turn.

Hall and Ames put it this way:

> The focus-field model results from understanding one's relation to the world to be constituted by acts of contextualization. The self is focal in that it both constitutes and is constituted by the field in which it resides. The field is the order constituting its relevant environs. By definition, the focal self cannot be independent. The structure and continuity of the focal self is immanental, inhering in and continuous with its context. . . . The openness of the self is guaranteed by the indefinite reservoir of potential perspectives offered by familial, social, cultural, and natural environs.[48]

Hall and Ames argued that Confucian philosophy sees this focus-field self as unique rather than distinct, as connected rather than isolated, as social rather than solitary. This is the point of 'ancestor veneration'. By venerating one's ancestors one recalls that one is part of a long social chain, extending into the past and leading in to the future. This is also the point of the 'mandate of Heaven', which put the relationship between the rulers and the common people at the center of political life. The ruler is responsible for the well-being of the *mín*; they, in turn, honor their superiors, especially the ruler. In the Confucian way of seeing things, correct rule is a matter of relationships rather than of one individual exercising autonomous, isolated power.

* * *

In sum, the central elements of traditional Chinese religion emphasize the relationalism that Confucians see at the heart of human life. How does this solve the question with which I started this section: of whether I am overgeneralizing when I refer to 'traditional Chinese thought' or even to 'Confucian ways of thinking'? Just noting that Rosemont, Hall, Ames, and Tu use their philosophical analyses of Confucian texts to elucidate the differences between the ways that traditional Chinese and modern Western civilizations see the world may not be enough.[49] Are they on good ground in doing so? Or are the many Confucianisms of the past two and a half millenia, and the many competing philosophical schools, too complex to allow them to treat the social self as a characteristic outlook of Chinese civilization?

Though there are certainly differences between the ways in which various Chinese eras have understood the *rú jiā* ('tradition of the scholars'), these differences are minor compared to the vast similarities. None of these Confucianisms has been individualist, in the Western mode. Neither have been the competing schools. All have recognized the intimate, mutually constituting connection between the individual and society. All of them have seen a close connection between the moral development of the individual and the moral development of the social order. Each has seen the importance of right relationships.

Bryan Van Norden has made a useful distinction between what he calls 'thin' and 'thick' accounts of various philosophies. He wrote:

> We can give a 'thin' description . . . which can be shared by a broad range of participants in a discussion, who might disagree significantly over many other matters. . . . In contrast, a 'thick' description is a detailed account framed in terms of the distinctive concepts and commitments of a participant in that discussion.[50]

Summarizing his example, we can speak of the sun as 'a large bright thing in the sky' without deciding whether it is really a god (Hesiod), a hot stone (Anaxagoras), the essence of the *qi* 氣 of fire (the view of the Chinese classic *Haui-Nan-Zi*),[51] or a mass of hot hydrogen and helium. All these views allow the 'large bright thing' as a thin description of what they think is really going on.

The scholars on whom I have built my account—Lakos, Yao, Rosemont, Hall, Ames, and others—have, I think, demonstrated that the social, relational self is at least a thin description of the dominant traditional Chinese view of how selves and others are connected. The key matter is that neither Chinese philosophy in general nor Confucian philosophy in particular begins with an isolated self. They begin with a social self that is connected in its very being to the people around it. The key question is how a person is supposed to relate to those connections, and the consequences of that relating both for the person and for the social field in which she or he lives.

We have one more step to go before we can see how to use this self/other relationalism in our own studies of religion.

Ritual Propriety

Lǐ 禮—the third of the Chinese religious terms that I promised to elucidate—is usually translated into English as 'ritual propriety'. This translation contains two terms: 'ritual' and 'propriety', which seem foreign when combined. Westerners associate ritual with formal actions, often (but not always) religious and public: "the priest gave a ritual blessing," "the president laid a ritual wreath at the Tomb of the Unknown Soldier," and so on. Propriety involves personal actions: decorum, good manners, courtesy, moral rectitude, etc. Both are formal and proper, but one is public, the other private, one has to do with matters of religion or state, the other with personal virtue. What ties them together?

The connection is clearer in classical Chinese. The term lǐ 禮 is an old one, used long before Confucius to describe the family rituals surrounding the veneration of ancestors. These were religious but were not transcendent, unlike most religion in the West. In Lakos's words,

> Chinese culture was one which concerned itself more with its people than with great gods; it was humanist more than idealist. The fundamental purpose of ancestor rituals was the incorporation of the family and its extension to kin and to state [and] society; it was a strategy for the continuation of Chinese culture.[52]

Private rather than public, lǐ rituals helped "to regulate a person's daily life and their [sic] interaction with others." Lakos cited Kai-wing Chow's comment that traditional Chinese ritual "channels emotions properly, distinguishes civilized patterns of behavior, and maintains the political order."[53]

Ancestor ritual is not, here, primarily a public event. Instead, it is simultaneously a way to connect with one's ancestors and develop one's good character. The 'propriety' part of the English phrase highlights this latter task; the 'ritual' part reminds us that good character, for traditional Chinese thinking, had a sacred quality. This makes sense of Confucius's statement that "a man without virtue (*dé*) had nothing to do with ritual (*lǐ*)."[54] Virtue and ritual are intimately connected.

Appropriately for a civilization in which particular relationships were more important than universal ones, what specifically counted as virtue varied according to one's social position. All people could attain good character, but they did so by fulfilling their specific social roles rather than by absorbing an abstract set of attributes. Lakos again:

> Every individual has a particular position or station in life (their *fèn*), which is arrived at according to a number of criteria such as age, kinship, and social status. An important element of *lǐ* is to differentiate the socio-political positions of individuals and to ensure that each has their [*sic*] allocated resources required for their station in life. Ritual was the means by which an appreciation of these rules and their underlying value as virtues was most readily inculcated to society.[55]

The early Confucian Hsün Tzu connected *lǐ* with *fèn* 分 as follows:

> The ancient kings hated [social] disorder, and hence they established *lǐ* (禮, rules of proper conduct) and inculcated *yi* (義, a sense of rightness) in order to make distinctions (*fèn* 分) and boundaries of responsibilities for regulating men's pursuit, to educate and to nourish men's desires, to provide opportunity for their satisfaction. They saw to it that desires did not overextend the means of satisfaction, and material means did not fall short of what was desired. Thus, both desires and goods mutually support each other. This is the origin of *lǐ*.[56]

In any case, ritual propriety (*lǐ*) was intimately connected with achieving virtue and one's personal potential (*dé*)—remembering, of course, that the Confucian self is not isolated but is intimately tied to others.

Here is Confucius's own statement of the matter:

Yan Yuan asked about perfect virtue (*dé*). The Master said, "To subdue one's self and return to [ritual] propriety (*lǐ*), is perfect virtue. If a man can for one day subdue himself and return to *lǐ*, all under heaven will ascribe *dé* to him." . . . Yan Yuan said, "I beg to ask the steps of that process." The Master replied, "Look not at what is contrary to *lǐ*; listen not to what is contrary to *lǐ*; speak not what is contrary to *lǐ*; make no movement which is contrary to *lǐ*."[57]

Lǐ is thus not just a matter of ritual, in the Western sense of the word. We need to remember that it is also the proper treatment of others. Such proper treatment makes social life possible, which to a relational self means that it makes the virtuous self possible as well. Self and other are integrated: connected by mutual proper conduct that takes on ritual dimensions. In doing so, it partakes of the sacred.

Like all concepts, *lǐ* developed over time. By the Song and Ming dynasties, it had come to mean 'principle' as well as 'ritual'—combining the homophones *lǐ* 理 and *lǐ* 禮 into a single concept. Wing-tsit Chan wrote:

Lǐ (principle) originally meant to "put in order" and can therefore be understood as "pattern" and order, but in the long evolution of the concept it came to denote principle, and it has been in this sense that most Chinese philosophers have used it.[58]

The 11th-century neo-Confucian philosopher Cheng Yi further connected *lǐ* as 'ritual/principle' with the earlier notion of Heaven to create *tiān lǐ* 天理: the idea that the rituals that support the social order have cosmic significance. The 20th-century neo-Confucian Qian Mu tied this cosmic ideal back to concrete social relations:

The *lǐ* that are the standards for the family—its internal relations, its external relations, birth, marriage, death—are equivalent to the *lǐ* that are standards for the workings of government and state ceremonies—internal relations, relations between state and society, recruitment, treaties, successions.[59]

Both are, he wrote, cosmically grounded. *Lǐ* thus involves a ritual care for human relationships as a sacred duty.

What can we take from this discussion? Simply that Chinese thinking connects rituals, manners, ethics, and social order to each other, rather than treating them as disparate phenomena. *Lǐ* as 'ritual propriety' emphasizes each individual's duty toward the social connections that make the self—in the Confucian sense—possible. As Rosemont pointed out, that self is constructed by its social connections. Those connections make individuals unique, without separating them from family, community, society, and the state. *Lǐ* tells us that the path to achieving one's personal virtuous potential involves fulfilling one's duties to others.

Lǐ as 'principle', moreover, emphasizes these relationships' cosmic dimension. If Confucius himself deemphasized *lǐ's* religious aspects ("while respecting the spirits to keep away from them"[60]), the 11th-century neo-Confucians restored them. Both would say that *lǐ* creates virtuous individuals—divine, semi-divine, and human—by helping them realize their interconnectedness. Without this connectedness, neither persons nor the world would exist. There would be only chaos.

The bottom line is that 'ritual propriety' is as relational a concept as are 'ancestor veneration' and 'the mandate of Heaven'. Traditional Chinese thinking taught that humans are far more intimately connected with one another than Western thinking realizes. Lakos expressed this particularly well:

> The rituals and ceremonies which have underpinned Chinese society, dominated . . . by ancestor worship, are not important simply because they are a link with the past, but because they celebrate and reinforce core social relationships and values in the present lives of the Chinese people and they mirror the social world and the concerns of the living.[61]

Lǐ 禮 is more than just *personal* behavior; it is *interpersonal* ritual. Maintaining one's relationships with the others that constitute oneself is a sacred matter.

Herbert Fingarette famously arrived at this realization by another route—one that I recommend you read but that I do not have space to summarize here. He wrote:

> Thus, in the *Analects*, man as an individual is not sacred. However, he is not therefore to be thought of as a mere utensil to serve "society". For society is no more an independent entity than is ceremony independent of the participants, the holy vessels, the altar, the incantations. Society is men treating each other as men (*jen*), or to be more specific, according to the obligations and privileges of *li*, out of the love (*ai*) and loyalty (*chung*) and respect (*sbu*) called for by their human relationships to each other. The shapes of human relationships are not imposed on man, not physically inevitable, not an instinct or reflex. They are rites learned and voluntarily participated in. . . . To "be self-disciplined and ever turning to *li*" ([*Analects*] 12:1) is to be no longer at the mercy of animal needs and demoralizing passions, is to achieve that freedom in which human spirit flowers.[62]

As Confucius is recorded as saying: "Virtue does not exist in isolation: there must be neighbors."[63]

Sociology of Religion from a Confucian Point of View

It is time to bring this conversation back to the sociology of religion. I enjoy exploring other civilization's philosophies, but that's not this book's point. Its point is to expand sociology's conceptual toolkit, by seeing what kind of sociology we can build from the insights of non-Western civilizations. What can we gain if we use those civilizations' ideas to analyze the religions that Western sociologists think we know well? How might *li* 禮, *dé* 德, *tiān ming* 天命, *rén* 仁, and the rest transform the way we think about religions everywhere?

First, it is clear that in the traditional Chinese view, religion does not just happen in churches. While there are religious specialists, temples, public rituals, and the like, most 'religion' is fully integrated into daily life. Family-centered ritual is private, and the assorted healers, geomancers, and so on—all of whose work involves the sacred on some level—are hired for private ends. Traditional religion certainly does not center itself on weekly public worship. Though there has been a recent rapid growth of Chinese Christianity, it has supplemented, not altered, popular religious practices. In short, to study religion in China is to study what we in the West call "popular religion." A sociology of religion with Chinese characteristics would have to organize itself accordingly.[64]

Second, from the Confucian point of view, the unit of religious analysis is not the individual: neither the individual's beliefs, nor the individual's actions, nor the individual's choices (rational or otherwise). A sociology of religion based on Confucian principles would begin from relationships and would ask how religions—both popular and institutional, both private and public—create and sustain the relationships that constitute human social life. It would look at the place of ritual propriety and the attention to the others who are an intimate part of our selves, in the web of social life that reaches seamlessly from human to divine. How is each being in this web constituted, and what are the consequences of this mutual constitution for daily life? How are their relationships—which means also their selves—sustained? The exact questions are less important for our purposes than the traditional Confucian premise that individuals come second, not first.

Third, the Confucian approach undercuts the distinction between the 'secular' and the 'religious' spheres. Early Confucianism posited an integrated world of mutual relationships, each involving ritual propriety (*lǐ*) and virtue (*dé*) vis-à-vis others; the sum of these relationships constitutes the person. As such, religiosity or secularization is not the core issue. The universe is neither enchanted nor disenchanted, but oriented toward *lǐ* and *dé*, under the aegis of *tiān míng*. As the recent Communist Chinese efforts to reembrace Confucianism show, not all that much has necessarily changed over the centuries.[65]

Confucian thought is thus neither secular nor religious, but denies the validity of these conceptual categories. Neither religious belief nor religious institutions have ever had hegemony in China. This does not mean, however, that religion is not present nor that Chinese thought cannot tell us anything about the religious sphere. The Chinese parts fit together into a different whole. Secularization theory asks the wrong questions, from the traditional Chinese point of view. The same is true of rational choice theories of religion. They both posit the individual as the metaphysical unit of analysis—exactly the reverse of where a sociology of religion built on Chinese principles would begin.

In the next chapter, we shall see what kind of sociology this might be.

Church Supper. Photograph by Nehrams2020, 2006 (Creative Commons BY-SA 3.0.

4

China Applied

Feeding the Holy Community

What might a sociology based on Confucian principles show us about religion that we currently do not see? What parts of the religious landscape would *lǐ* and *dé* illuminate? Obviously, I cannot develop a full alternate sociology of religion in a single chapter. I can, however, take up a simpler question: What do we learn about religions by beginning with relationships, not with individuals? More specifically: How do religions of various kinds create and sustain the relationships that constitute human social life? Western sociologists could ask these questions, but they do not often do so. That's because these questions do not automatically arise from sociology's default view.

Let us keep things simple by focusing on American religious congregations. These are the local churches, synagogues, mosques, and so on, where ordinary people meet to satisfy their religious needs. This is not the only way to organize religious life, but it is ubiquitous in my country. Even recent immigrants create congregations, and some sociologists argue that this one way they learn how to be American.[1] I've done field research in three congregations, participated in several more, and have read widely in the congregational literature. I know the patterns. A Confucian perspective on them would highlight two questions:

- Who does the (sacred) work of maintaining the social ties that turn a congregation into a community?
- Whose attention to *lǐ* creates the *dé* that makes American congregational religion possible?

Spoiler alert: it's largely the women, not the pastors, priests, rabbis, imams, or other religious specialists; the men, however, typically get credit for bringing religion into people's lives.

Then, we will explore the recent sociological attention to individual religion in the work of several prominent scholars. We will pose the questions that a Confucian sociologist would ask of this research and will see what answers we can find.

In both cases, a Confucian sociology of religion would highlight quite different aspects of religious life than do the sociological treatments based on the default view.

Who Makes Congregations Possible?

Congregations are the dominant form of religious organization in the United States and also in some other parts of the world. Congregations run worship services, hire pastors, own or rent worship spaces, and often work collectively on projects of local concern. My college town of sixty-nine thousand people is home to over fifty such groups: one Catholic, two Jewish, a dozen or so from the Protestant Mainline, and the rest mostly Evangelicals. Someone has to tend these flocks, and the job is more than any paid staff can manage. Even the largest congregations depend on volunteers to keep themselves running.

We can take my own congregation as an example, even though it is an outlier on the American religious scene. I am Quaker, and my local Quaker Meeting is of the 'unprogrammed' variety. This means we have no liturgy, no fixed order of worship, and no clergy to lead us. We sit together in silence for about an hour each Sunday morning, waiting for the Spirit to move us. We seek mystical communion, deep thought, and occasionally the inspiration to speak. Some sessions are completely silent; others are not. Nothing is directed, however, and there are no religious specialists among us. Looked at another way, we are all religious specialists. I sometimes joke that Quakers did not abolish the clergy but abolished the laity. We are all responsible for maintaining our collective religious activities.[2]

How, exactly, do we do this? There are times when I want to say "not particularly well," but that is not the direction I am heading. (Like every organization, we have our dysfunctional moments.) There are, of course, committees that manage our finances, repair our building, staff the children's program, and so on, but 'maintaining the congregation' requires more than that. Someone has to pay attention to people. Church is not compulsory in the U.S., and unattended people often leave. Someone has to make sure that people feel welcome, honored, and heard. That's not a job that committees do well.

Let me give you an example. Some years ago, my local Meeting finally decided to build a Meetinghouse. We had rented space for years from a series of other groups, including a local arts organization and a Methodist community center. We had grown enough that we needed a place of our own.

Unfortunately, building a Meetinghouse was a contentious matter. Not only do Quakers value helping others more than we like spending money on ourselves; we are traditionally 'plain people' who like well-designed architectural simplicity. If you've ever built a house, you know that 'well-designed' and 'simplicity' seldom go together. Add in the fact that Quakers decide everything by consensus,[3] and you know how hard it was for us to proceed. Tempers flared, feelings were hurt, and long-term members left for elsewhere. It was not a pretty picture. To use our in-group language, it was a "most un-Quakerly" time.

Just as the construction began, an older couple retired to our town. They became active in Meeting and, given their skills and experience, were quickly tasked with various bits of committee work. The husband was put on the Building Committee and the wife was appointed to Ministry and Oversight—the committee that is supposed to run the Meeting. In those roles, they quickly saw that some healing needed to be done.

Each of them found a way to do so. The husband, in the guise of building-related issues, reached out to those who had either opposed the Meetinghouse design or had been alienated by others' behavior. He went out of his way to consult with everyone, making sure that they all felt that their views were heard. He treated each person with respect and care. Gradually, several of those who had been offended returned to help with the building process. The wife, in the meantime, made sure that there were Meeting activities beyond just construction. She supported spiritual discussion groups, informal get-togethers, multi-generational potlucks, and so on. She, too, gave people a sense that they were valued.

This couple's community-building is a fine example of how to restore a congregation's fractured relationships. They saw that the Meeting needed interpersonal care and they figured out how to encourage it. They were not the only ones to do so, but they were remarkably effective. They saw what they were doing in religious terms: as nurturing the congregation's religious life. In a Confucian view, they were re-creating right-relationships by paying attention to the value of each Meeting participant. By attending to *lǐ*, they helped restore the group's sense of unity.

Let's take an example from another tradition: Methodism. To understand it, you need to know that in the United States, rural and small-town Methodists used to have strong anti-Catholic views. You would never find a Methodist church named after a saint; that was Catholic business. Yet in 1939 a congregation in rural West Virginia renamed itself Saint Mary's Methodist Church. How did this happen?

It turns out that three Methodist denominations combined in that year, leaving two churches in town with the same name. One had to change, and the church that was to become St. Mary's drew the short straw. Laurence Stookey reported that, as they talked through what name to choose,

> the men of the church confessed: "During the Depression we were ready to close this place down and join one of the other Methodist congregations in town. It was the women who insisted otherwise; and they kept us alive by bake sales, quilting bees, bazaars, and church suppers. Perhaps we should name our church after a woman."[4]

So they did: after the mother of Jesus. The name celebrated the women who had kept the congregation alive by tending to the relationships that made them a community.

Church Food

"Bake sales, quilting bees, bazaars, and church suppers." These community activities have long been a part of American congregational life. Fundraisers, social events, or both, they let congregations get together outside of the worship service. They let people talk, work side by side, and get to know each other. They create a sense of relationship.

I am going to focus on church suppers, in part because they are typically seen as secular events, not religious ones. They are also stereotypically American, especially for White Protestants from the Midwest (though Midwestern Catholics enjoy them as well). Daniel Sack told the story, "snatched from the Internet," of a second-grade class doing a project on comparative religion, for which each child was supposed to bring a religious symbol. He wrote:

The first child stood up and said, "My name is Joshua. I go to Beth Sha-lom. I am Jewish, and this is a Star of David." The second child . . . said, "My name is Marguerite. I go to St. Mary's. I am Catholic, and this is a crucifix." The third child . . . said, "My name is Fred. I go to Grace Church. I am a Protestant, and this is a casserole."[5]

Casserole, crispy fried meatloaf, tuna hot dish, green beans, jello salad, pies, weak coffee; these define Midwestern church food. Other regions have their own cuisines. A recent listing of Southern White favorites included hot chicken salad casserole, baked spaghetti, crawfish rice, jambalaya, baked beans, strawberry cake, sock-it-to-me cake, pecan pie muffins, banana pudding, and all the sweet iced tea you can drink. Add in some fried chicken and some "Shout Hallelujah Potato Salad" and your church will have a meal.[6]

Sack devoted an entire chapter of his *Whitebread Protestants: Food and Religion in American Culture* to what he calls "social food"—mainly potlucks and coffee hours. He noted that most Protestant churches have a church kitchen, often a large one, and many have church halls able to seat several hundred people. He traced their attention to food to the early Protestant camp meetings, but noted that it blossomed after the Civil War, with the rise of what historian Brooks Holifield called the "social congre-gation." Rural churches were already social centers for their communi-ties, but urban churches responded to industrialization and its social ills by trying "to provide alternatives to the city's tempting entertainment." Food became a way of solidifying the church community.[7] (Sack focused on Protestants, but Catholic congregations engage in similar activities.)

Food was particularly important for immigrant congregations, includ-ing the one that Sack studied most closely. Chicago's St. Pauls United Church of Christ was founded by German immigrants, as a congregation

where people could both feel at home and experiment with assimila-tion. It preserved ethnic solidarity and tradition against the homogeniz-ing forces of the larger culture. And it provided opportunities for young people to meet and court, encouraging marriage within the community.[8]

Church suppers were a prime way to do this. Sack described the compli-cated set of such events at St Pauls, from the formal Men's Club Annual

Dinner (which "in 1913 was a four-course banquet, featuring trout and beef tenderloin and concluding with cigars") to the Dorcas Society luncheons (for women) with their "dainty, delicious sandwiches." The 1961 Easter Monday luncheon included, according to the church bulletin, "potato salad, jello molds, pickles, olives, meat balls, ham, fried chicken, and all the rest of the goodies." Father-Son and Mother-Daughter banquets, Western night "Chuck Wagons," family nights, and a whole host of special events gave families plenty to do. This large congregation did more than most, but the pattern was typical.[9]

Who did all this cooking? It certainly was not the men of the congregation, not in that highly role-divided age. St Pauls' Frauenverein ("Women's Union") handled kitchen affairs. At the 1918 Men's Club Dinner "forty gracious young ladies waited on the tables, while twenty more women, some young and others not so young, worked like Trojans in the kitchen." The 1923 reunion of the church's confirmation classes was prepared "by the willing members of the Ladies Aid Society."

> The Mothers' and Daughters' Banquet in 1928 became a bit more chaotic when a hundred more people than expected turned out. But "Mother" Pister, wife of the pastor and head of the Frauenverein, [said the church bulletin] "was not to be flustered. . . . Orders flew quickly and decisively. Everyone obeyed. There were no men to interfere, not fathers and brothers to give a lot of advice . . . the sudden rush delayed the beginning just a little."[10]

Sack noted that that the Frauenverein women knew that their kitchen work was important "and they reminded the congregation of it at every opportunity." Writing in a 1940 church newsletter, one woman estimated that over the preceding twenty-five years, "We have served 86,950 cups of coffee, together with 29,850 pounds of meat, 5000 pounds of turkey and chicken, 500 bushels of potatoes, and many other foods."[11] Women were certainly important to keeping this congregation together.

That's the point. As much as this congregation may have depended on its pastors for spiritual guidance, its governing board for financial decisions, and its Sunday School teachers for educating its youth, the women in the kitchen were the ones who made the "social congregation" possible. They put in the hours that gave the congregation a sense of community. They did it together, which itself created a sense of belonging to something important. Whatever else they may have done—from tending the babies and toddlers, to teaching the young, to helping new mothers learn the ropes, to visiting the sick, to aiding the bereaved—women's kitchen ministry turned congregations into communities. They made their churches strong.

I doubt that the women of St Pauls would have used that term, "kitchen ministry". It would have been a bit too challenging for most Midwestern Whites to put women on such a par with men. Barred from the pulpit and from most formal church offices, they stayed in the background. Perhaps that's why sociologists of religion have not always realized their importance in American religious life. Yet the "kitchen ministry" term has long been used in another sector of the U.S. religious scene: by African Americans. There, too, women have traditionally been excluded from formal leadership. Yet as Jualynne Dodson and Cheryl Gilkes have written, women's roles in the African American church have often been seen as ministry, too.[12]

Dodson and Gilkes wrote that "food is a central part of the African-American Christian experience." They noted that food

> is taken very seriously in both positive and negative ways. It is sung about. It is worried over. It is prayed over. It is the subject of church meetings. Permanent committees are formed to ensure that food is provided by the church at appropriate times: receptions for new ministers, funerals, home-comings, watch nights, and visits from sister churches. Indeed, it is not unusual for congregations and visitors to purchase dinners from a church auxiliary or club after morning worship service. The dinners provide a source of income for the church and at the same time, on-site diners take an opportunity to sit and share while reconstituting community.[13]

Dodson and Gilkes pointed out that scholars have long agreed about "the social and communal importance of the Black Church" for African Americans, but they have not often identified the means by which those churches create the sense of community itself. In fact, though,

> the voices of enslaved Africans and their descendants singing of their deter-mination "to sit at the welcome table" and exhorting one another to "break bread" and "drink wine together on our knees" point to food as an impor-tant mytho-poetic element in the process of community formation.[14]

They cited the work of Melvin Williams, who wrote that "food is a basic theme in the idiom of [the congregation he studied]—as nourishment, as an instrument of solidarity, as a mechanism of communication, and as a means of solidarity."[15]

For example: many African American congregations provide a formal meal to the congregation after the Sunday service. Given the several-hour length of African American services and the emphasis on a hot meal—often chicken (called "gospel bird")—members of the "kitchen team" have to cook while other church members are attending the sermon and praying. Some churches solve this by installing speakers in the kitchen so cooks can hear the service. They are thus part of the service while preparing for the community-building that comes afterward.

Food is so important in the Black Church, Dodson and Gilkes wrote, that it is even used to describe sermons. "That preacher really fed us" is a remark of praise. In parallel, preparing food is "kitchen ministry," which feeds both body and spirit. African American Christians see it is a vital and religious part of their lives together.

Finally, food in the African American church is a means of comforting the bereaved. "Deaths in the congregation bring outpourings of food."

> Many church members who have lost loved ones comment upon the fact that, for quite some time after the funeral, they are able to open their refrigerators and be reminded of the community's concern for them and their well-being.[16]

Care for grieving people is community-building *par excellence*.

This last point is not unique to African American congregations: many White congregations also donate food to their bereaved members. One difference, however, between Sack's description of White Protestant church cooking and Dodson and Gilkes's account of the Black Church is that the latter, despite its history of sexism, includes men as kitchen ministers. Many African American men have been employed in the restaurant industry, often out of sight of the public. They, too, turn their skills toward creating church community. The title and content of Gilkes's solo book, *If It Wasn't for the Women*, made clear the central role that women have played in African American religion. In her joint article with Dodson, she affirmed the cross-gender solidarity that has been so important to the African American community as well.[17]

In short, both Whites and African Americans build religious community through food. Kitchen ministry is a core, if under-recognized, part of North American church life. A Confucian sociologist would pick this out immediately, because of the sacred importance of maintaining human ties. Western sociology has been too focused on belief and on formal church organization to notice what is going on.

One final note before moving to another example. Just for fun, I googled "kitchen ministry" while I was writing this section. The top entry was from New Hope Baptist Church, in Sacramento, California. Over eighty years old, this Black Baptist church is now led by Reverend Gary W. Young, "Pastor-Teacher." The website tells us that the kitchen ministry

> is to support and further the cause of being servants for the people in the Oak Park area. Our purpose is also to unite New Hope members as a responsible and dedicated group of worshippers.

They promise to prepare good, wholesome meals for the community and for the sick and shut in, to provide "a short biblical lesson and prayer before each meal," and to "welcome and fellowship with our guests."[18] The ministry is led by two women. Community-building is alive and well in this congregation.

(Googling "church suppers" turns up more references to "salmonella" than to "sociology"—further proof that sociologists have ignored this important part of congregational life.)

Los Pastores

American Catholics, of course, stage similar events—and also others. Let's turn to an example of this, from the West Side of San Antonio, Texas. This is a largely Mexican American part of town, heavily Catholic, with its own women-led celebrations that also involve food. This example comes from the work of anthropologist Richard Flores, who did significant fieldwork in this community.

Flores noted that Latina Catholics do not attend Mass as often as do their White counterparts. That has led sociologists to treat them as if they are less religious. He documented this, but he also documented these women's other religious activities, particularly those beyond Church control. Specifically, West Side Latina women put much effort into maintaining home altars and preparing ritual feasts. Flores studied one of those feasts, given on the occasion of a Christmas play, *Los Pastores*. This is a reenactment of the story of the shepherds seeking to worship the baby Jesus. It is a very important ritual to the Mexican American women of San Antonio's West Side.[19]

Los Pastores has a long tradition in Spanish and Spanish American culture. Medieval Spain was host to many Christmas-time folk-plays, the majority of which made their way to the New World. As Flores described it,

> The narrative begins with the shepherds keeping watch over their sheep when the Archangel Michael appears to them, announcing the birth of the Messiah. Upon deciding to journey to Bethlehem, to bear offerings for the new Messiah, the shepherds encounter Luzbel (Lucifer) and his legion of devils who attempt to thwart their efforts in a series of comic routines. In the end, the Archangel defeats Luzbel, banishing him into the dungeons of hell, and the shepherds arrive in Bethlehem offering their humble gifts to the new-born King.[20]

The missionary Catholic Church used such plays as ways to teach Christianity to Mexican Indians. Local communities in Mexico and the American Southwest later embraced them as a means of self-evangelization. The current San Antonio *Pastores* was brought north in 1913 by Don Leandro Granado, who founded the troupe that performs each year in the city's predominantly Latino neighborhoods.

> The performers are Mexican working-class men and women, both young and old. Many are supported by government pensions like social security, disability, or various forms of welfare subsistence. Mostly, however, they share their common devotion to *El Niño Dios*. They all have their special stories of how—in times of crisis, sickness, and other moments of human crisis—supplications to *El Niño Dios* were responded to in ways that provided comfort, solace, and miracles.

Troupe members perform in local churches and in one of the city's five historic missions, but they also perform in the backyards and driveways of homes in San Antonio's many *barrios*. Home-cooked food plays a big part in these latter events.

Each year brings a different set of home locations. Women typically volunteer to host the event as part of a *promesa* or ritual promise to *el Niño Dios* (the Child God). A *promesa* can be a thank-you for healing, for deliverance from legal troubles, for the safety of family members, and so on. One promises to put on the play and give a feast in return for good fortune. The play is important, but feeding the cast and attenders is equally important. It highlights Latino women's roles as nurturers and as carriers of family and community. It also highlights the central importance of the kitchen in Latino households. To quote sociologist Ana María Díaz-Stevens,

> It is there, in the kitchen, where the women of the household and other women from the extended family and community often gather and, over a cup of *café con leche*, reminisce about the past, give each other counsel and consolations, discuss the events of the community, and plan for family and community celebrations which most often are also religious celebrations.[21]

Food preparation typically begins several days in advance. Women from the extended family work together to build a home altar and decorate a backyard stage, and to prepare food for thirty to fifty people, under the host woman's direction. The altar is important, for on it the host puts symbols of her *promesa*, both sorrow and succor. So is the food, for it is a culturally central way for women to give gifts to their community and also to show their religious devotion and culinary skill. To quote Flores, "In some ways, the meal compliments the work of the home altar—one being a shrine to the saints, the other to those who attend."[22]

On the night of the performance, the host recounts her *promesa* and gives her thanks to God for the blessings she has received.

> Hace dos años que hice una promesa al Niño Dios. Si curaba a mi mamá, le prometí tender una pastorela en mi casa. Peus, la salud de me mamá majoró, y me siento feliz que ya llegó este dia. [It has been two years since I made a vow to the Christ Child. If he cured my mother, I promised to hold a pastorela in my house. Well, my mother's health improved, and I feel happy that today has arrived.][23]

Others recount similar stories, for such problems are common among West Side Latinas. Finally, the performance begins, is enjoyed, and ends; then people eat together. As Flores put it:

> These narratives function to . . . gather those present into a common social body by building on experiences that affect everyone. . . . The personal narrative ceases to be an individual invocation, but [becomes] a means through which the audience engages the experience as one collective body.[24]

Simply put, the event creates community. A Confucian sociologist would highlight this as a core part of Latina religion. Most Western sociologists of religion, on the other hand, ignore it because it happens outside of the church setting.[25]

That is the point: a sociology of religion primed to pay attention to *lí* and *dé* would see congregations as ritual communities and put community-building at the heart of religious activity. Western sociology puts community-building on the side. I am not saying that Western scholars cannot notice such things; Sack, Dodson, Gilkes, and Flores are as Western as I am. Their work is unusual, however. Most scholars classify church suppers and religious plays as "popular religion," which they see as at best a sideshow to the main event. They do not see them as mainstream religious activities. I think they seriously underestimate the importance of community-building in congregational and parish life. They do not realize that the attention to relationships is a religious matter.

That is what a Confucian sociology of religion would bring to the table. I am not claiming that relationship-work is the only thing going on in religious settings. I do claim, however, that our discipline's current disregard of it grows directly from sociology's default view: that religions are, at root, focused on beliefs and centered in formal church organizations. That view simply cannot imagine that anything else is important.

Women's Work

It is no surprise that these cases involve women. White, Black, or Latina, women are central to North American religious life, even if sociologists have too often overlooked their contribution. Cheryl Gilkes's comment about African American churches is true of other groups as well. As she put it, "the tendency to view black churches only as agencies of socio-political change led by black male pastors . . . obscures the central and critical roles of black women."[26] To the extent that sociology focuses on religions' official leaders, it fails to notice all women's community-building efforts. Their efforts make church life possible.

Sack made this clear in his account of White Protestant women's kitchen work. He noted that volunteer cooking declined steeply after the 1960s, as women had more out-of-home responsibilities. Often, this was paid work to keep their families going. While only 32% of adult women had paid employment in 1948, over 46% were employed in 1975 and nearly 58% were employed in 2012 (the latest year for which we have figures). These include retired women, so a perhaps better comparison is between the figures for mothers with children at home. Employment rose from 47% to 71% between 1975 and 2012 for those with children under eighteen, from 39% to 65% for those with children under the age of six, and from 34% to 61% for those with children under age three. These women clearly had much less time for church volunteering.[27]

As a result, larger churches gradually turned to professional kitchen staff. Sack reported a 1997 interview with Carolyn Clayton, the executive director of the National Association of Church Food Services, Inc. Her group had some two hundred members, mostly in the Southeast, mostly churches with over a thousand members, and mostly Baptist. "'Fifteen years ago the group would have been all 60-year-old white women,' [Clayton said], but now it has almost 50 men, and is about one-quarter black. Now that men are getting into the field, Clayton notes, salaries are going up." Clayton's own church, Peachtree Road United Methodist in Atlanta, "hasn't had a covered dish supper for years. 'In this area people don't want to cook,' she says; the women work or are volunteers in the community."[28]

Willow Creek Community Church, the famous megachurch in suburban Chicago, takes this one step farther: it has installed a professional food court. This "ministry" does solicit volunteers and its Internet site carries the tagline "Creating community through an atmosphere of delicious food." Still, it is a far cry from St. Pauls' former food events. It treats food as an opportunity for religious conversion. Sack quoted its food director as saying, "Many times walking through these aisles we see people, over a meal, getting saved." Yes, this is human connection, but of a very different kind. Sack put it well:

Whatever the cause, this move from volunteer to professional food preparation also changed the relationship between the church and its members. When members of the church provided the volunteer labor to cook a meal, the church was a community, a place to work together. But when paid cooks prepared the meals, the church was simply a place to eat together, a service provider.[29]

Something was clearly lost.

Without referring to food, Penny Long Marler showed the importance of women's activities to Christian church life in the U.S. and the United Kingdom. She used church participation figures to trace the decline of Christian denominations and congregations to long-term changes in women's roles. She noted that shifts in family structure and patterns of employment had driven the industrial-age expansion of religious organizations. So, too, the post-industrial shifts in both family and work made it harder for those organizations to thrive.[30]

Her argument was rather simple. The earlier era shifted the family from a unit of economic production (the farm or home crafts center) to a unit of consumption that purchased goods with wages. Men worked outside the home; women's unpaid domestic work and childcare supported the wage economy. "At the same time, women's unpaid religious work supported the expansion of religious institutions."[31] Women were particularly charged with socializing the young, including religious socialization. Marler presented figures stretching back to the early 20th century to show the close relationship between attending church as a child and attendance in later adulthood. Once women stopped taking their children to church, the churches began to wither.

Why did they stop? First, they had fewer children. Fertility rates declined by a bit under half between 1960 and 2003 in both the U.S. and the U.K. This was particularly true among Anglicans and the Protestant Mainline.[32] A generation later, these churches were aging and in trouble. Second, women had careers and work. They lacked time for the volunteer work that kept congregations running. Their move from being religious 'producers' to religious 'consumers' meant that fewer people were available to produce the side-activities that encourage religious involvement.

Together, these changes reduced women's willingness and ability to maintain their church communities. As the sense of community declined, so did congregational strength and resources. Marler's subtitle, "Watch the Women," reminds us that religious decline is not an impersonal, mechanical process, as it has been portrayed in much secularization theory. It stems directly from shifts in family and work life that prevent women from maintaining the relationships that make congregations thrive. As women turn to other things, churches will continue to decline.

A Confucian sociologist of religion would have seen this pattern instantly. Western sociologists of religion have mostly not. True, Catholic News Service reporter Nancy O'Brien did quote sociologist Robert Putnam as recommending that church pastors should "spend less time on the sermons and more time arranging church suppers." His survey research showed a direct relationship between the strength of church friendship networks and personal life satisfaction. Church suppers build intra-congregational relationships rather well.[33] Putnam underscored for *all* congregations what Dodson and Gilkes revealed about African American congregations and Flores showed about San Antonio's West Side. Sacred work occurs not just in the church sanctuary but in the maintenance of community. It is relational work, a ritual attention to human relationships (the Confucian *lǐ* 禮) that creates a circle of virtue (or *dé* 德). This community-work sustains religious groups. Had the sociology of religion been founded on Confucian principles instead of Western Christian ones, we would have noticed this long ago.

I see the irony here. Chinese culture, in general, and Confucianism, in particular, are not known for their good treatment of women. Besides the house god, my grandfather's artifacts included a set of foot-binding shoes, from the era when upper-class Chinese women's feet were deliberately deformed to make the women decorative and 'beautiful'. Married women venerated their husband's ancestors, not their own. Male children were favored while female children were often neglected—sometimes fatally so.[34]

It is women, however, who have traditionally sustained the interpersonal relationships on which American religious congregations depend. A Confucian sociology of religion would not miss this. It would highlight this as sacred work, central to religion. It would not have let Western religion's attention to belief and doctrine (and to its own forms of male superiority) keep women's central role in congregational life in the dark for so long.

Nor, on the other hand, would it assume that relationship-work always belongs to women. Who does this work varies from time to time and place to place. Like so many things, the details matter.

Individualized Religion?

What else might a Confucian sociology of religion accomplish? Among other things, it might deepen the recent explorations of 'spirituality' in advanced industrial countries. Many studies have tracked the current rejection of formal religion in favor of personal spirituality. Most describe this as a form of religious individualism, which they often see happening beyond church walls.

For example, Robert Bellah and his co-authors of the famous *Habits of the Heart* wrote about an extreme approach to religion in which each individual gets to claim her or his own truth. This is "Sheilaism," a term coined by "Sheila Larsen," their pseudonym for one of their interviewees. As they described her religious life:

> "I believe in God," Sheila says. "I am not a religious fanatic. I can't remember the last time I went to church. My faith has carried me a long way. It's Sheilaism. Just my own little voice."

They commented:

> Sheila's faith has some tenets beyond belief in God, though not many. In defining what she calls "my own Sheilaism," she said: "It's just try to love yourself and be gentle with yourself. You know, I guess, take care of each other. I think God would want us to take care of each other." Like many others, Sheila would be willing to endorse few more specific points.[35]

This trend clearly worried Bellah and his team. They wrote that Sheilaism "suggests the logical possibility of more than 235 million American religions, one for each of us." This implied to them a religious solipsism, a religious privatization, a withdrawal of religion from the public sphere into the individual heart. In a later lecture, Bellah described this as a threat to democracy:

radical autonomy . . . pushed to its extreme . . . leads to authoritarianism. This is Tocqueville's teaching. Society reduced to its constituent individuals, each isolated and alone, shut up in the solitude of their own hearts, as he said, automatically becomes a despotic society, because people cannot effectively, through corporate action, make a difference in their government. And so they will be ruled, whether they like it or not or even whether they know it or not, by powers entirely out of their control.[36]

Bellah saw this as an attitude of churchgoers, not just of the unchurched. As he put it in the just-quoted lecture, "many people sitting in the pews of Protestant and even Catholic churches are Sheilaists," who do not think their personal religion should be constrained by the historic church, the Bible, or tradition. This, he said, partly explained American churches' declining public influence.

The problem, of course, is that we are given no data about Sheila Larsen's actual religious practices and specifically nothing about her religious relationships. Bellah and his team presented her as a religious individualist, but their data forced them to do so. They interviewed her as an individual about her individual religious views. They did not report asking her about any communal religious life, nor even any communal secular life. We know nothing about the nest of relationships in which she probably lives.[37]

A Confucian sociologist would ask about such things. A Confucian sociologist would not assume that someone who says that religion is a private, personal matter is, in fact, an isolated individual. We are, in the Confucian view, all shaped by our social surroundings. Pulling an interviewee out of those surroundings and interviewing her about her personal views emphasizes her individualism. Perhaps it partially creates it. Bellah and his team did not give us the data, so we do not know.

It gets worse. Jeffrey Stout noted that the interviews that formed the basis for *Habits of the Heart* often seemed to push respondents toward an individualism that they may well not have embraced. Of their opening interview with "Brian Palmer," for example, he wrote:

When [Anne] Swidler [the interviewer] asks Brian why he finds the outcome happy, he says that he just finds "more personal satisfaction from choosing course B over course A" (p.8). . . . Bellah and his coauthors treat these remarks as if Brian were advocating a moral principle of the form, "One ought always to choose the course that will maximize one's own satisfaction." Brian can, however, just as easily be read as offering his own experience as evidence for the claim that one course is objectively better than the other. He may be saying, in effect, "I have lived in each of these ways. The first way made me miserable. The second way, with its shared goals and mutual respect, made me happy."[38]

Stout's point was that interviewers can easily think people are moral individualists if they fail to ask the questions that might reveal otherwise. They can just as easily think people are *religious* individualists, if they fail to ask about the social ties that connect them with others or about the degree to which they find those ties meaningful, even sacred. This failure comes naturally to sociology's default view of religion, because that view focuses on religious beliefs and participation in formal religious organizations.

A Confucian sociologist would begin quite differently. She or he would assume that people live in a nest of social ties and would automatically ask about them. We would see clear pictures of Sheila's, Brian's, and the rest of the interviewees' connections with others. We would see how these work in practice, and particularly what sustains them. Of course it is possible that nothing does; Bellah and his colleagues did not give us enough data to tell. Yet the Confucian starting point would tell us for sure.

This is not the only example of the default view shaping sociologists' conclusions. Operating at a quite different level, Paul Heelas and Linda Woodhead explored a shift from theistic religion to what they called "subjective-life" spirituality in Britain and the United States. Heelas has long written about 'New Age' religion and individual spirituality. In their jointly run empirical study, they looked at the decline of church religion and the growth of individualistic spiritualities in the Lake District town of Kendal, England.[39]

The Kendal study aimed to gauge the extent of what the authors called various "patterns of the sacred" among this market town's thirty thousand inhabitants. They distinguished two patterns: a "congregational domain" and a "holistic milieu." The congregational domain was made up of groups, mainly centered in the established churches. The holistic domain contained some groups but more of its practitioners worked one-on-one with clients. These included chiropractors, homeopaths, osteopaths, aroma therapists, Tarot specialists, and other non-mainstream consultants. Groups included yoga classes, meditation classes, and the like.

> By way of several methods, including use of British Telecom Archives of the Cumbria and North Lancashire Yellow Pages running back to 1969, we established that there were virtually no holistic, mind-body-spirit activities in 1970. At the time of our research, however, there were 126 separate activities provided by 95 spiritual practitioners—41 practitioners served 63 different groups and 63 practitioners worked with individual clients (9 practitioners served both groups and individual clients).[40]

That's quite a bevy, though the total number of people active in the holistic milieu in a given week amounted to just 1.6% of the Kendal population. Many times more than that were involved in congregational religion. Numbers are not the issue, however. Nor is the fact—raised by David Voas and Steve Bruce—that "nearly half of the respondents to the questionnaire sent to all the participants of the holistic milieu did not consider their activities to be of spiritual significance."[41] The issue for us is what Heelas and Woodhead's *a priori* opposition between organized, institutional church religion and individualistic forms of spirituality prevented them from seeing.

Heelas later acknowledged one such blindness, writing: "I am now firmly convinced that the either-or approach . . . was something of an un-avoidable mistake."[42] Some, perhaps many people participated in both domains, something that the original research was not designed to discover.

More serious, however, was the choice to focus on the individual beliefs and practices of the people involved in the holistic domain. The emphasis on beliefs made the holistic spiritualities seem more individualistic than was likely the case. So did the study's emphasis on things people did alone or in small groups.

Heelas and Woodhead focused on the ways that individuals found meaning in such activities. They did not ask about the network of relationships that (probably) sustained them as they did so.

A Confucian sociologist would likely ask different questions about this data. Rather than opposing religious groups to spiritual individuals, a Confucian sociologist would likely look for the relational ties that make both kinds of religion possible. In my own observation, for example, the friendship networks among yoga practitioners in the U.S. turn this 'individualistic' client-based activity into a social network. Such relationships sustain participants far more deeply than would be possible if individualism ruled. This might not be the case in Kendal, but that in itself would be an important finding.

Can what Heelas and Woodhead called the "holistic milieu" develop relational networks like those that let American congregations thrive in the first half of the 20th century? Or is 'spirituality' so much an individual matter that it becomes a mere way-station on the road to religious oblivion? A sociology of religion based in traditional Chinese thought would attempt to trace these relational networks and would ask how (or whether) they are maintained. Heelas and Woodhead did not focus on this, nor has either of them done so in their very interesting subsequent work.[43] A Confucian sociology of religion would suggest that someone do.

This is, by the way, no small matter. Woodhead's work, in particular, constitutes a leading edge of the contemporary sociology of religion. She, Tuomas Martikainen, and François Gauthier are doing very creative work on non-traditional spiritual and religious practices, particularly those shaped by neo-liberal politics and consumer culture. Other scholars are exploring what they call a 'digital religion': religion on the Internet, the religious use of digital social media, and so on.[44] These are creative endeavors, in which I have participated, but they too seldom examine the ways in which relationships are maintained—or are not—in these new circumstances.

I have publically worried about the degree to which the new spiritualities that Heelas, Woodhead, and others study lack the organizational resources to engage in effective social criticism.[45] Let me add here that their peculiar organizational form could also hinder the development of the kinds of sacred relationships discussed in the previous chapter. This may or may not happen, but standard sociology has not encouraged us to gather the kind of data that would tell us for sure. It is something that Confucian sociology of religion would want to explore.

The point is: Chinese religion is not church religion, so a Confucian sociology of religion—like Heelas and Woodhead—would see formal religious organizations as only part of the religious landscape. She or he would not, however, simply assume that non-church religion is an individual matter. She or he would instead assume that non-church religion, like other kinds, requires someone to attend to sacred relationships.

Lest you think that no contemporary sociologist is doing so such work on alternative religious communities, let me suggest that you read Douglas Ezzy's recent study of a contemporary Pagan festival.[46] Ezzy described "Faunalia," a four-day, three-night set of rituals designed to "restore Soul" to its mostly Australian participants. He focused on two main rituals: the "Underworld" and "Baphomet," each of which was designed to "provide an experience of the frailty of humanity at the limits of our ability to understand and communicate." The first helps participants overcome their fear of death, by means of a ritualized capture, burial, and resurrection. The second helps them transcend their fear of erotic desire by presenting them naked to a hybrid animal/human, male/female, goat-headed deity that represents the animalistic and sexual side of being human. Though focused on individual experiences and deeply supportive of personal interpretations of the divine, the rituals simultaneously create a keen attention to ethical relationships. In Ezzy's words,

> In moments and experiences that are "beyond words," participants at Faunalia engage with a threatening other that is also desired and loved. In a moment of mutual recognition, they both pursue their own authenticity and an ethical concern for the other.[47]

Ezzy shows that in this case, one cannot separate the individual from the festival's relational context. As difficult as it is to picture Confucius dancing naked before a hermaphroditic goat-headed god, it is not at all difficult to imagine a Confucian sociologist seeing individualism and community happening at the same time. That is the genius of the Confucian approach: seeing that individuals and sacred relationships cannot be separated.

Rethinking 'Tradition'

A Confucian sociology could do other things, as well. Specifically, it could free us from sociology's default view that 'traditional society' is deficient compared to 'modern society'. This is the great heritage of sociology's 19th-century origin. It is also a particularly unfruitful way of seeing the world.

In Chapter Two, I criticized Max Weber for treating 'tradition' as a matter of inertia. For him, traditional action was 'doing what has always been done'. I pointed out that this made the concept 'tradition' a mere placeholder: a theoretic foil for Weber's real interest, the roles played by various kinds of rationality in producing the modern world. Rationality was modern, so doing things by rote had to be tradition. Progress was modern, so tradition had to be static. Despite Weber's ambivalence about living in an overly rational world, these attitudes are at the root of his sociology. This exemplifies the default view.

In that chapter, I also outlined an alternate approach to tradition, based on H. Richard Niebuhr's ethics of responsibility. In this view, tradition is based in relationships. Like the early Confucians, Niebuhr saw the self as inherently social. We are all born into a nest of relationships, to which we have responsibilities. Where the Weberian goal-oriented self starts from the pursuit of personal ends and the value-oriented self starts from personal values or rules, the traditional self begins with the relationships and responsibilities into which she or he has been born. In this view, one follows traditional authorities not out of inertia but because one has ongoing relationships with them. Likewise a traditional leader acts out of an established, ongoing relationship with her or his followers. Tradition is no mindless habit. Instead, it consists of the ongoing social ties that are built into our very selves.

This is, at root, a Confucian view. Like Niebuhr, a Confucian sociology of religion would not assume that all action is relational but it would understand relational action far better than does the Weberian approach. It would not produce the one-sided 'dilemmas of institutionalization' that we find in Thomas O'Dea's famous predictions about religious development.[48] Better put, it would not regard such dilemmas as inevitable. Their presence or absence would vary according to the strength or weakness of the interpersonal relationships that shape the religious community. A Confucian sociology of religion would particularly focus on the ways in which the maintenance or non-maintenance of those relationships shapes the character of the people involved.

Traditional Chinese society was 'traditional' not because it hewed to established patterns but because it placed great emphasis on nurturing the web of relationships that constitute both social life and individuals. Weberian sociology misses this, to its loss.

There are other ways besides Confucian philosophy to get to this conclusion. Niebuhr's is one, though he created a relational ethics, not a sociology of religion; it was I who nearly twenty years ago suggested how to extend it into our discipline.[49] Another would be to use feminist responsibility ethics, such as Nel Noddings's "ethics of care."[50] These are also relational, emphasizing the socially engrained tendency of women to take responsibility for relationships, and not just in Western societies. Noddings distinguished between "natural care," in which all humans engage, and an "ethics of care," which asks people to take responsibility for others, even when they do not wish to. Unlike Kantian deontology, this is not a responsibility that rests with individuals *qua* individuals; instead it arises from their status as social beings who are constituted by their ties to each other. The result is an ethical system that treats relationships as primary and individuals as secondary. This, too, could generate a different notion of tradition.

However, neither of these ethical systems produces as clean a rethinking of 'tradition' as does a Confucian sociology. Sociologists already consider Confucian thought to be traditional. Were they more familiar with its features, they would see that its traditionalism has nothing to do with inertia and everything to do with social ties. The shift from tradition to rational modernity is, in the end, a rupture of such ties. This insight is not new to sociologists. However, a Confucian approach would give them a new appreciation of the relational texture of traditional life and better grasp on what the shift from that traditional world means.

That is the point. Had sociology emerged from a Confucian context, it would automatically see some things that the Western view misses and miss some things that the Western view sees. Each sociology would remain shaped by its historical-cultural context. Every intellectual discipline is so shaped, would we only admit it. Having two such sociologies to hand, however, would let us see religion with an additional set of eyes. We would understand better some aspects of religious life than we do now.

Ibn Khaldūn Image from Tunisian 10-Dinar Note. Photo by Getty Images.

5

To North Africa

An Arab Judge Looks at History

Now for something completely different. The previous two chapters have explored Chinese civilization, to see what new perspectives it can give us on religious life. This chapter does not attempt to summarize a tradition, much less a civilization. Instead, it explores the writings of a single man.

Walī al-Dīn Abū Zayd 'Abd ar-Raḥmān Ibn Muḥammad Ibn Khaldūn al-Tūnisī al-Haḍramī[1] was born in Tunis, in North Africa, in 1332 CE (734 AH). Known by his clan name, Ibn Khaldūn, his work is more popular today than it was when I was a student. Yet it is still under-appreciated. A politician and court advisor as a young man and the chief judge (qadi) of the Maliki school of Islamic law in his middle and old age, Khaldūn wrote an encyclopedic history of the Arab conquests and of the rise and fall of its dynasties and kingdoms. He covered nine centuries of events ranging across the Middle East from Iran to Moorish Spain. That work, the Kitāb al-'Ibar ('Book of History'), was the first analysis of the socio-political dynamics of a multi-ethnic, multi-religious society. Together with its introduction, the Muqaddimah, it contains ideas that can help us understand certain religious dynamics today.[2]

We moderns think we live in a chaotic world. The 20th and early 21st centuries have been filled with wars, genocides, and abject brutalities. They have also been filled with great efforts for human rights, social progress, and world peace. Yet we cannot forget the millions of soldiers and civilians killed in World War II, the millions more who died during Stalin's and Mao's famines, the Holocaust, the genocides in Armenia, Rwanda, and Cambodia, and the civil wars over land and resources in Central America, West Africa, Angola, and elsewhere. Nor can we forget the current collapsed states in much of the Islamic world. We who have lived through these times often imagine that earlier eras moved more slowly than ours, and were thus more stable. They were not.

Ibn Khaldūn's century—the 14th of the Common Era—was even more chaotic than ours. His was the century of the plague: the 'Black Death' that carried off as much as 60% of Europe's population. North Africa suffered similar death rates and also much political instability. Armies invaded, common people rebelled, and kingdoms collapsed in both Christian and Muslim lands. This constant disorder shaped Ibn Khaldūn's views just as much as Europe's stability during the 'High Middle Ages' had shaped Thomas Aquinas's hopeful views.[3]

Image yourself a fifteen-year-old boy in 1347, living in Tunis under the Hafsid dynasty, which ruled what was then the most powerful state in North Africa. You are the son and grandson of scholars and the great-grandson and great-great-grandson of court diplomats. You study politics, literature, Qur'an, and jurisprudence with some of the best teachers of your day. Some were refugees from Moorish Spain, or the descendants of refugees, for by the time of your birth, the centuries-long Christian Reconquista had left only Granada in Muslim hands. Your forebears, too, had left Spain more than a century ago; they had been prominent in Seville. You are bright and well connected. Life is promising for such an intelligent son of a distinguished family.[4]

All of a sudden, things fall apart. The armies of Abul-Hasan, the Merinid ruler of Fez, conquer Tunis and send the Hafsids into exile. The new court brings you new teachers, but an Arab tribal revolt drives out Abul-Hasan's troops the following year. Then the plague hits. Your parents, other of your relatives, and several of your most esteemed teachers die. The city is in chaos. What future does an ambitious boy have in a place like this?

Ibn Khaldūn did not stay. Though offered a minor post by the returning Hafsids, he soon followed one of his remaining teachers westward: first to Bougie, on the North African coast, then to Fez. There, he became part of a scholarly circle set up by Abul-Hasan's son and successor, Abu 'Inan. He stayed eight years. For a time he was Abu 'Inan's secretary, but that ended when the ruler decided to retake Tunis. He put Khaldūn in jail, perhaps not wanting a resourceful Tunisian at large while he was gone.[5] Khaldūn remained in prison for twenty-one months, until Abu 'Inan's death. The new ruler made him minister of state, but after that man's death in a revolt, Khaldūn moved to Granada. There he was made an ambassador to the court of Pedro the Cruel, the Christian king of

Castile. Intrigues at both the Moorish and Spanish courts drove him again to North Africa, where he became prime minister to Abu 'Abdallah, the Hafsid ruler of Bougie. That post lasted a couple of years. Then, the Hafsids fell into dynastic bickering and Ibn Khaldūn thought it best to find work elsewhere.

I could go on, but you see the pattern. Franz Rosenthal, who translated Ibn Khaldūn's masterwork into English, recounts the story in great detail. For our purposes, it is the pattern that matters. North African and Spanish/Moorish politics were chaotic and deadly. Theirs was a civilization in decline, in which few thought that all Muslims ought to work together. Factionalism, intrigue, and personal aggrandizement were the rule, not the exception. Ibn Khaldūn saw this. He could not manage this as a politician, so his task as a scholar was to explain why it happened.[6]

He soon got his chance to do so. In 1375 he was asked to lead a political mission to some Arab tribes in what is now central Algeria. He persuaded one of their leaders to give his family protection at Qal'at Ibn Salamah, a rural castle in the province of Oran. He spent three years there in quiet and comfort. He later wrote in his autobiography,

> I completed the Introduction *(Muqaddimah)* [to the *Kitāb al-'Ibar*] in that remarkable manner to which I was inspired by that retreat, with words and ideas pouring into my head like cream into a churn, until the finished product was ready.[7]

It is this *Muqaddimah* for which Ibn Khaldūn is now remembered. Despite its title, it is more than a mere 'introduction'. It lays out a set of principles for a new approach to history. In some passages, he called this *'ilm al-'umrān al-basharī* ('the science of human organization') and in others *'ilm al-ijtimā al-insanī* ('the science of human society'). He meant these terms to distinguish his project from ordinary history, which he saw as a record of events that float on history's surface *(ẓāhir)*. In the *Muqaddimah*, he sought to lay out history's inner meaning *(bāṭin)*. To him, an historian ought to provide a "subtle explanation of the causes and origins of existing things, and deep knowledge of the how and why of events."[8]

This is why Ibn Khaldūn is frequently called the world's first sociologist. To use a phrase often applied to 19th-century European thinkers, he tried to uncover the 'motor of history'. Hegel famously found this motor in the dialectical movement of ideas; Marx found it in the internal contradictions of the economic order. Ibn Khaldūn found it in the dynamics of *al 'aṣabiyyah*, a term usually translated as "group-feeling," "esprit de corps," or "spirit of kinship." The term comes from the Arabic root *'aṣab*, "to bind." It is a force for social solidarity. Societies with well-developed *'aṣabiyyah* are strong and capable; those whose *'aṣabiyyah* is weak divide easily and are quickly conquered. The *Muqaddimah* outlines the aspects of social life that strengthen and weaken *'aṣabiyyah*. The rest of the *Kitāb al-'Ibar* applies this analysis to the pre-Islamic Mediterranean world, to early Arab and eastern Muslim history, and to the history of the Muslim west.[9]

Three Key Ideas

Ibn Khaldūn built his work around three key ideas. The first was a basic distinction between nomadic and sedentary peoples, rooted in the differing requirements of their ways of life. The second was the importance of *al 'aṣabiyyah* to a group's ability to organize itself and to stay united. The third was the role of Islam in augmenting or transforming this group-feeling. Together, these ideas let Khaldūn trace the interactions between kin ties, economics, and religions as they influenced the rise and fall of the various groups that shaped the history of North Africa and the eastern Mediterranean. We'll take up each idea in turn.

Tribes and Cities

Ibn Khaldūn saw history as a cyclic struggle between barbarism and civilization—or 'tribes and cities', to use a popular shorthand. He saw nomads as typified by "*badāwah*"—"bedouinity" or "desert attitude." Their sparse surroundings force them to move their herds to find grass and water. Wet years bring good grazing and their animals increase, though they still must move to find fresh feed. Dry years bring privation: lands dry up, water disappears, and sand covers what little vegetation remains. In these times, no one can afford to be generous. Groups battle over resources. In short, dwelling in an unstable natural environment gives tribes a rude and savage life. They endure with little and work hard for what they get.[10]

This life has consequences for tribal social relations. To put it bluntly, tribes can survive only if they stick together. Tribal peoples, wrote Khaldūn,

> are alone in the country and remote from [protection by civil] militias. They have no walls and gates. Therefore, they provide their own defense and do not entrust it to, or rely upon others for it. They always carry weapons. They watch carefully all sides of the road. They take hurried naps only when they are together in company or when they are in the saddle. They pay attention to every faint barking and noise. . . . Fortitude has become a character quality of theirs, and courage their nature. They use it whenever they are called upon or an alarm stirs them.[11]

In such a situation, the tribe is everything. Individuals cannot survive alone, and if a tribe starts bickering, it risks being overrun by others. The tribe has to work as a unit, both to master its environment and in response to outside threats. Compelled to courage and fortitude, its members support each other against all comers

"*Hatharah*"—"sedentarization"—on the other hand, typifies settled peoples. Relatively speaking, these people are stable and rich. Agriculture, trading, and similar livelihoods let them accumulate wealth. They spend this on better living, which, Khaldūn argued, softens their characters. They think more of themselves and less of their neighbors, because they can afford to do so. They ask magistrates and rulers to defend them both against their fellow citizens and against hostile outsiders. They depend on institutions for support—on laws, not on persons. In short, their living makes them less able to take care of themselves. As Khaldūn put it:

> sedentary people have become used to laziness and ease. They are sunk in well-being and luxury. They have entrusted defense of their property and their lives to the governor and ruler who rules them, and to the militia which has the task of guarding them. They find full assurance of safety in the walls that surround them, and the fortifications that protect them. No noise disturbs them, and no hunting occupies them. They are carefree and trusting, and have ceased to carry weapons. Successive generations have grown up in this way of life. They have become like women and children, who depend upon the master of the house. Eventually, this has come to be a quality of character.[12]

Clearly, Ibn Khaldūn exaggerated this picture to make a point. In doing so, he was merely creating what Max Weber would later call *ideal types*. These are logically distinct cases by which an analyst seeks to capture the range of social possibilities. No particular society corresponds completely to either *badāwah* or *hatharah*. The distinction between them, however, illustrates something important.[13]

Specifically, Khaldūn proposed two principles. First, he claimed that everyday life shapes people's character; second, he claimed that different patterns of character are typical in different societies. Some groups live in rigorous circumstances, which call forth personal fortitude and a devotion to the group. Other groups find easier living, because their circumstances let them accumulate wealth. The former suppress individuality, the latter encourage it. Both kinds of society need order, but the former calls on everyone to help each other while the latter lets people delegate key tasks to others. Ibn Khaldūn was interested in the consequences of these situations for various societies' development.

> Since . . . desert life no doubt is the reason for bravery, savage groups are braver than others. They are, therefore, better able to achieve superiority and to take away the things that are in the hands of other nations. The situation of one and the same group changes, in this respect, with the change of time. Whenever people settle in the fertile plains and amass luxuries and become accustomed to a life of abundance and luxury, their bravery decreases to the degree that their wildness and desert habits decrease. . . . [T]he more firmly rooted in desert habits and the wilder a group is, the closer does it come to achieving [military] superiority over others.[14]

This is Ibn Khaldūn's central point about these two social types: they produce a cycle of conquest and dissolution. Harsh life makes tribes strong and fierce, which enables them to conquer softer city dwellers. On doing so, they become rulers, who settle down and take on the civilized habits of their subjects. After a couple of generations of sedentary life, they lose their unity and fortitude and so fall to the next wave of barbarians. Khaldūn saw the history of his native Maghreb, of Islam, and indeed of the Mediterranean world since Roman times as a cyclical history of conquest. Tribes overwhelmed cities, became civilized, and were overwhelmed by other tribes in their turn.[15]

Some contemporary scholars have taken up this contrast. Daniel Pipes, for example, calculated that Muslim armies were disproportionately made up of soldiers from the steppes, deserts, and mountains from the time of Islam's 8th-century expansion until 1823, when Egypt's Muḥammad ʿAlī conscripted Nile valley peasants to make a national army. He thus supported Khaldūn's point. On the other hand, Pipes argued against Khaldūn, saying that pre-Muslim armies were not so dependent on soldiers from marginal areas. Yet under Islam, he agreed, troops that came from a hard life were far more successful than were those raised in gentler circumstances. Benjamin Barber similarly opposed tribes and cities in his popular analysis of current political events, *Jihad vs. McWorld*. His contrast, however, was not closely attuned to Khaldūn's work, in that he treated "jihad" as a reaction to globalization, not as the natural result of harsh tribal life.[16]

Al ʿAṣabiyyah

For Ibn Khaldūn, there is a deeper motor to this process. He did not think that military success is the result of just individual fortitude; more importantly, it depends on group unity. Other things being equal, unified peoples will conquer those who are less able to cooperate. Tribes and city people, in his view, differ in the amount of feeling they have for one another. He used the term *ʿaṣabiyyah* to describe the emotion that leads group members toward mutual support. Tribal people have a strong group-feeling, which to leads them to support each other, even at the cost of their own lives. City folk have less group-feeling, so they are less apt to sacrifice themselves for the common good.

Ibn Khaldūn wrote that group-feeling has several sources, of which kinship is the strongest. In his words:

[Respect for] blood ties is something natural among men, with the rarest exceptions. It leads to affection for one's relations and blood relatives, [the feeling that] no harm ought to befall them nor any destruction come upon them. One feels shame when one's relatives are treated unjustly or attacked, and one wishes to intervene between them and whatever peril or destruction threatens them. This is a natural urge in man, for as long as there have been human beings. The direct relationship between persons who help each other is very close, so that it leads to close contact and unity.[17]

Different social settings, however, can emphasize or deemphasize these ties. Tribal peoples live with and depend on their kin, while settled folk live with kin and non-kin alike. It makes sense that kin group-feeling is stronger among tribes than elsewhere. Tribes, wrote Ibn Khaldūn, will fight to the death for their group. They thus readily prevail over those for whom the group is not so important.

In Ibn Khaldūn's telling, group-feeling is, at first, external or defensive. It is the functional equivalent for nomads of the fortresses and armies of city folk. Lacking economic resources and even a secure livelihood, nomads must depend on their group or die. Some scholars thus see in al ʿaṣabiyyah a substitute for the strength and security that richer societies provide.[18]

Yet Ibn Khaldūn did not see complex societies as having something that nomads lack. On the contrary, he saw just the opposite. City dwellers not only lack the personal fortitude found among nomads, they also lack their strong group-feeling and common will. They are not used to looking out for one another, which makes it harder for them to respond to emergencies. This leads to their eventual defeat. Law and armies compensate somewhat for sedentary people's weak aṣabiyyah, but they cannot replace it. Nomads' superior group-feeling and lack of regard for outsiders allows them a single-minded brutality that ultimately prevails.

There is, however, a catch: it does not prevail for long. The nomads' victory brings booty, wealth, and rich living. This weakens their aṣabiyyah, for which they substitute laws, mercenary armies, and so on. Ultimately, they become weak enough to fall to others.

When a tribe has achieved a certain measure of superiority with the help of its group feeling, it gains control over a corresponding amount of wealth and comes to share prosperity and abundance with those who have been in possession of these things [for a long time]. . . . As a result, the toughness of desert life is lost. Group feeling and courage weaken. Members of the tribe revel in the well-being that God has given them. Their children and offspring grow up too proud to look after themselves or to attend to their own needs. They have disdain also for all the other things that are necessary in connection with group feeling. This finally becomes a character trait and natural characteristic of theirs. Their group feeling and courage decrease in the next generations. Eventually, group feeling is altogether destroyed. They thus invite [their] own destruction.[19]

Ibn Khaldūn thought this process took at most four generations.[20]

Let's step back for a moment. Clearly, Ibn Khaldūn focused on kin ties, though he wrote that these need not be actual blood connections. Master-client relations, close friendships, longstanding relationships with neighbors, and so on can also produce strong group-feelings. The issue is not whether people have common ancestors; the issue is the degree to which a group holds together based on a sense of mutual commitment. As Khaldūn put it, "A pedigree is something imaginary and devoid of reality. Its usefulness consists only in the resulting connection and close contact."[21] Other social ties can be equally strong.

Read even more generally, however, Ibn Khaldūn is giving us a theory of ethnic solidarity—a theory of how and when ethnic groups hold together. Modern social science knows that ethnicity is not rooted in biology or descent but in social identification and attribution. Your 'ethnicity' depends on what others think you are and what you claim to be. Ibn Khaldūn said much the same. Biology and descent are mere metaphors. Ethnic groups form because others treat them as groups and also because people see themselves as connected with one another. Ibn Khaldūn emphasized the second of these. His work contains a centripetal (or center-focused) theory of group solidarity. For him, groups unite by mutual attraction, which can be either strong or weak. He traces both the causes of this strength or weakness and also its consequences.

We can illustrate this with some contemporary examples. First, people can, and do, take on non-relatives as family. The Irish American adopted 'son' of the Corleone family in the *Godfather* films is a fine example. He acts out of family loyalty as much as do the 'real' Italian sons. His group-feeling is strong. Second, ethnic ties are variable. One of my graduate professors often challenged us to identify his ethnic background. We could not, in that pre-Internet age, and his looks did not give us a clear reckoning. Nor did his behavior: he hung out with and was accepted by Whites, African Americans, Asian Americans, and even a few Latinos (though that was not the name-of-choice in that era). What was he? He seemed to be able to move across 'ethnic' borders with ease.

Similarly, Paul Spickard and Rowena Fong showed how Pacific Islanders are able to shift ethnic identities across their lifetimes. Most are of mixed ethnicities and the Islander kin system lets them actualize whichever of their varied identities they need. Depending on how they can trace their relatives, they can become Tongan while in Tongan communities, Samoan in Samoan communities, generic 'Islander' among Islander Whites, and so on. Spickard and Fong speculate that perhaps such flexible ethnicities will become more common in an increasingly mixed-race world—a city-world, in which Ibn Khaldūn would expect group-based *aṣabiyyah* to be weak.[22]

Here is one more example. I have a colleague who grew up 'White', in the United States, but became 'Black' when he moved to London. He has spent much of his professional life trying to become 'Asian'. How does this work? His parents were from Pakistan. The U.S. counts Pakistanis as 'Caucasian', but in Britain they have been popularly lumped with West Indians, Africans, and other immigrants from the former empire. All are termed 'Black'. The last thirty years have seen a vigorous identity movement among British South Asians, who have sought their own category. They have demanded the right to choose their own ethnicity. Their social and political struggle has largely worked, in part because several decades of British leaders have realized that the United Kingdom is no longer made up just of pale English speakers. The U.K. is now a multicultural society. The question is how to make sure that this society does not fragment. Leaders of all political stripes recognize that forcing White British identity on everyone is out of the question.[23]

This is a useful example, because it shows how ethnicity can be a matter of both attribution and choice. My colleague used to have an attributed identity: one to which he was assigned. Now he has chosen—and agitated for—a different one. Not everyone gets to do this, especially in societies riven with ethnic conflict. My colleague's educational and class privilege gave him leverage that other people do not have.[24]

As Ellis Cose showed in his interviews with successful African American professionals, however, even knowledge and accomplishment do not erase some ethnic barriers. The White police officer who accosted African American Harvard professor Henry Louis Gates in 2009 for 'breaking and entering' into his own house, and then arrested him on his own porch for 'disorderly conduct', clearly thought that this Black man was out of place. The case made headline news, while proving that some ethnic attributions are harder than others to erase.[25]

Ibn Khaldūn has two things to add. First, his theory of group-feeling highlights the fact that the strength of group identification is variable, not constant, and that it depends on the circumstances of daily life. He wrote that tribal peoples have strong 'aṣabiyyah because their situation demands that they stay unified. If they do not, they are overrun by others. He wrote that city peoples have weaker 'aṣabiyyah because they do not depend on their group for day-to-day protection and sustenance. If this is right, the opponents of British multiculturalism should stop worrying. Britain's ethnic diversity is a city phenomenon, which Khaldūn thought meant easy living. He wrote that easy living always undercuts in-group loyalties.

Here's where Khaldūn may need some correction. At least part of Britain's ethnic landscape puts some ethnic groups in poverty. The U.S. is not the only place where minorities have less access to jobs, education, and prospects. City police forces in both countries often target them for special treatment, from formal 'stop-and-frisk' policies to informal patterns of arrest that result in fines that pay the cities' bills. Ethnic youth gangs are one response to this kind of oppression. They protect their members and give them a sense of unity that looks an awful lot like the aṣabiyyah that Khaldūn attributed to desert dwellers. In this sense, cities can generate group-feeling too.

Khaldūn's point is about the rigors of life, however, not whether one lives in a rural or a built-up environment. Group-feeling varies according to that rigor: high where life is hard, low where it is not. That makes it a variable. Measuring group-feeling is something that social analysts need to do, as they seek to understand particular situations.

Ibn Khaldūn's second point is about how ethnic ties form. He proposed a centripetal (center-focused) theory. For him, groups are strong or weak based on the ties that members have with each other. Strong 'aṣabiyyah comes from strong internal ties, and it lets groups prosper. Weak 'aṣabiyyah keeps them from uniting. Khaldūn's approach is all about internal attraction: members either feel connected to one another or they do not. The feeling they have for each other makes their groups rise or fall.

This is not the only way to conceive of group cohesiveness. It is one of two basic models, the other of which argues that groups are formed by conflict with outsiders. Such conflict leads each party to consolidate out of fear and for self-protection. These are edge-focused theories, not center-focused ones. Many contemporary scholars focus on edges, em-

phasizing either the role that actual attacks play in creating group support networks or, more abstractly, examining groups' reactions to such
things as the 'pressures of modernity'. In both cases, the idea is that outside stresses lead groups to unite.[26]

The distinction is relatively simple. On the one hand, groups can
unite by mutual attraction—in Ibn Khaldūn's case because of the feeling they have for one another. On the other hand, they can be forced
together by outside circumstances: oppression, war, or maltreatment.
Both clearly occur, but Ibn Khaldūn argued that only inwardly generated group-feeling could create the kind of solidarity that keeps groups
strong. Were outside pressure the only factor, then groups would fall
apart as soon as the pressure lifted. He emphasized, however, that
group solidarity is active, not just reactive. Yes, Bedouins had to band
together for safety, but they also banded together because they depended on each other for survival in a harsh environment. Raised to
be mutually supporting, they developed the habit of watching out for
the group's well-being. It took, he said, up to four generations of easy
living for them to forget this habit of mutual care. Only then does
group-feeling decline. For him, al 'aṣabiyyah's centripetal attraction is
crucial for group unity.

Religion

Ibn Khaldūn made one further turn that contemporary theorists of
ethnic solidarity do not. He saw a role for religion in generating and
regulating al 'aṣabiyyah.

As noted above, Ibn Khaldūn thought that city dwellers had a problem. Settled life lowered their sense of group-feeling and encouraged
them to put themselves above others. It turns out that he thought that
tribes had a problem, too. They were sometimes so group-oriented that
it was hard for them to work with outsiders, at least for very long.

He best described this in his discussion of the nomadic pre-Muslim
Arabs.[27] They were, he wrote, extremely warlike and also extremely successful at conquering others. He called them the most barbarous of peoples, because their life as camel herders kept them in the most nomadic
condition. They thus had strong 'aṣabiyyah, courage, and fortitude, but
were the most remote from civilization. Their loyalty was limited to

blood relations, and their warfare produced only pillage and ruin. He described them as

> a savage nation, fully accustomed to savagery and the things that cause it. Savagery has become their character and nature. They enjoy it, because it means freedom from authority and no subservience to leadership. . . . On account of their savage nature, [they] are people who plunder and cause damage. They plunder whatever they are able to lay their hands on without having to fight or to expose themselves to danger. They then retreat to their pastures in the desert.[28]

Though he admired their strong group-feeling, he did not think it provided any basis for continued lasting success:

> [The Arabs] care only for the property that they might take away from people through looting and imposts. When they have obtained that, they have no interest in anything further, such as taking care of [people], looking after their interests, or forcing them not to commit misdeeds. . . . Under the rule of [the Arabs], the subjects live as in a state of anarchy, without law. Anarchy destroys mankind and ruins civilization. . . . It is noteworthy how civilization always collapsed in places the Arabs took over and conquered, and how such settlements were depopulated and the [very] earth there turned into something that was no [longer] earth. The Yemen where [the Arabs] live is in ruins, except for a few cities. . . . [B]ecause of their savagery, the Arabs are the least willing of nations to subordinate themselves to each other, as they are rude, proud, ambitious, and eager to be the leader.[29]

There is, however, a way out of this situation: religion. Ibn Khaldūn argued that religion—specifically Islam—could counteract such a group's particularism, lending it the strength and unity that it needs to triumph.

> When there is religion [among them] . . . , then they have some restraining influence in themselves. The qualities of haughtiness and jealousy leave them. It is, then, easy for them to subordinate themselves and to unite. This is achieved by the common religion they now have [Islam]. It

causes rudeness and pride to disappear and exercises a restraining influence on their mutual envy and jealousy. When there is a prophet or saint
among them, who calls upon them to fulfill the commands of God and
rids them of blameworthy qualities and causes them to adopt praisewor-
thy ones, and who has them concentrate all their strength in order to
make the truth prevail, they become fully united and obtain superiority
and royal authority.[30]

In Khaldūn's view, Islam expanded Arab 'aṣabiyyah to encompass more
than kin. This allowed the growth of royal authority and proper kingship, which he saw as a healthy result of well-developed group-feeling.
A society needs 'aṣabiyyah to stay together, but it also needs to be able
to extend that group-feeling widely across the society; narrow group-
feeling tears societies apart. Uniting behind kings, who organize their
followers to look out for the common good, makes healthy social life
possible.[31]

The problem is, the establishment of royal governments normally
lowers 'aṣabiyyah, as governments soon come to depend on laws, not
on the group. How to prevent this? Religion provides the answer. Ibn
Khaldūn showed how Islam kept Arab 'aṣabiyyah high, enabling the
growth of Muslim civilization. The group-feelings of various tribes and
clans did not vanish, but they were submerged into a wider unity that
made the Arab empire possible. Prophetic religion thus proved a better
unifier than kinship. It ensured that the nomadic Arabs would become
a stronger force than city dwellers' armies and laws.[32] Here's how he described the process:

Religious coloring does away with mutual jealousy and envy among
people who share in a group-feeling, and causes concentration upon the
truth. When people [who have a religious coloring] come to have the
[right] insight into their affairs, nothing can withstand them, because
their outlook is one and their object one of common accord. They are
willing to die for [their objectives]. [On the other hand,] the members of
the dynasty they attack may be many times as numerous as they. But their
purposes differ, in as much as they are false purposes, and [the people of
the worldly dynasty] come to abandon each other, since they are afraid
of death. Therefore, they do not offer resistance to [the people with a

religious coloring], even if they themselves are more numerous. They are overpowered by them and quickly wiped out, as a result of the luxury and humbleness existing among them.

This happened to the Arabs at the beginning of Islam during the Muslim conquests. The armies of the Muslims at al-Qadisiyah and at the Yarmuk numbered some 30,000 in each case, while the Persian troops at al-Qadisiyah numbered 120,000, and the troops of Heraclius, according to al Waqidi, 400,000. Neither of the two parties was able to withstand the Arabs. [The Arabs] routed them and seized what they possessed.[33]

In essence, Ibn Khaldūn saw religion as another source of 'aṣabiyyah. Historically, it made the Arab conquests possible. Yes, the nomads' fortitude contributed, but Islam kept kin-feeling under control. It gave the Arabs a wider sense of purpose. The point, for us, is that religion and kinship can both increase 'aṣabiyyah.

However, the cycle did not end there. Despite Islam, the natural decline of group-feeling soon set in. Having conquered, the Arabs took on civilized habits and lost their 'aṣabiyyah. City life lowered their common will below the point that Islam made any difference. Their empire split into kingdoms, whose dynasties rose and fell with the rise and fall of various tribal solidarities. Seljuqs, Almoravids, Turks, Berbers, and others came to power and then were absorbed or swept away in the pattern of invasion and conquest that Khaldūn traced back one thousand years. Religious group-feeling came to be but one among scores of group-feelings that typified the ethnically and territorially diverse Muslim world. Regimes rose or fell, peoples conquered or faded away in a complex dance of these many 'aṣabiyyaht. This is the pattern that Ibn Khaldūn saw lying beneath history's surface.[34]

Comparing Khaldūn and Durkheim

How does Ibn Khaldūn compare to standard Western sociologists, especially in his analysis of the role of religion in social life? Among the classical theorists, Émile Durkheim provides the most interesting point of contrast. Like Khaldūn, Durkheim was concerned with what holds societies together; both also thought that religion plays a role in creating social solidarity. Their two theories are, however, quite different. Their contrast sheds light on some ways that Ibn Khaldūn's approach might show us something new.[35]

Durkheim famously divided societies into two types, according to the complexity of their divisions of labor. In simple societies, everyone does pretty much the same kind of thing. They all herd, or farm, or hunt, or fish, or gather, or whatever it takes to keep life going. He recognized that such societies often have clear gender lines, but one man's work is a lot like another man's and the same is true for women. Roles are limited and stable. Young people grow up knowing what they will do as adults. There are, of course, small variations, but one peasant farming family is pretty much like another. Everyone has to develop the same skills and abilities.

A complex society, on the other hand offers lots of different professions, and people have to specialize. This is more than the just "butcher, baker, and candlestick maker" of the children's rhyme. Try accountant, ballerina, coach, development officer, engineer, firefighter, geneticist, on through politician, quality inspector, real-estate agent, stevedore, etc., all the way to zookeeper. They all have different skills. Their jobs require different levels of education, different mental and physical abilities, sometimes even different personality types. People end up being not at all like one another, though many can (and do) form friendships across their various divides.

Durkheim wondered what held each of these societies together. He argued that the simple societies are particularly prone to splitting. Left to themselves, the people in them do not much need each other. They all hunt, grow, or gather the same things. Except for repelling enemies or finding non-consanguineous mates, they could easily split into several groups without it making much difference for people's lives. Complex societies, on the other hand, are much less apt to splinter. Their extensive division of labor keeps them together, because no one can produce all the goods she or he needs to live.

As a result, Durkheim said, each kind of society has a different form of solidarity. Simple societies have to be held together 'mechanically': by means of externally enforced common ideas and customs. Like his British precursor Henry Sumner Maine,[36] Durkheim tracked shifts in law to show how simpler societies mainly use laws to enforce conformity and keep people in their place. Complex societies, however, hold themselves together 'organically'. Like an organism, all the parts contribute to the whole. They thus do not need so many laws to regulate specific norms of behavior. Their laws focus on enforcing contracts and keeping their division of labor running smoothly. Not that modern societies lack criminal law, but there is proportionally less of it than there is in the traditional world.[37]

In Durkheim's view, this did not end the matter. Read together, his 1893 *Division of Labor in Society* and his 1897 study of *Suicide* show how each form of social solidarity creates its own social problems. Simpler societies require external pressure to tie people together; when this pressure is too high, their suicide rates increase as people sacrifice their lives for the group ('altruistic suicide'). Or they kill themselves when they see so little difference between themselves and others that there is no point in living ('fatalistic suicide'). Complex societies, however, suffer from excessive individualism. Their suicides result from a lack of social ties ('individualistic suicide') or a dearth of moral support in times of confusion ('anomic suicide'). Durkheim advertised *Suicide* as a study of how society shapes even the most personal of acts. It is also, however, a study of the consequences of the shift in social structure that he had tracked in his earlier work. The very nature of suicide changes as societies move along the path from simple to complex.[38]

In both cases, Durkheim found a role for religion. In simple societies, he argued, it can enforce common beliefs and customs, producing a solidarity of sameness. Everyone stays together because they all believe and do the same things. Religious deviance is heavily punished. In complex societies, on the other hand, religion can give individuals a sense of meaning that they too often cannot find in the other parts of life. It can also give them a way to connect with others. Churches, synagogues, and the like are all places where people go both to find the meaning of life and to develop the social ties that an overly individualistic society fails to nurture.

In short, for Durkheim, everything changes according to the social structure. Religion changes too.

It is easy to see the similarities and differences between this and Ibn Khaldūn's work. Both scholars concerned themselves with social solidarity, and both posited two polar types of society based on people's means of livelihood. Ibn Khaldūn agreed with Durkheim that tribes were much more uniform than cities and that city life encouraged individualism.

Yet where Durkheim saw simpler societies tied together by external laws and compulsion, Khaldūn saw tribes as knit from within—by their group-feeling. Where Durkheim saw complex societies as strengthened by their internal interdependence, Khaldūn saw them as weakened by their lack of common will. Most notably, where Durkheim found social solidarity problematic for simpler peoples, tracing what solidarity they have to common ideas, Khaldūn saw tribes as stable and tied together by feelings, not philosophies. Durkheim did not wrestle with solidarity's emotional side until his later work, where he wrote that it supports the sacred ideas that he says prop up the social order.[39] Even then, its precise outlines are not clear. For Khaldūn, the emotional bond to the group always came first; shared ideas may support it, or they may undercut it. Ideas are secondary in any case.

The contrast between the way that Durkheim and Ibn Khaldūn approached religion is particularly strong. Durkheim identified religion most particularly with simpler societies, where it establishes unity among groups that might not otherwise cohere. Khaldūn found tribal solidarity unproblematic, but saw a role for religion in energizing settled life. Islam, he said, could accentuate even a settled group's *'aṣabiyyah*, lending it the strength and unity that it otherwise lacks. Further, Durkheim saw religion acting on a group from without while Ibn Khaldūn saw it enhancing mutual attraction from within. In essence, the two disagreed about just how to approach the issue of solidarity. Though Durkheim did not espouse a completely boundary-oriented approach, he was much less centripetally focused than was Khaldūn. The latter insisted that group solidarity requires strongly felt emotional attachments between members.[40]

The final contrast centers on each theorist's treatment of ethnicity. This is relatively simple: Durkheim ignored ethnicity; Ibn Khaldūn found it central. Throughout his work, Durkheim focused on social structure as well as on the moral sentiments that he thought made social life possible. Like most Euro-American social theorists of his time, he did not consider race and ethnicity to be central to the social transformations of the industrial age. W.E.B. Du Bois was the only theorist of sociology's founding generation to do that, and he was long marginalized by the profession.[41]

Ibn Khaldūn, however, not only placed ethnicity and ethnic solidarity at the center of his theorizing. He also used the same set of concepts to capture both its role in society and the role of religion. Both ethnicity and religion are important as carriers of al 'aṣabiyyah. In his view, each of them generates feelings of social solidarity. They do so in much the same way. The two forces interact to produce the particular patterns of solidarity found in a given place and time. Put bluntly, for Ibn Khaldūn, religion and ethnicity are the same sort of thing. Yes, they have different attributes; anyone can see that. Yet in his schema both work by means of the same mechanism. They work by generating group-feeling, which builds group strength. They are both centripetal emotional forces that tie groups together. His core concept connects two things that standard Western sociology (and the sociology of religion) typically keeps apart.

Let me pause briefly over that last sentence, for it is an important one. When I was growing up in the United States in the 1950s and 1960s, the general consensus was that race and ethnicity were biological and fixed—i.e., something that you were given and could not change. Religion, on the other hand, was a matter of identity and ideas: something you could change. These two things operated very differently in the public consciousness.

For example, the Civil Rights Movement of my youth did not try to make people race-less. It merely tried to have people of different races and ethnicities treated equally. My African American friends did not want to become White; they just wanted the same respect that White folks took for granted. After all, Irish Americans did not lose their ethnicity as they joined 'native' Anglo-Saxons to constitute the racially dominant White race. The same was true for Italian Americans a bit later on. Their biology did not change; the boundaries of what was considered White just shifted to include them. There was no way that racial boundaries were going to erase the difference between White and Black—that difference was too embedded in American history to disappear.[42] In any case, race and ethnicity were seen as biological, not as matters of personal choice; the Civil Rights Movement's goal was to make human biological variation stop influencing social and political structures.

In the same years, Will Herberg wrote an influential book on the sociology of American religion. Titled *Protestant, Catholic, Jew*, it argued that 19th-century America's multiple religious divisions had reduced themselves to three. There was, he argued, no longer much difference between Methodists and Episcopalians, between Presbyterians and Congregationalists, nor between these and the other groups that were part of what scholars called the American Protestant Mainline. People switched from one to another rather easily. Catholics were becoming more and more like Protestants, though they had not (at that time) begun to give up their own religious brand. Jews, too, were giving up their particularity—especially the Conservatives, who were becoming more and more open to liberal ideas. In addition, intermarriage was beginning to grow between these three religious streams. All were regarded—at least by educated people—as being of equal moral worth.[43]

The 1970s, of course, saw the decline of the Protestant Mainline, Catholic dissatisfaction with *Humanae Vitae*, and the first expansion of Jewish-gentile intermarriage. They also saw the rise of American Evangelicalism—a religious movement for which conversion is both conceptually and institutionally central. Each of these events enhanced these sense that religion is a matter of personal choice. My students today cannot imagine anything else. Being young and Californian, many of them choose to have no religion at all.[44]

The point here is not that race and ethnicity are or are not really fixed, nor that religion is or is not really a matter of personal decision. The point is that standard thinking treats the two as being fundamentally different. Sociology textbooks put them in different chapters. That is how they were looked at when I was being trained.

This is beginning to change. As I write this passage, the Middle East is in the midst of a multi-sided war, whose fault lines no one can quite understand. Some of the conflict is portrayed as religious: Iraqi Sunnis attack Iraqi Shiites and are attacked in turn. Yazidis are massacred by Sunni fundamentalists for their supposed religious apostasy. These Yazidis are, however, also treated as an ethnic group and are defended by the Kurdish *peshmerga* (Sunnis), who see them as ethnic kin. Syrian Druze and Alawites are often called religious minorities but act like ethnic groups—and are occasionally persecuted like them. Are religion and ethnicity so separable here?

As we shall see in the next chapter, there is a lot to gain by seeing religion and ethnicity through the same set of conceptual lenses. That is this book's purpose: to show us things that standard ways of doing the sociology of religion miss. This is one of Ibn Khaldūn's strengths: he saw that religion and ethnicity have a lot in common, especially in the ways they tie people to one another.

In any event, Ibn Khaldūn's work is more than just a history of nomadic conquest. It is the first sociology of a multi-ethnic society, one in which religion played a key but varied role. Khaldūn saw religion as a parallel means of solidarity, alongside kinship, ethnicity, and so on. All were active in both tribes and cities, but in different strengths and combinations. As we shall see in the next chapter, putting religion and ethnicity in the same picture lets us see relationships that would otherwise be invisible.

Ibn Khaldūn's Islam

So far, I have presented Ibn Khaldūn as if he were a secular sociologist. That is not the case. This is not just because sociology was only invented five centuries after his death. It is because his social analysis is inseparable from his religion. Unlike the 19th-century sociologists we encountered in Chapter Two, Ibn Khaldūn was a convinced believer. Indeed, he spent the last twenty-four years of his life as a Muslim judge in Egypt, much of it as the head (*qadi*) of the Maliki school of Islamic law. He was, in fact, rather devout. What are we to make of Ibn Khaldūn's Muslim side? How did it shape his writing about the core patterns he saw underlying social life?

Though contemporary scholars separate (or claim to separate) their personal religious views from their research and writing, the same was not true in earlier eras. Thomas Aquinas, for example, was both a Catholic and a scholar; one cannot read his work without seeing how both shaped his intellectual vision. Baruch Spinoza was similarly enmeshed in science, in philosophy, and in mystical Judaism. Both Immanuel Kant and Karl Marx outgrew their religious upbringings (and in Marx's case, his teen Christian fervor), but one can see those upbringings in their mature work. Why should Ibn Khaldūn be any different?

In fact, he was not. It is something of a commonplace to remark that the *Muqaddimah* and the *Kitāb al-'Ibar* were simultaneously masterpieces of scholarship and a way for a jobless politician to advertise his skills to prospective employers. It is less often noticed that the *Muqaddimah*, in particular, contains an argument for the importance of Islam in political life. I described this above as his expressing an appreciation for the role of religion in creating al 'aṣabiyyah, but that is not precisely what he did. He did not write about just any religion; he wrote about Islam. Nor was the Islam he praised just any Islam. It was a particular variety of Islam, focused on bringing people together for common purposes. It was decidedly unmystical. In fact, it bears some resemblance to present-day Salafist Islamism, though not with the same exclusive fervor and not with the same disregard of actual history. He portrayed an Islam grounded in the early years of unity and expansion. It was this Islam that could generate al 'aṣabiyyah. No other.

I am not the only scholar to have seen this. James Morris noted that many passages in the *Muqaddimah* criticize certain movements in Mahdist Sufism that Khaldūn thought were un-Islamic as well as politically disastrous. Morris wrote:

> One of the most common targets of Ibn Khaldūn's criticism is the common popular belief in a redeeming "Mahdi"-figure (or other related forms of messianism), which is typified in his long section [of the *Muqaddimah*] (Q 2: 142–201) debunking both the hadith foundations of such beliefs and their further development in Shi'ite and Sufi contexts. The main aim of his criticisms there is not so much the intellectual pretensions underlying that belief as it is the recurrent political delusions following from the popular spread of such ideas among those he calls "common people, the stupid mass," which have led many Mahdist pretenders—both sincere and fraudulent—into fruitless uprisings and revolts without any hope of successful and lasting political consequences.[45]

In Morris's telling, Ibn Khaldūn thought that such Sufism was responsible, in part, for the political and material decline of Islamic states in Andalusia and the Maghreb. Where he wrote of early Islam as bringing people together across their differences, thus creating tremendous group-feeling and a sense of holy mission, he described Mahdists and folk-messianists as dividing Muslims, one from another.[46]

This may explain why Ibn Khaldūn portrayed contemporary Sufi leaders in such a negative light. Morris notes that his accounts of them clearly do not match those of other contemporaneous writers. He wrote so as to mobilize his readers against them. Morris reminds us that,

We should never imagine that Ibn Khaldūn—at least in his *Muqad-dimah*—is speaking simply as a disinterested, objective historian and mere describer (or "encylopedist") of the Islamic intellectual, artistic, cultural, and religious traditions that he discusses. Machiavelli did not write his *Discourses on Livy* for scholars of Latin philology.[47]

Ibn Khaldūn was thus, in a deep sense, an apologist for a particular kind of political Islam. He thought that Islam, rightly conceived and maintained, could reverse Muslim civilization's declining fortunes. He saw group unity as the best way of reinvigorating Muslim civilization. He also saw it as better Islam than the Sufi variety: Sufism's honoring of individual holy men and their revelations undercut Islam's core message of submission to Allah alone.

We will revisit this matter in the next chapter. It will help us see what Ibn Khaldūn might be able to tell us about the contemporary rise of ISIS—the Islamic State in Iraq and Syria—a phenomenon that has been hard for Western scholars and politicians to understand.

Virgin Mary. Drawing by Fractalbee, 2012.

ISIS Flag. Drawing by J. Spickard, 2016.

6

Ibn Khaldūn Applied

Medjugorje and the Islamic State

How might a Khaldūnian sociology work in practice? There's no better test of theory than using it to unravel a complex case, and there's no place where religion and ethnic identity have been more intertwined than in the former Yugoslavia. Almost everyone knows about the wars that tore through that region in the 1990s, as Croats, Serbs, Bosniacs, and Kosovars fought over territory. Some people also remember a set of religious events that took place a decade earlier: the visitations of the Virgin Mary to a group of teenagers on a hill outside Medjugorje, a small village in southwestern Bosnia-Herzegovina. Are these related? Or are they separate? We shall see what a Khaldūnian sociologist might say about these events and then evaluate that interpretation's strengths and weaknesses. Then we'll consider a more recent case: the current civil war in Syria and the growth of the Islamic State.

Case 1: The 'Miracles' at Medjugorje

On June 24, 1981, six young people claimed to have seen and conversed with the Virgin Mary, the mother of Jesus, on a hill behind Medjugorje, whose name means "between the mountains." Members of the local Franciscan priest's catechism class, they encountered "the Gospa" (Our Lady) while returning home after evening Mass.

> After a few heartening remarks and the promise to return the following
> evening, the figure vanished. . . . By that evening, the whole village knew
> about it. Accompanied by a rapidly growing crowd of villagers, the seers
> went back to the hill the following evening. The Madonna, who was said
> to be seen and heard only by the young visionaries, gave messages to pass

on to everyone. Peace and forbearance among God's people, the priests, and all the people of the world.[1]

The apparitions continued daily, first on the hillside, then later in the church rectory, during which the Virgin transmitted teachings to her believers. Calling herself the "Queen of Peace," she typically urged people to pray, fast, confess, and take communion. Within a short time, the evening meetings on 'Apparition Hill' had grown to a few thousand people, mostly locals. Villagers reported miraculously swift healings, similar to those experienced in the Catholic Charismatic Renewal, which was at that time growing in influence in both America and Italy. Indeed, the parish priest, Father Branko, had attended a Renewal meeting in Italy just two years before. While there, he supposedly received visions of the special relationship between the Holy Mother and his parish.[2]

Yugoslavia in 1981 was still a Communist state, under a good deal of central control, so official repression started almost immediately. The six visionaries were investigated, access to the hill was closed, parish religious services were disrupted, and the church collection was sometimes confiscated. This had the unwanted effect of publicizing the apparitions, so that ever larger numbers of people heard about them and made pilgrimages to the village. Franciscans from abroad began organizing visits, which brought a tremendous amount of money into the previously backward region. Recognizing this, the authorities relented; they ultimately built their own tourist complex at the edge of town. By the early 1990s, an estimated ten million pilgrims had visited the site, sometimes over one hundred thousand in a day. Travel agents set up package tours, which included Masses in English and visits with the visionaries.[3]

From the first, scholars generally treated the reports of these apparitions as religious phenomena. The visionaries were all staunch Catholics, their visions corresponded to Catholic beliefs, the content of the teachings was orthodox, and the local church was in an area of a long-standing Franciscan mission work. The millions of pilgrims who visited the site in the 1980s, along with journalists, Vatican religious inspectors, and others framed the apparitions in a language of "miracle," "charism," "prophecy," and "renewal." Sociologists, at least those writing up to the early 1990s, used the language of "pilgrim-age," "religious organization," "religious competition," and "religious revitalization."[4]

Not all of this reportage was positive. It turned out that there was a good deal of behind-the-scenes conflict between the visionaries, the local priests, and diocesan officials. This was perhaps inevitable, given the sheer numbers of visitors. Much was made (by the sociologists) of the split between the local Franciscans and the ecclesial hierarchy, especially after the latter declared the apparitions "unsubstantiated." Michael Sells reported:

> The increasingly wealthy Franciscans refused to cede control of several disputed local parishes to diocesan authorities. The Bishop of Mostar denounced the Medjugorje visions as a fraud. At one point militias attached to the Medjugorje Franciscans seized the bishop, held him overnight, beat him, and ceremonially stripped him of his ecclesiastical insignia. The Medjugorje Franciscans were accused by critics of engaging in cult practices and sexual exploitation. The Franciscans accused the Bishop of similar depravities, threatened to blow up the cathedral of Mostar, and barricaded a disputed church in nearby Capljina against any effort of the Bishop to assert diocesan control.[5]

This was heady stuff, seemingly suitable for B movies, the tabloid press, or American daytime television, were it not for the context: beginning in 1992, an ethnic war tore apart this region of the former Yugoslavia. Serbs, Croats, and (so-called) "Bosnian Muslims" struggled for control of Bosnia-Herzegovina from March of that year until late 1995. NATO intervention and the Dayton Accords finally brought an end to the fighting.

Ethnic War

The wars that dismantled Yugoslavia during the 1990s are complicated and have multiple sources, about which scholars have argued at length.[6] For many sociologists, and also in the popular press, the 1992–1995 war in Bosnia was cast as an ethnic conflict—albeit one that split on inherited religious lines. Serbs, Croats, and Bosniacs were recognized as being divided by religious background, but their rather slack religiosity was seen as a marker of ethnic primordialism, not of religious practice and belief. As the joke went at the time, the only difference between the three groups was which religion they did not practice. Still, people would kill for these differences. As Michael Sells noted, "some survivors . . . had not viewed themselves as religious or even thought about their religious identity until they were singled out for persecution because of it."[7]

Though not primordial, inter-ethnic conflict in the region extends at least to the founding of the Yugoslav state after World War I. The conflict was mainly between Serbs and Croats. Serbs had had their own state before the war, while Croats had been part of the Austro-Hungarian Empire. Their division was actually a matter of state identity, not biology or deep history. However, as Benedict Anderson famously wrote, late-19th- and early-20th-century nationalist ideologues imagined that language, biology, and history were coterminous. One 'people' were supposed to have one language, one body-type, one history, and one culture, and deserved their own state.[8]

Croat dissatisfaction with Serbian dominance in the Yugoslav kingdom, and especially with the king's attempts to strengthen central control, led to various ethnically charged political assassinations. After invading in 1941, the Germans divided the country, setting up a puppet state in Croatia controlled by the nationalist Ustaše militia. In the next several years, and in the context of a bitter war against both Serbian royalist 'Chetniks' and Tito's Partisans, the Ustaše killed several hundred thousand Serbs plus tens of thousands of Jews and Roma. The victorious Tito government set up a memorial to these dead on the site of the Jasenovac concentration camp. Despite Tito's rhetoric of "Fascists" and "Partisans" to describe the wartime conflicts, this memorial was read by many as a Serbian commemoration of Croatian atrocities—and also a disregard of the atrocities that had been committed by other sides.[9]

The fact that Tito was himself a Croat dampened ethnic tensions for a while, as did the disproportionate economic development of Yugoslavia's north, where the bulk of the Croats and Slovenes lived. This balanced Serbian political control, exercised through a Communist Party formally open to all. By the 1960s, however, the government succumbed to pressures to recognize the Yugoslavia's various ethnic components, both demographically (through identification on the national census) and institutionally, by devolving some power to Yugoslavia's regions. The categorization of Bosniacs as "Muslims"—a 1968 constitutional change—was the first formal identification of religion with ethnicity. The category "Bosniac" was not made available, but the category "Yugoslav" was; it was mainly chosen by urbanized elites and by those who had married across ethnic lines.[10] These categories shifted with Yugoslavia's disintegration during the 1990s. After the civil war, for example, Montenegrin 'Muslims' were reportedly evenly split about whether to identify themselves as "Bosniac" or "Muslim." The first term connected them to a country in which they did not live, and the second connected them to a religion that most of them did not practice. Such are the choices that people were forced to make in this region.[11]

Medjugorje was no stranger to these pressures and to this conflict. Though located quite close to a Bosniac-dominated part of Bosnia-Herzegovina, Medjugorje is also only a few kilometers from the Croatian border. The village served as an Ustaše stronghold during World War II and, Sells wrote, "was the site of some of the most gruesome atrocities." Beginning in 1992, Croatian Army and civilian militias launched a concerted attack on Bosnian Muslims and Serbs living in the region. Their destruction of the town of Stolac, for example,

> was systematic, methodical, and precise. Catholic homes, businesses, and shrines remained untouched, but the non-Catholic heritage and property were thoroughly destroyed. Foremost among the mosques destroyed . . . was the Emperor's mosque . . . one of the three most ancient in B[osnia-]H[erzegovina]. . . . Eight other mosques were destroyed, including other historic works from the Ottoman period. Also . . . the Orthodox church of Holy Assumption . . . as well as ten residential areas, four urban neighborhoods, the bazaar area, . . . three main libraries, two public galleries of paintings . . . [and so on]. As in other campaigns by Catholic and Orthodox militias, the precision with which the target heritage was sought out and destroyed indicated the participation of an educated elite as advisors, including, according to reports, local Catholic art historians and professors.[12]

Bosnian Serbs launched similar attacks on Catholics and Muslims in other areas, including killing several thousand Muslim men at Srebrenica and scattering their bodies in the surrounding fields. Such ethnic cleansing goes beyond mass murder; it amounts to the systematic erasure of a people's cultural heritage and being.[13]

Religion and Ethnicity

As we saw in the previous chapter, the contemporary world typically sees 'religion' and 'ethnicity' as being fundamentally different sorts of things. Religion is imagined to be a matter of beliefs and of personal participation in religious life, and, in the views of many writers, is increasingly a matter of personal choice.[14] Ethnicity, on the other hand, is typically treated as a given: as a matter of biological breeding and tribal allegiance. Objectively, it was hard to distinguish between the three warring Yugoslav groups. All spoke the same language, possessed the same blood, hair, and skin types, and had interbred for hundreds of years. The few linguistic differences that existed were invented in the 1920s; biological difference was an illusion. Nor were the various groups divided by residence, though different villages had differently balanced populations. Even their pasts were not as separate as later nationalist ideologies led outsiders to believe. That's what surprised the world: that generations-long neighbors would turn on one another, murderously. This was not supposed to happen in modern times.[15]

Historically, sociology has admitted a tie between religion and ethnicity, but one that is intrinsic to neither of them. Put succinctly, it saw them both as artifacts of a 'traditional' past. As we saw earlier in this volume, 19th- and early-20th-century sociology was born out of an effort to understand Europe's industrialization and did so by distinguishing 'modernity' from 'tradition'. This took various forms in the sociological classics: Marx's "feudalism" versus "capitalism," Maine's "status" versus "contract," Tönnies's "Gemeinschaft" versus "Gesellschaft," Durkheim's "mechanical" versus "organic" solidarity, and Weber's efforts to describe the uniqueness of the West. By the mid-20th century, American sociologist Talcott Parsons had systematized this difference with his famous 'pattern variables': social characteristics on which traditional and modern societies were supposed to diverge. Among them, religion and ethnic particularism were firmly on the traditional side.[16]

On the religious side, institutional differentiation and state expansion were supposed to have moved religion to the private sphere, while increasing interreligious contact was supposed to make supernatural belief less plausible. On the ethnic side, group-based identity and intergroup discrimination were believed to interfere with needed economic development. Several sociological theories argue that a modern economy needs people to be individualistic, cosmopolitan, universal in outlook, tolerant, oriented toward rationality, self-reflective, and willing to break traditional ties for the sake of personal advancement. Add in the sense that industrial and post-industrial economies create ties between formerly unlike peoples, and it is easy to understand why many sociologists—along with other scholars—thought that religious and ethnic groups would vanish as the traditional world waned.[17]

The eruption of religio-ethnic conflict in Yugoslavia and elsewhere produced a crisis for the proponents of a smooth transition to an individualized, secular, post-ethnic world. Eastern Europe was supposed to be 'on the road to modernity', where ethnic and religious ties were thought to be no longer important. Some observers tried to salvage their basic theories by treating religious and ethnic resurgence as anti-modernist responses to the social disruption that modernity brings. Others took refuge in talk of ethnic primordialism, though why this would have religious overtones was left unexplained. Yet, even on this score, ethnic violence should not have erupted in Medjugorje, which had played host to so many outside visitors. The religious tourism that had so connected that village to the outside world should have inoculated the villagers against conflict. Clearly, the reigning sociological view failed to predict events on the ground.[18]

What Would Khaldūn Say

Unlike Western sociologists, Ibn Khaldūn applied the same conceptual categories to religion and to ethnicity, seeing them both as potential sources of "group-feeling." He focused not on tribal peoples' supposed traditionalism, but on their willingness to sacrifice for one another. He saw religion not as a matter of belief, organization, and rite but as a force that similarly encouraged people to cooperate. Both ethnicity and religion could accentuate group-feeling. Both could sustain group identities in the face of conflict and change. Most notably, they could do so at any point in history—for his was a cyclical theory, not one imagining 'progress' from the 'traditional' to the 'modern'.

A Khaldūnian sociologist would argue that it makes sense to see the Marian apparitions at Medjugorje and the ethnic violence of the 1990s as part of the same social process. Despite their overt message of peace, the apparitions heightened Catholic identity and solidarity at a time of disintegrating state power. Coming in a border region, economically backward and ethnically mixed, the apparitions amounted to a supernatural affirmation of Catholicism's special status. Precisely because the region was backward before the influx of tourist money, clan groups were stronger. Farming was hard and resources were scarce, which forced families and clans toward self-reliance. Prior events had presented inhabitants with a conceptual world in which "Croat" and "Catholic" were seen as synonymous, even if this was not historically accurate. Is it any wonder that group-feeling was heightened as Catholicism became more important?[19]

As Michael Sells pointed out, "the original messages attributed to [the Virgin] contained an anticommunist subtext"—an appropriate dividing line, given the nature of the existing Yugoslav regime. Later messages dropped this theme in favor of calls for prayer, fasting, and the conversion of unbelievers. It is not hard to see how the latter might justify the forced expulsion of Serbs and Bosniacs, who were increasingly defined by their non-Catholic status. Heightened Croat/Catholic group-feeling mobilized this opposition to "outsiders" in the context of a declining Yugoslav state. As that state evaporated, religio-ethnic conflict burst into the open.[20]

The issue here is group-feeling, not 'tribes' conquering 'cities', though that was where Ibn Khaldūn focused his history of the Muslim world. For Khaldūnian sociology, the question is about the extent to which various groups are tied together, and about the sources and results of that centripetal solidarity. The rigors of life in southwestern Bosnia united families and clans but did not bind them into larger groups. Indeed, we know there was considerable hostility between the various Croat-

Catholic clans; a Khaldūnian sociologist would look for similar conflict among Serbs and Bosniacs. Among the Croats, at least, clan group-feeling was high but of limited scope. This is where religion enters the picture.[21]

The "miracles at Medjugorje" made Catholicism more important in this region, and Khaldūnian sociology would expect this to create greater intra-clan cooperation. This was apparently the case. The events themselves were framed in a Catholic idiom, under the supervision of the local Franciscan order. Various local clans and families worked with outside Catholic groups to develop the tourist trade. They presented themselves as Catholics to the pilgrims, such that this became their public master identity. The net result was to highlight the equation of Catholicism with Croatian ethnicity—exactly the submerging of particular loyalties into religion that Ibn Khaldūn found so important for Islam's triumph.

A Khaldūnian sociologist would also highlight a further development: the effect that the apparitions and the subsequent deluge of pilgrims had on local Catholicism. Prior to the 1980s, Medjugorje was mostly a village of women. As was the case in several of Yugoslavia's economically less-developed regions, many of its men lived in Italy and Germany as migrant workers, sending home remittances to support their families. Village religious life revolved around women's prayer groups, not around the church. Women held religious status, and, according to anthropologist Mart Bax, "It was widely felt that without their efforts . . . the Virgin Mary would not have appeared." As is true in many places, popular Catholicism was not uniquely church-centered, which means that it was a much more eclectic than during the later pilgrimage period. It was, in fact, less oriented both to orthodoxy and to boundaries, though no village woman would have said this to church officials directly.[22]

The massive influx of pilgrims did more than bring wealth to the region; it also re-centered popular Catholicism on the church. Women's status declined, both because economic opportunities brought men back from abroad and because outsiders focused their attention on the visionaries, the priests, and other local officials. They portrayed the region as more uniformly (and orthodoxly) Catholic than it had been, heightening local Catholic identity. Non-Catholics could not participate in the economic boom, so were displaced. All this heightened Catholic *'aṣabiyyah*, in Khaldūnian terms.

This is not to say that the Marian apparitions are responsible for, much less caused, the ethnic cleansing. That is not how a Khaldūnian sociologist would put the matter. Instead, religious solidarity and ethnic solidarity are of a piece. This is particularly so where ethnicity is defined along religious lines, whether or not the people involved are "religious" in terms of their personal beliefs, prayer life, and so on. It is the feeling that matters, and the sense of group identity. Unlike the standard Western approach, a Khaldūnian sociology would not be surprised by the eruption of communal violence. Intense group-feeling can stimulate conflict with outsiders. It does not matter whether the feeling comes from religion or from ethnic ties.

In short, a Khaldūnian approach is not surprised by the eruption of ethnic conflict at a religious pilgrimage site. The 1980s religious fervor heightened group-feeling, which then set locals against their ethno-religious 'enemy'. Ibn Khaldūn's ideas reveal central elements of the events at Medjugorje, both ethnic and religious, that standard Western sociologies hide.

Is It True?

This is a plausible picture, but we have to ask ourselves: Is it true? First, is it actually the case that both religion and ethnicity were sources of group-feeling in this region? Second, did this group-feeling contribute to the massacres, ethnic cleansing, and other events about which I have spoken? Despite the appeal of the Khaldūnian interpretation I have laid out, I am afraid that the answer is split.

Based on what I have described in the previous section, the first question deserves a qualified "yes." The 'miracles' at Medjugorje did heighten Catholic identity in the region and religion did serve as a source of group-feeling for those involved. Overall, previously divided clans co-operated with one another. "Catholic" and "Croat" became more closely identified than before, even interchangeable. This fits the Khaldūnian model. The qualification stems from some residual inter-clan competition over business opportunities and from divisions between the local

Franciscans and the diocesan authorities.[23] Catholic group-feeling did not seem to stifle such rivalries in full.

However, the second question deserves a decisive "no." Let me explain why.

As we saw in the previous chapter, there are two ways to describe group formation. Groups can form by attraction: the center-focused force to which I referred earlier in this chapter. Alternatively, they can form by division: as a result of group conflict, which leads each party to consolidate out of fear and for self-preservation. Was the Bosnian conflict in and around Medjugorje primarily a result of centripetal solidarity—i.e., forces that bind people together? Or was ethnic division there fed by violence in a self-perpetuating spiral? An analysis of the role played by elite actors in creating the conflagration indicates the latter. We can address this issue in four related points.

Point One: As the Yugoslav state imploded in the late 1980s, various leaders played up ethnic divisions as a way to hold onto power. Slobodan Milošević notoriously parlayed an ultra-nationalist 1987 speech in Kosovo into election as president of Serbia, leading that country throughout the 1990s wars. Franjo Tudjman was similarly elected Croatian president on an extreme nationalist platform. Each financed and armed ethnic militias in Bosnia that carried out much of the 1992–1995 killing. Milošević was indicted by the International Criminal Tribunal for the Former Yugoslavia for war crimes and genocide, and was still standing trial at the time of his death. Tudjman reportedly would have been similarly indicted, had he not died before the Tribunal was convened. Both were political instrumentalists, "who used their cultural groups as sites of mass mobilization and as constituencies in their competition for power and resources." 'Playing the ethnic card' has long been a route to political success in countries with histories of ethnic division and where electoral systems and/or electorates do not reward cross-ethnic connections. It was especially tempting in Yugoslavia, where access to the political power was suddenly up for grabs.[24]

Point Two: Both Serbs and Croats used religion as a means to create divisions. The 1989 anniversary of the 1389 Battle of Kosovo was heavily ritualized by the Serbian Orthodox church and state, being treated as the "Serbian Golgotha"—complete with a Mary Magdalene figure ministering to the fallen Serb warriors. This highlighted Serb-Muslim divisions, which fed both the atrocities in Bosnia and the later conflict in Kosovo. Croatian Catholic nationalism had long centered on the campaign to canonize Cardinal Stepinac, a church leader tied to the Ustaše and opposed to the Communists and Serbs. It is worth noting that Croatia declared its independence from Yugoslavia on the tenth anniversary of the first Medjugorje visions. This was clearly a ploy to give Croatian separatism a supernatural imprimatur. Serb and Croat militias were both said to identify their victims by religiously identified surnames and by asking about the prayers they had learned in childhood. In doing so, they made what Michael Sells called "religion identity" a dividing line, imposing it on people whose actual religious identity was sometimes quite different. Sells reported that Croats in the Stolac-area HVO (Croatian Defense Union) militia even murdered their fellow Muslim militia members, creating a divide where none had existed before. This is certainly group formation from without, not the kind of solidarity that Khaldūnian *'aṣabiyyah* would generate.[25]

Bosniac 'Muslim' leadership, on the other hand, did not use religion as a rallying point, though the regime did attract some outside *jihadi* fighters who came to support their imagined 'Muslim brothers'. These outsiders were reportedly often appalled at the religious slackness of the population they sought to defend. Today's Bosnian Islamism appears to be a post-war phenomenon, driven at least in part by the West's failure to protect Bosniacs and by the disproportionate death toll that Muslims suffered during the war. Resurgent Bosnian Islam—and it is not very resurgent—is a result of the dividing lines drawn by others, not their cause.[26]

Point Three: Conflicts in and around Medjugorje did not always divide on religious lines. Mart Bax's 1995 report of a 1992 murderous intra-Catholic clan feud appears to have been at least overblown and at worst invented,[27] but the conflicts between Medjugorje's Franciscans and the Mostar bishop were not. Sells reported that this was mainly a struggle over property and influence—one that led the bishop to denounce the visions as false and led the Franciscans to refuse to cede authority over their villages. At the height of this struggle, the bishop was kidnapped by Croatian militias, beaten, and held captive overnight in a Franciscan chapel.[28] Reality on the ground does not allow us to embrace any neat Khaldūnian picture of religion enhancing group-feeling.

Point Four: The Communist state had long used "Serb" and "Croat" as categories by which to administer the Medjugorje region. It originally called them "Partisan" and "Fascist," rewarding and punishing locals for their parents' actions during the Great War. Croats paid taxes to Serb officials, saw new development channeled to Serb villages, and suffered official depredations at the hands of Serbian police. They were unofficially barred from public employment, which meant that many were forced to emigrate for work, either to Western Europe or to the United States. Is it any wonder that they resented this treatment, based solely on their ethnic status? Or that they welcomed the Marian apparition as a source of both pride and cash? Or that they used their newfound independence to retaliate across the ethnic lines that governing elites had drawn around them?[29]

We are not dealing here with an ethnic primordialism. 'Serbs' and 'Croats' have not been fighting for centuries, as was claimed in the media at the time. 'Catholic', 'Orthodox', and 'Muslim' have not always been firm lines drawn around various groups in the region, nor have they always been the most salient social barriers. Yes, there have always been lines of separation here, but the various divisions usually cut across one another, and they were of differing strength in different eras.

Still, at this place, at this time, 'ethnic' and 'religious' divisions were available as tools that regional and national elites could use to expand their political power. The Yugoslav wars of the 1990s are a classic case of how such elites can set groups against one another. Medjugorje's divisions were not simply the grassroots result of Khaldūnian group-feeling; they stemmed from deliberate elite policies. Group identification was actively created, which led to war crimes, ethnic cleansing, and even genocide. Religiously and ethnically based 'group-feeling' is not the whole story.

Where does this leave our attempt to expand the sociology of religion's intellectual toolkit by adding Ibn Khaldūn's concept of al 'aṣabiyyah or 'group-feeling'? The answer is mixed. Clearly, the Khaldūnian approach—with its roots in the history of Islam, not Christianity—has the merit of placing the Medjugorjian miracles and the inter-ethnic fighting in the same field of view. It is one of the few approaches that does so, forcing scholars to gauge their empirical relationship. Religion and ethnicity are related intimately in this case; seeing exactly how this works itself out represents considerable scholarly progress. That is one point in its favor.

Here is another: Khaldūn's approach also recommends against sociology's historic representation of 'tradition' as static and 'modernity' as dynamic. Both are dynamic, because both involve shifting degrees of group-feeling. Simple traditionalism-versus-modernity is an inappropriate way of understanding Bosnian events.

On the other hand, Ibn Khaldūn's concept of *al 'aṣabiyyah* fails to account for many of the events at Medjugorje, particularly during the fighting. Though the 'miracles' likely heightened Catholic solidarity during the 1980s, later social solidarity seems to have been more a matter of heightened group boundaries than of attractive group centers. During the war, Serbs, Croats, and Bosniacs were defined more by their divisions than by their central ties. Indeed, religion appears to have heightened these divisions while shifting the balance of power within groups as well as between them. This would not have surprised either Max Weber or Vilfredo Pareto, each of whom focused on the actions of elites. It should not surprise us, either.

We would not, however, expect Weberian sociology to explain all aspects of social life, and neither should we expect this of a Khaldūnian approach. It is, I believe, useful to look for the presence or absence of centripetal group-feeling in social conflicts; we should just not expect to find that it always important. In this case, groups were shaped from the outside, through conflict, rather than from an inwardly generated sense of solidarity. I suspect that Ibn Khaldūn himself, the hopeful (and not totally successful) politician, would draw useful conclusions from seeing exactly how these elites accomplished their task.

For sociologists of religion, however, there is an additional reward. We saw in Chapter Two how 19th-century sociology formed itself in intellectual opposition to Ultramontane Catholicism. Early sociology portrayed itself as scientific and progressive; thus it portrayed religion—its opponent—as part of an intellectually irrelevant past. Following Manuel Vásquez, I argued that this created a tendency among sociologists to disvalue the study of religion: Why spend time investigating something that is about to disappear?

Events of the last forty years have made it clear that religion is not disappearing. Yet institutional sociology has not really noticed. The sociology of religion is often seen in the profession as an intellectual backwater. Few graduate schools offer significant training programs. Few academic job openings list it as a first or second acceptable sociological field. More than a few of the major current scholars in the sub-discipline teach other subjects, because that is what their universities say they need.

Race and ethnicity, class structures, globalization, conflict, and the transformation of communities are, on the other hand, seen as core sociological concerns. Yes, they should be. Religion, however, figures into each and every one of these topics in the contemporary world. A Khaldūnian sociology would not closet the study of religion, as does much of today's institutional sociology. It would trace the various roles that religion plays in the creation and maintenance of social solidarity, intertwined with these other factors. Khaldūn would certainly not treat religion as something relevant only to the past.

Case 2: The Islamic State

Events, of course, often force scholars out of their shells. We live in a new political era, in which religion refuses to play the part in which sociology once cast it. As I am writing this (in 2015), the news is filled with worries about Islamic militants overrunning the Middle East as well as attacking Western targets in the rest of the world. Islamists set off a truck bomb at New York's World Trade Center a bit over twenty years ago.[30] Eight years later, a group used airplanes as flying bombs to bring down its towers. This sparked a U.S. invasion of Afghanistan and Iraq, neither of which has turned out well. Islamist attacks in Sudan, Kenya, Yemen, Spain, Britain, Indonesia, Nigeria, and elsewhere have left hundreds dead. A few years ago, Islamic militants captured (and were later driven from) Mali's capital. Libya descended into civil war.

As I write, vast swaths of Syria and Iraq have been conquered by an armed organization that goes by various acronyms: IS, ISIL, ISIS, Daesh, and who knows what by the time you read this. The "I," of course, stands for "Islamic" and "S" stands for "State." ISIL stands for "Islamic State in Iraq and the Levant," ISIS stands for either "Islamic State in Iraq and Syria" or "Islamic State of Iraq and *ash-Sham*"—the latter term denoting the northern reach of the 7th- and 8th- century Muslim conquests. In Arabic, that's *ad-Dawlah al-Islāmiyah fī 'l-'Irāq wa-sh-Shām*—the name that the Islamic State itself prefers.[31]

In any case the Islamic State claims to be establishing a new Caliphate and has won recognition from Islamist groups in several countries, including Libya and Nigeria. It is certainly imposing Islamic law on the people it has conquered. Can Ibn Khaldūn's analysis of *al 'aṣabiyyah* teach us anything about these events?

I have already said a lot about the interactions between ethnicity and religion. These are certainly active in the current struggle. The Islamic State's fighters (mostly Arab proponents of Sunni Islam) attack Yazidis as 'devil-worshippers', while the latter are defended by Kurds (also Sunnis but non-Arabs), who see the Yazidis as ethnic kin. Turks (Sunnis by religion and Turkic by ethnicity) attack Kurds while claiming to attack the Islamic State and frequently attacking the Shiite-supported Syrian government as well. Alawites (an ethno-religious group from northern Syria) side with the government, as do some Syrian Christians (also from the north), fearing that an Islamic State victory will destroy whatever tolerance once existed in that country. Lebanese Shiites under Hezbollah defend the Syrian government, a task supported by Iran (Shiite but Persian). Druze (another ethno-religious group, but largely Arab) oppose both the Islamic State and the government, mainly wanting to be left alone. Druze living in Israel side with Israel's Jews. All but the Jews, Kurds, and Turks are ethnically Arab, though that does not prevent divisions along religious lines. Clearly, religions and ethnicities both divide people and unite them. Ibn Khaldūn's idea that the two factors work similarly certainly seems to be true here. Beyond that general principle, however, the details are still unfolding. The situation is an even better example than was Bosnia of how religion and ethnicity can complicate conflicts.

Khaldūn would also be interested in some other factors underlying the conflict. One in particular is the mega-drought that drove somewhere between a quarter and a half of Syrian farmers from their land, crowding them into cities that quickly became ungovernable.[32] Add in the U.S. invasion of neighboring Iraq and the mass of refugees it generated, and social chaos is no surprise.

For our purposes, however, the most interesting Khaldūnian contribution would be an analysis of who joins the Islamic State and why. We are not dealing with desert folk, nor tribal folk, nor people who are trained from birth to fight for their kin. As of this writing, we do not have a full demographic picture of contemporary *jihadiya*.[33] We do know that the forces that have declared a new Caliphate in Syria and Iraq include volunteers from many different countries—including the United States and Germany—who have rallied to aid what many call 'Islamic fundamentalism'.[34] In Syria, they have joined long-time opponents of the Assad regime. In Iraq, they have been joined by disaffected Baathists (a former political grouping) and purged members of the former Iraqi military.

This is an unstable coalition, but it is not a horde riding out of the desert to overwhelm softer city-folk. That part of Ibn Khaldūn's theory does not hold. None of these are barbarians. They demonstrate a technological and strategic savvy on a par with any city dwellers. They recruit widely and intelligently, raise cash by selling oil, extracting ransom, and taking over banks, plant sleeper cells throughout the region, and maintain an active Internet presence.[35]

On the other hand, for some of these, at least, there is a possible role for group-feeling. We can leave aside the Baathists, the former Iraqi officers, and the lower-class Iraqi Sunnis who, as Lydia Wilson discovered, are fighting to settle scores with their Iraqi Shiites oppressors.[36] Their solidarity is born of division, like that in the Balkans. We can also leave aside the recruits from the Muslim Caucasus: Chechnya, Ingushetia, Dagestan, and similar regions. Dangle a few thousand dollars in front of unemployed young men from impoverished families and you'll find a lot of takers.

The *jihadi* recruits from Europe, the U.S., Australia, and other developed states are another matter. They come from rich countries with strong welfare systems. They travel long distances to be trained and to join the fighting. Just like prior Western recruits to Al-Qaeda, they join for ideological, not practical reasons.[37] If the new Islamists' willingness to die for their cause does not stem from the conditions of desert life, is it rooted in a religious vision that—to use Ibn Khaldūn's words—lets "them concentrate all their strength in order to make the truth prevail, [so that] they become fully united and obtain superiority and ... authority"?[38]

The French scholar Olivier Roy has explored the social origin for those proclaiming an Islamist identity, particularly those engaged in contemporary *jihad*. Though the Islamic State is too new to fall under his lens, his analysis of earlier *jihadiya* gives us some clues to the role that Islamism plays in their lives.[39]

Roy pointed out that the 2001 Trade Center bombers were all highly educated professionals, many of them from scientific and technical fields. They mostly lived in Western countries as part of a transnational Muslim elite. They were not in the top elite, and so had little political influence, either in the West or in the countries from which they or their families came. Yet they were privileged when compared to the bulk of their countrymen. They were the kind of city people whom Ibn Khaldūn would scarcely imagine giving their lives for a cause.

Their problem, Roy wrote, was that these men's mode of existence gave them no secure identity. First, they lived as Muslims in the secularized West. That made them not just a minority, but an unaccepted minority, particularly in Europe, where the fear of 'Muslim invasion' is rife even in the mainstream press. Second, their conditions of work took them from one country to another as job opportunities opened and their professions called. They had nowhere stable to set down roots, even had those roots been welcomed, which they were not. Could they look to a homeland? Not likely, given Middle East's moribund economies. To use Roy's term, they were "deterritorialised."[40] Having no other way of defining themselves, they turned to Islam as a core identity.

> Far from representing a traditional religious community or culture, on the margins of which they lived, and even rejecting traditional Islam, most of these militants broke with their own past and experienced an individual re-Islamisation in a small cell of uprooted fellows. Here they forged their own Islam, as shown by Muhammad Atta's will.[41]

Jihadi Islam looks backward to its imagination of the first Muslim conquests, forgetting the centuries of tolerance and diversity that came afterward to mark Islam as a high civilization. Identifying with the early fighters, it creates a global *jihad* to defend *Dar al Islam* ('the house of Islam') against what it sees as a decadent secularism. Until recently, this took place on Islam's borders (the U.S., Spain, Britain, Kenya, Bali, etc.) or against perceived 'crusaders' (Afghanistan, Iraq). Only in Syria and perhaps Libya has the main fight been against fellow Arabs. There, ISIS battles regimes that it sees as either secularist or heretical.

Those are the leaders. The followers, wrote Roy, are often also from the West, but from the unemployed immigrant and post-immigrant working classes.

> The radicals are often a mix of educated middle-class leaders and working-class dropouts, a pattern reminiscent of most West European radicals of the 1970s and 1980s (Red Army Faction in Germany, Red Brigades in Italy, Action Directe in France.) Many became born-again or converted Muslims in gaol, sharing a common marginal culture. . . . Twenty years ago these men would have joined a radical leftist movement, but such movements have disappeared from the spaces of social exclusion. . . . For a rebel, to convert is to find a cause.[42]

This explains how disaffected Chechens, Saudis, Kosovars, Pashtuns, Turkish Germans, Black Americans, Balochis, and the like can take up arms for Islam. Late-modern globalized society could not give them a reason for being, so they found their own. These fighters are clearly driven by a form of group solidarity: one of ideology, not origin. It is not the *al 'aṣabiyyah* that Ibn Khaldūn attributed to backward desert peoples. Is it an analogue of the religious *'aṣabiyyah* that he said could substitute? I think so.

Remember that Ibn Khaldūn traced the presence or absence of *al 'aṣabiyyah* to the concrete situations in which people live their lives. Desert life was hard, so groups needed to stick together. City life was comparatively easy, so individualism could flourish and groups could weaken. What Roy has done is surprisingly similar. He has noticed that *jihadiya* come from social strata that do not have a secure place in the late-modern world. They are rootless. They are alienated. Their societies give them no positive sense of self. Islamic radicalism is one way to get a sense of purpose. As he put it, "They are fighting at the frontiers of their imaginary *ummah* ['Muslim community']."[43] Their allegiance to Islam gives them a sense of mission—something that otherwise they would not have had.

To my knowledge, Roy has never mentioned Ibn Khaldūn in his writings, and why should he? He has, however, made a similar theoretical move. He has looked to people's concrete social situations to see what kind of social solidarity they can develop. He has seen that Islamism is a way to find personal identity and overcome weak social connections. Ibn Khaldūn said the same. Islamism creates a religious group-feeling, even as that version of the religion is rejected by the vast majority of Muslims.

This is not, however, a religion of sweetness and light. In 2000, Mark Juergensmeyer published a prescient book about religious violence: *Terror in the Mind of God*. In it, he examined recent cases of violence in five religious traditions, from Christian bombers of abortion clinics in the U.S. to Jewish and Muslim suicide attacks in Israel and the West Bank, to the Aum Shinrikyo attack in Tokyo's subways. He also interviewed some of the perpetrators: the Reverend Michael Bray, who firebombed seven American clinics; Mahmud Abouhalima, the 'mastermind' of the 1993 World Trade Center bombing; the Sikh militant Simranjit Singh Mann; and others. He found, unsurprisingly, that these men saw themselves at the center of a cosmic war. They saw themselves involved in a spiritual battle against the forces of darkness, one fraught with moral significance. Above all, their struggle was embedded in the social tensions of the present era. Radical religious ideas, in Juergensmeyer's view,

> have given a profound and ideological clarity to what in many cases have been real experiences of economic destitution, social oppression, political corruption, and a desperate need for the hope of rising above the limitations of modern life. The image of cosmic struggle has given these bitter experiences meaning, and the involvement in a grand conflict has been for some participants exhilarating. . . . [It helps assuage] the sense of personal humiliation experienced by men who long to restore an integrity

they perceive as lost in the wake of virtually global social and political shifts.[44]

Here, militant religion provides a path forward to those seeking to escape social chaos and moral decay by turning back the clock to a purer era. It is not the only path available, but it is by no means rare in the contemporary age. Ibn Khaldūn would likely agree.

Sand Painting. Photograph by Mullarky Photo, ca. 1900.

7

To the American Southwest

Navajo Ritual and the Experience of Time

We began by visiting a great civilization, to see if it could teach us to see religion in new ways. Then we immersed ourselves in the writings of a single man. Now we shall take a middle road: we shall see what a traditional indigenous religion has to show us. Like all religions, this one is complex. It is, however, unified enough for us to pick out certain patterns. Those patterns highlight aspects of religious life that Western sociologists often neglect.

The Navajo Nation covers more than 27,000 square miles of desert and mountains in the American Southwest. This "domestic dependent nation" has its own government, judicial system, electoral politics, and so on. Five-sixths of its three hundred thousand members live within the Nation's boundaries. Like most of North America's First Nations peoples, poverty is high on what used to be called "the Reservation"; it has recently hovered above 35% with unemployment even higher (45–60%), though the official figures fail to count work in the underground and subsistence economies. About a third of the Nation's residents live in rural areas. Few follow a full traditional life, since herding and bottomland gardening produce no more than a marginal livelihood. Mining once employed some but it polluted the landscape, particularly mining uranium (now banned) and coal. In the mid-2000s, the tribal government reluctantly authorized building casinos and has recently explored building wind farms. Navajos work for the tribal government, teach in the schools, staff the police forces, own and tend shops. Making crafts for the tourist market provides income for a few.[1]

The Navajo Nation hosts a number of religions. Some Navajos are Christian, some are Mormon, some belong to the Native American Church, and some practice the traditional Navajo religion, which will be this chapter's focus. Numbers are hard to come by and are not very useful. The Association of Statisticians of American Religious Bodies, for example, provides membership data for the various Arizona and New Mexico counties that overlap Navajo Nation land. Their latest figures show 40% of residents affiliated with a Christian or Mormon congregation, but they do not list figures for the Native American Church nor for those participating in traditional practices. D. L. Birchfield cites an unnamed 1976 survey to claim that "twenty-five thousand Navajos belong to the Native American Church, and thousands more attend its peyote ceremonies but do not belong." Such numbers mean something for the Christian and Mormon groups, because formal church membership matters to them. The concept is foreign to traditional Navajo religion, however—it is not something that one joins, certainly not exclusively. Leland Wyman, who was one of the foremost scholars of traditional Navajo ceremonies, pointed out that, at least through the 1970s, leaders of the Native American Church participated in traditional religious practices, and "a good number of traditional Navajo medicine men had become Roadmen in the Native American Church." Other crossings are not uncommon. The point is, membership numbers do not tell us much about Navajo religious ways.[2]

In fact, as Wyman wrote, "there is no word or phrase in the Navajo language that can be translated as 'religion' in the sense of that term in European languages." He added, however, 'religion' is still

the most convenient label for Navajo beliefs concerning the dynamics of the universe and their techniques for controlling them when rational means fail, and for their belief in what may be called the "supernatural," although Navajos do not place such matters in a separate category of experience.[3]

The difference between traditional Navajo religion and Christianity is not limited to belief. Traditional Navajo religion does not have church buildings. It does not have congregations. It has no ministers, no choirs, no youth chaplains, no holy books, nor most of the other things that defined 'religion' for my parents and for the world in which I came of age. It does have gatherings: times when people come together for religious purposes. It does have rituals: ceremonies held over multiple nights that aim to repair the world, which traditional Navajos think periodically comes undone. It does have ritual leaders: well-trained *Hataɬii* ('singers', 'chanters') who are adept at carrying out the "chantways" that restore the world's order. Their role is, however, quite unlike that of Catholic priests, Protestant ministers, Jewish rabbis, and Muslim imams. The rituals, as well, are unlike those with which most Americans are familiar.

At root, traditional Navajo religion is oriented toward maintaining life and health—both individually and communally. Its main event is the "chant," a ceremony several nights and days long designed to reorder one's relationship with the powers of creation. There are many different types of chant. Wyman counted twenty-four aboriginal "chantway systems" used for curing, plus Blessingway and Enemyway (and their sub-varieties). These last two, respectively, bring luck and exorcise alien ghosts. Each system can be conducted according to one of three ritual modes, depending on its intent. Holyway mode invokes the *Yeibicheii* or "Holy People"; Evilway mode wards off native ghosts; Lifeway mode treats victims of accidents. Most chants have two-night and five-night versions; some can be spread over nine nights. The permutations and combinations of chantway type, mode, and length make many different rituals possible.[4]

These multiple systems are not random; they have a very clear purpose. Again quoting Wyman:

> Ceremonialism is the system the Navajo have developed to cope with the uncertainties and dangers of their universe. They regard the universe as an orderly, all-inclusive, unitary system of interrelated elements. The tiniest object, being, or power, even minute insects; the most stupendous, the great mountains that bound the Navajo country and the thunder and lightning that crash above them; and man himself—all have their place and significant function in the universal continuum. . . . Evil and danger come from disturbance of the normal order, harmony, or balance among the elements of the universe.[5]

Families choose to sponsor chants at times of crisis or potential disorder. A family member may be ill; someone may be leaving for or returning from a journey among foreigners; perhaps a person has had a run of what Westerners would call 'bad luck', but which Navajo, with their belief in an orderly universe, think must have a cause. That person—

the patient or "one sung over"—is the focus of the ceremony. For that person's protection or healing, the family will engage a *Hataɫii* who specializes in the particular chant deemed proper for the occasion. Learning each chant requires memorizing several days' worth of prayers and activities, so few *Hataɫii* have mastered more than a handful.

Let's take an example: one of the Holyway chants that invokes the Holy People for curing. A typical Holyway chant begins in the evening by consecrating the hogan (the Navajo traditional circular house) in which it is to take place. The patient's body is painted with pigments, cornmeal, and pollen. The *Hataɫii*'s helpers make "unravelers"—bundles of herbs and feathers that are placed on the patient's body, then unraveled, symbolizing release from evil, danger, and harm. This is followed by songs and prayers that last most of the night. The family participates, neighbors come, clan relatives travel long distances to take part.[6]

After dawn a large fire is built on the hogan's floor, and the *Hataɫii*, the patient, and any family members who wish then disrobe and sweat. The patient is given an herbal emetic and washed; this is accompanied by more singing. After breakfast, the *Hataɫii* makes offerings to the Holy People, so they will come and render aid. Prayersticks are placed outside the hogan in specific spots where they will attract the Holy People's attention. In Gladys Reichard's description, they are placed

> under a rock, near an arroyo, under a tree at the south, in a branch of a pine tree at the west—where the gods must see them. . . . If the sticks are made properly and deposited according to deific decree, and if the prayer is repeated without a mistake, the gods cannot refuse to come.[7]

Depending on the particular chant and its length, this pattern may repeat for as many as four days. The point, wrote Reichard, is to exorcise evil and invoke the deities. On the fifth day for nine-night ceremonies, but earlier for shorter ones, the sand painting begins.

Most Americans have seen pictures of Navajo sand paintings. Also called "dry paintings," these are complex designs made by pouring powdered pigments onto a smooth bed of sand. Colored sand, crushed minerals like gypsum (which makes a white powder), pollen, cornmeal, powered roots, and so on can be combined to produce the needed colors. Simple paintings may depict just one or two figures, like the "Blue

Horned-Toad and Anthill" painting that Wyman used to illustrate the Red Ant Holyway ceremony in his contribution to the *Handbook of American Indians*. Or they can be complex, like the painting of "Four Holy People" or the painting of "Whirling Logs Myth," both part of the Nightway ceremony, which he described in the same article. In each case, the sand painting either depicts in symbols the spirit beings who are being asked for assistance, or it depicts the mythic journey that resulted in this particular chant being given to the people. In the latter case, the figures represent the Holy People encountered along the way.[8]

Before dawn on the morning when sand painting is to begin, the *Hataɫii* opens a medicine bundle and lays its contents on a mound/altar a few yards from the hogan's door.

> As each piece of ritualistic property is placed, the chanter [*Hataɫii*] utters the appropriate sentence of a prayer and the patient, as a symbol, takes hold of the property. The altar is there to announce the preparation of a sandpainting inside the house, to inform the gods that they are expected, to warn persons not concerned that they should stay away.[9]

Sand paintings are made by carefully trickling dry pigments onto the hogan floor. Depending on their size, they can take up to several hours to complete. The *Hataɫii* directs the work, assisted by any man who knows how to help. The patient usually rests until the task is finished.

When the sand painting is finished, the patient sits in its center and the *Hataɫii* applies medicine objects to various parts of the Holy People depicted in the painting. Then he touches the patient in the same places, intoning ritual prayers and songs. The patient is in this way identified with the Holy People, for his or her protection. The accompanying prayers retell the myth by which the world was created and through which sand painting was given to the People.

After this part of the ceremony, the patient goes outside and the sand painting is destroyed. The sand—now supernaturally dangerous—is removed and strewn far from the hogan. The whole process is repeated for four days, in a nine-night chant, three days, in a five-night chant, and so on. Each day uses a different painting and a different myth. The last night is devoted to singing, culminating in the dawn songs, which greet the first faint streak of light in the east.

Of course, I have left out much. Besides the unravelings, the medicine bundle, the sand paintings, and the sweats, a chant may specify more than one hundred prayers and songs the *Hataɫii* must repeat exactly if the ritual is to have effect. These are highly repetitive and display a detailed imagery. On the surface, they contain a simple message. Each invokes a Holy Person, then seeks identification between the patient and that Holy Person's powers. In some chants this leads to a request that the Holy Person remove and disperse the malevolence that besets the patient. Often the language models this removal. As one prayer from the Enemyway chant says to Pollen Boy:

> Nicely you shall put my foodpipe in its [former] condition again!
> Nicely you shall put my windpipe in its [former] condition again!
> Nicely you shall put my heart in its [former] condition again!
> Nicely you shall put my nerves in its [former] condition again!
> Nicely I shall walk about, without ailment I shall go about, unaffected
>   by sickness I shall be going about!
> Without monsters seeing me I shall be going about!
> Without beings which are evil seeing me I shall be going about!
> With monsters dreading me I shall be going about!
> With monsters respecting me I shall be going about!
> Governed by this I shall be going about!
> After conquering monsters I shall be going about!
> After accomplishing this with monsters I shall be going about!
> Pleasant again it has become.
> Pleasant again it has become.
> Pleasant again it has become.
> Pleasant again it has become.
> Pleasant again it has become.[10]

Symbolic? Or Something More?

What can we say about these prayers? Some observers focus on their images. They either treat them as magically compelling, as did Reichard in her early work, or they treat them as texts out of context, separated from the religious performances of which they are a part. Reichard's later work was more thorough, but it still subordinated ceremonies to their symbolism and attempted to shape the disparate acts and attitudes she found in the ceremonies into a more-or-less unified theology.[11]

Reichard's monumental *Navaho Religion: A Study of Symbolism* (1950) was a *tour de force*. In line with its subtitle, it focused on what ritual symbols mean to the Navajo and on how rituals reflect underlying Navajo religious beliefs. To take an example almost at random, here is a passage from her analysis of color symbolism:

> The sequence *b-y-u-p* [black, yellow, blue, pink] represents The Twins in flint armor, Flint Boys acting as hogan posts (in which case the center pole was white), Thunders, Sky People (when all four colors were represented in one picture), the talking prayersticks of the prayerstick branch of the Shooting Change (when sung for men), and the curing herbs of the Place-of-emergence.[12]

She compared *b-y-u-p* with other color combinations, noting their associations with particular objects, directions, size, places, and so on. Summing up, she wrote:

> Chart I [titled "Creation of the Earth"] was set up to show how dogma synchronizes different types of symbol with the making of the world, especially the placing of the mountains. There is an association between mountains, stones, day skies, jewels, birds, vegetation, sound, body-parts of the personified earth, inhabitants, power of motion, special gifts, and physiography. . . . [O]ther associations may be made in schematic form to tell a story.[13]

Note that 'dogma' has pride of place. Reichard saw Navajo rituals as good to think with. The fact that her book's three main sections are titled "Dogma," "Symbolism," and "Ritual"—in that order—suggests a latent Christian origin to her interpretive scheme. Despite the lack of a Navajo theological tradition, religious belief was, for Reichard, the root of everything. In her words, "Navaho mythology is to Navaho chanters what the Bible is to our theologians."[14] Though she stated clearly that the *content* of Navajo belief is very different from Western religious worldviews, she treated Navajo religion as having a parallel idea-centered *form*.

Some later interpreters followed this lead, albeit differently. Louise Lamphere, for example, interpreted symbols as systems rather than focusing on isolated symbolic elements. As she wrote in one early publication, "In the Navajo case, it seems most appropriate to analyze chants as a system of symbolic objects and actions" rather than taking each symbol in isolation. For her, Navajo religion had a two-fold focus. It could both "express cosmology and provide a means of dealing with individual illness." It accomplished the latter "through [the] symbolic manipulation of [both] man-to-god relationships and the patient's body state."[15]

Here, ideas about the world are just one part of the picture. Navajo religion is about both cosmology and healing. This is, I think, closer to what the Navajo themselves would say. For example, the just-quoted Enemyway prayer is not, primarily, a theological statement about the nature of the world. It is a step-by-step description of a person coming back to health. The first four lines describe the body being returned to its rightful order, so that the patient can walk about without ailment. Lines six through nine describe the patient gathering strength, moving from becoming safe from monsters (by being invisible) to having earned those monsters' dread and respect. Lines eleven and twelve describe the patient as strong enough to conquer monsters. The last five lines express how pleasant it is to be well and strong again.

Yes, this is symbolic healing. It is, however, a particular type of healing, in which the ritual guides the patient back to health by expressing his or her growing strength. Navajo ritual consists of a set of acts that symbolically connects the patient with the Holy People, then uses those Holy People's strength to expel the illness and evil that the patient suffers. It does so by declaring that the move from sickness to health is coming to pass.

At this point, it is helpful to introduce the work of Sam Gill, who took a decidedly non-symbolist approach to Navajo religion. He agreed with Reichard's emphasis on ritual, but he wrote that Navajo ritual is better seen as performance than as text. When seen from the point of view of the ritual's participants, prayers such as the one just quoted "evoke and structure the images . . . in such a way that they create the power that can expel malevolent influences and that can reorder, and hence restore to health and happiness, a person who suffers."[16]

Gill noted that "prayers are never texts, in the Navajo view: they are always acts that are performed for someone for some felt need." Put otherwise, Navajo prayers are not messages, nor are they primarily designed for communication, as are the petitions to God common in Christian rituals. They are, instead, meant to accomplish something: in this case, the patient's cure. They use what the linguistic philosopher John Austin called the performative power of words. Austin noted that the sentence 'I nominate John Smith for Governor' creates the very situation that it seems to describe. So does a judge's statement, 'I sentence you to thirty days in jail.' Gill argued that Navajo prayers are similarly oriented toward action. Indeed, the whole ritual is a process of creating (or re-creating) a harmonious world.[17]

> Sand-painting rites are meaningful curing acts because of the Navajos' recognition of the performative powers of ritual representation. . . . Properly prepared and used, the sand painting has the power to cure. It reestablishes for the sufferer the proper relationships with the forces of life on which his or her health and happiness depend.[18]

Navajo religion is particularly oriented toward ritual and prayer, because ritual and prayer are believed to have created the world in the first place. On a conceptual level, we can see this in the Blessingway myth, which is retold at all major creative events. It is used when building houses, before journeys, at marriages, and as part of many other rites. Literally translated, it means "the way to secure an environment of perfect beauty."[19] The myth recounts the occasion of the first ceremony, by which the world was made.

At the beginning of this world, the story goes, all was chaos. The lower worlds had fallen into disorder and been destroyed. All that was left was a medicine bundle, a collection of objects and powers from which the world was made. Thought and speech emerged from this bundle, taking the form of a young man and woman, too beautiful to behold. As Long-life Boy and Happiness Girl, they thought and talked about how the world was to be. Then they built a ceremonial hogan held up by the cardinal directions: East, South, North and West. They entered the hogan and spread the contents of the medicine bundle on the sand. They painted the life forms of all the living things that would be in the world, along with the months of the year, the stars, and the landscape. Then they sang through the night. At dawn the painting was transformed into the world the Navajo know.[20]

This story posits an unusual (to us) relationship between reality and language. In essence, it says that the world was created by speaking it: it was thought and spoken into being all at once, perfectly. As Gill put it, "When creation was completed, the world was beautiful. All things were formed and set in place, and proper relationships existed among them."[21] The anthropologist Gary Witherspoon wrote that this fits with the Navajos' underlying presumption about the relationship between language and reality:

> Navajos do not postulate the possibility that language may distort reality or the perception of reality. Such a proposition goes directly contrary to the Navajo scheme of things. This world was transformed from knowledge, organized in thought, patterned language, and realized in speech. . . . [R]eality was created or transformed as a manifestation of language. In the Navajo view of the world, language is not a mirror of reality; reality is a mirror of language.[22]

Quite literally, tradition-oriented Navajos believe that speech creates the world that it describes.

This has practical consequences. For one thing, Navajos are very careful not to voice negativity for fear of creating it. To use Witherspoon's example, 'saving for a rainy day' brings about 'rainy days'. More directly, talking badly about other people can make them ill—one of the reasons that Navajos worry about witches, whose very thoughts can harm those around them. On the other hand, wrote Witherspoon, "If one thinks of good things and good fortune, good things will happen."[23] Ritual, in particular, can be powerfully beneficent.

> Ritual language does not describe how things are; it determines how they will be. Ritual language is not impotent; it is powerful. It commands, compels, organizes, transforms, and restores. It disperses evil, reverses disorder, neutralizes pain, overcomes fear, eliminates illness, relieves anxiety, and restores order, health, and well-being.[24]

In the Blessingway chant, speech does so formulaically, by retelling the myth of the world's origin. The world was perfect at its creation, so retelling the story in ritual actually restores this original perfection. This is essentially Gill's point. As he put it, "rather than reenactments or dramatic performances, [Navajo ceremonies] are the actual creation of reality."[25]

This sought-after reality is *hózhǫ*—a Navajo term that means 'good', 'harmonious', 'orderly', 'happy', and 'beautiful'. Witherspoon analyzed the key phrase *'sǫ 'áh naagháí bik'eh hózhǫ*, which appears in nearly every song and prayer in all Navajo ceremonies, used much like Christians use a benediction. Literally, it combines the names of the two spirit beings who emerged from the Blessingway bundle: *sǫ 'áh naagháí* ('long-life') and *bik'eh hózhǫ* ('happiness'). Translating this as "may you have a long happy life" is inadequate, though, because while the root *-zhǫ* indeed means 'beauty' and 'harmony', the prefix *hó-*

> refers to the general as opposed to the specific, the whole as opposed to the part, the abstract as opposed to the concrete, the indefinite as opposed to the definite, and the infinite as opposed to the finite.[26]

The phrase *'sǫ 'áh naagháí bik'eh hózhǫ* therefore does not refer just to individual long life and health. It refers as well to the communal well-being of Navajo families, to the health and harmony of their communities and, indeed, to the right ordering of all creation. Reichard agreed that, though the term was untranslatable, it also includes "the nature of the universe, the world, and man, and the nature of time and space, creation, growth, motion, order, control, and the life cycle." She suggested "according-to-the-ideal may-restoration-be-achieved" as the closest translation that captures this wider context.[27]

No matter how we translate this phrase, its importance to Navajo ritual helps us address a question posed to all healing rituals: Do such rituals objectively restore people to health? Do they actually cure? Many Navajos would say 'yes', though they recognize that ceremonies do not cure cancers nor make tumors disappear. Instead, they reinstitute the world's original perfection, of which the patient's long life and happiness is a part. They reorder a disordered universe. Navajo philosophy is realistic: we are all going to die. "The goal of Navajo life in this world," wrote Witherspoon,

> is to live to maturity in the condition described as *hózhǫ*, and to die of old age, the end result of which incorporates one in the universal beauty, harmony, and happiness described as *'sǫ 'áh naagháí bik'eh*.[28]

In this view, Navajo rituals do something much more important than curing patients. They restore the world's original perfection. Looked at from the point of their participants' subjective experiencing, they do so by reframing the original illness as the result of disorder. The ritual renarrativizes the situation, to use anthropologist Thomas Csordas's term. That is, it sets the patient's illness within a culturally meaningful story about an originally perfect world that has decayed, then been restored to its pristine significance. It does so by leading the patient through a multi-day event that recapitulates that perfect world's creation. In experiencing this restoration, the patient experiences the restoration of her or his health. Simultaneously, the community experiences the restoration of *hózhǫ* (beauty, harmony). Navajo ritual rebalances a world that has become out of kilter.[29]

There are many examples. Csordas showed how this renarrativizing affected one Navajo man who lost his power of speech as the result of a brain tumor. Derek Milne and Wilson Howard traced this process for Navajo diagnostic practices, in both the traditional and Native American Church traditions. The latter wrote: "For Navajos, diagnosis is not merely a prescriptive rite that passively initiates the therapeutic process . . . but can itself constitute a cure." Both Csordas and they showed how religious ritual language reshapes Navajo personal experience.[30] As Sam Gill put it in a slightly different context:

> The prayer act is therefore not simply a curing act, but a religious act of curing. When it is seen as a total integrated act, illuminated by the religious traditions, it becomes evidence that it is meaningful to those who perform it not simply because it cures physical ailments, but because it performs the acts which institute and maintain a particular way of life.[31]

Here lies the cultural importance of the Blessingway myth that I summarized above. Told in the context of ritual, it is self-referencing. The story says that thought and speech created the world at the beginning of time; in the ritual retelling, thought and speech create it once again. This time, however, the creation is inward, not outward; it is located in the experience of both teller and hearer. Every retelling is a new origin. As people hear the story again, they experience their world as reborn.

This experience is not vicarious. Though the ritual goes to great lengths to identify the patient with the Holy People, and to model his or her cure, its ultimate reference is not 'there-then' but 'here-now'. Specifically, the ritual experience is not, for the Navajo, a *copy* of the original world-creation. It *is* the world-creation. In Navajo cosmology, the ritual literally re-creates the world in the experience of its participants.

A Theory of Ritual

The foregoing invites us to think about ritual in a new way. Sociologists and anthropologists frequently treat rituals as symbolic constructions. They examine rituals as "texts" made from words, gestures, figures, and events, then they reveal the various meanings that supposedly stand behind them. This focus on cognitive meaning is one-sided. It treats ritual as head-stuff, forgetting that, like theater, poetry, and music, rituals unfold bodily and aurally in time. Navajo rituals certainly take time, as they shape their participants' flow of attention over the span of several nights and days. As described above, this process reorients them toward their world, but that reorientation is not just a mental process. Attentively, corporeally, and emotionally, rituals pick people up in one place and set them down again in another.

For most participants, experiencing rituals is more important than thinking them, though neither of these two aspects can exist in isolation. Rituals are multi-dimensional entities, of which symbolic analysis captures only a part. It helps, however, to know something about symbolic analysis, at least as a point of contrast. There is no better spot to begin than Clifford Geertz's famed definition of religion as

(1) a system of symbols which acts to (2) establish powerful, pervasive, and long-lasting moods and motivations in men by (3) formulating conceptions of a general order of existence and (4) clothing these conceptions with such an aura of factuality that (5) the moods and motivations seem uniquely realistic.[32]

Without being totally mentalistic, this definition emphasizes religion's cognitive side. Symbols clothe religious ideas in a way that both arouses religious moods and motives and makes them seem realistic. Like other cultural systems, religions embed their participants in a shared mental universe. Rituals are one means of doing so. Geertz famously analyzed many such rituals, from Javanese funerals to Balinese cockfights, showing the social and cultural messages underlying such formal acts.[33]

Victor Turner used a symbolic approach in his famous studies of Ndembu rituals. He treated rituals as symbolic performances that express socially valued meanings; he wrote that ritual analysis can provide insight into how participants see the world. He emphasized, however, that such meanings are always equivocal. No human society has a completely coherent worldview, and every society experiences social conflict. He identified two ways in which rituals expressed conflicting principles and conflicts in practice. First, he affirmed the functionalist claim that rituals smooth social conflicts by dramatizing and integrating them. Second, he also showed that ritual symbols themselves can carry multiple and contradictory meanings. In the Ndembu *Nkang* (female initiation) ritual, for example, the milk tree "stands for, *inter alia*, women's breasts, motherhood, a novice at *Nkang a*, the principle of matriliny, a specific matrilineage, learning, and the unity and persistence of Ndembu society."[34]

Turner wrote that such symbols are at once ideological and sensory. For example, white tree sap represents breast milk because they look alike, but the ritual situates the two so that they represent purity, fecundity, and the conflict between matrilineal descent and virilocal residence. As Turner pointed out, women are simultaneously central and peripheral to Ndembu social structure. Ndembu ritual both highlights and mediates this contradiction.

Other anthropologists have pursued a symbolic approach, quite fruitfully. Mary Douglas analyzed Hebrew food taboos as rituals that simultaneously symbolized and maintained inter-group boundaries. Luc de Heusch argued that ritual symbols can only be understood as part of a conceptual system in which each of the elements gets meaning from the others. Claude Lévi-Strauss defined a ritual as "words uttered, gestures performed, and objects manipulated; . . . [of which] gestures and objects are *in loco verbi*; they are a substitute for words." All three emphasized rituals' cognitive role in religious and social life.[35]

Turner did not lean so far. As Mathieu Deflem pointed out, "For Turner, studying symbols meant primarily 'studying symbols in action, in practice."' Despite his emphasis on symbolic meaning, Turner did not forget that rituals are multi-sensory experiences. In Deflem's words:

> Symbols are "good to manipulate" and the handling of symbols "works," because they are not just reflections of cognitive classifications, but [are] also "a set of evocative devices for rousing, channeling, and domesticating powerful emotions." Turner's view is here directly opposed to the structuralist approach because the latter would fail to draw attention to the whole person involved in ritual.[36]

Still, Turner, like Geertz, emphasized rituals' symbolic meanings for their participants, showing us what we, as outsiders, might miss, because we do not know the symbolic codes available to 'the natives'. While we can often understand rituals' overt words, outsiders need to have someone translate the gestures, colors, movements, and images—both verbal and visual—before we can grasp the rituals' full meaning. Symbolic analysis does this, to great effect.

While acknowledging the value of such enterprises, the ritual theorist Catherine Bell noted some shortcomings with this approach. She observed, first, that 'ritual' is not an object that we can observe empirically. Ritual is not the particular 8, 9, or 11 a.m. Mass at St. Such-and-Such on Sunday mornings, nor any other event we might imagine. These are incidents—actions—that scholars comprehend by means of concepts like 'ritual'. 'Rituals' instead exist as mental constructs, for 'the natives' and for scholars alike. Like all constructs, 'ritual' draws boundaries around events, telling us which parts are important and which are not. For symbolists, 'rituals' are actions that have symbolic meaning. The construct thus co-creates the object of our investigations. Like all constructs, 'ritual' has a history and presuppositions. These have consequences for what we see when we examine the particular 'rituals' unfolding before us.[37]

Bell agreed that standard social-scientific approaches to ritual have treated it as mainly head-stuff.[38] They have, she wrote, explained rituals with three distinct intellectual moves. Their first move separates thought from action: symbolists see rituals as actions that 'have meanings'. Rituals are thought to encode messages, so the task of the observer is to decode the message and thus understand the ritual. Yet, she claimed, symbolic meaning does not exhaust ritual: a sermon is not the same as a Mass, though they may 'say' the same things. Thus a second move (common among these theorists) documents the ways in which rituals symbolically reunite thought and action: by generating moods and motivations that lead participants to accept the plausibility of their symbols (to use Geertz's formulation). Underlying this move—and indeed, making it conceptually possible—is a third pattern that separates the observer from the ritual participants. The participants *act* the ritual, while the observers *think* about it. Acting and thinking are seen as parallel here: both observer and participant are supposedly getting the same meaning.

As Bell pointed out, all three of these moves or patterns stem from the distinction between thought and action, which was presumed by the theorist *a priori*. Though step two sees ritual as reuniting thought and action symbolically, the contradiction itself is an artifact of the scholarly approach. In essence, she concluded, we as scholars set out to study other people's rituals; in the end we may well be studying our own minds, which constituted those 'rituals' as objects of study in the first place.

Bell set out to develop an approach to ritual practice which might avoid this theoretical circularity. Building on Bourdieu's notion of "habitus," but also influenced by Althusser's concept of "misperception" and Foucault's emphasis on "power," she focused on the socially generated "sense of ritual" by which "members of a society know how to improvise a birthday celebration, stage an elaborate wedding, or rush through a minimally adequate funeral." Rather than trying to construct a theory or model of such practices, which would again split thought from action, her approach attempted "to describe the strategies of the ritualized act by deconstructing some of the intricacies of its cultural logic."[39]

Specifically, Bell focused on what she called 'ritualization', as distinguished from 'ritual'. This is the process by which certain culturally specific notions are connected to other culturally specific notions, and then granted privilege over them. The Mass is a meal, for example, but it is a meal with a difference. Its key does not lie so much in its patterns and symbols as in the strategies by which its practices are made to contrast with (and made superior to) ordinary life. Thus the formal activities of gathering for a Catholic Mass distinguish this "meal" from daily eating activities, but the informality of a Mass celebrated in a private home with a folk guitar and kitchen utensils is meant to set up another contrast (the spontaneous authentic celebration versus the formal and inauthentic Mass).[40]

Of course, these particular differences are only salient for our own society. Other societies' rituals may involve meals, as does the Kwakiutl potlatch, but they differentiate themselves from normal meals in a different way. For Bell, this means that no ritual can be separated from its socio-cultural context. Every ritual is strategic. Every ritual is also practical, in so far as it is entered into with an intention to accomplish something in the socio-cultural world.

To be frank, Bell's solution interests me less than does her analysis of the problem, largely because her solution seems to me to be as head-oriented as are the positions she criticizes. She helpfully focused on ritual as a process rather than as an essence, and on the fact that ritual is performed by bodies, not just minds. She also noted that rituals often transcend their actors' intentions while still reframing their worlds intellectually, mostly in the direction toward which those actors originally aimed. Reviewing her volume some years ago, this sounded to me less earthshaking than it appears. I still think so, because her approach continued the previous focus on ritual meanings and treated rituals' results as largely intellectual matters. Yes, it is better to treat rituals as events rather than as objects, and they do occur in physical space, not just in imagination. Yet these are small steps. For all her references to Bourdieu, Foucault, and others, Bell's concepts do not seem to me to take us very far from the symbolists she criticized.[41]

Embedded in Time

Let us start at a different point: with the fact that rituals unfold in *time*. Whatever else they are, rituals are actions. All actions have a temporal side, and we can explore that side without imagining that it encompasses every aspect of the particular action under review. Indeed, rituals are sequences of acts, organized intentionally, for a purpose that varies according to the particular ritual we are investigating. A Catholic Mass is intended to be a worship service, but we can no more reduce its action to such purpose than we can reduce rituals to their symbolic meaning. Just stating the purpose or meaning of a ritual is not enough, no matter how complexly. We still have to perform that ritual on appropriate occasions, for it to exist. Rituals can only be experienced in time.

To underline the role of time-bound experience in human social life, Alfred Schutz appropriated a distinction common in mathematics and biology, between monothetic and polythetic phenomena. Monothetic phenomena are things that can be grasped all at once, conceptually. Polythetic phenomena cannot; they exist in multiple dimensions, of which concepts are only one. In general, ideas are monothetic. The idea standing behind the phrase 'two is two' could be equally well expressed as 'four is four' or 'John is John', 'Mary is Mary', etc. These all say that something equals itself. Schutz argued that once we grasp such an idea, the particular words by which we have grasped it lose their importance; they are not central to monothetic endeavors. This is why one can understand a scientific, mathematical, or philosophical conclusion without having continually to recreate its proof. Science, mathematics, and philosophy—indeed all conceptual thinking—are monothetic to the core.[42]

Unlike conceptual thought, Schutz argued, music is polythetic; it cannot be grasped all at once, because it has to unfold in time. Yes, one can speak about the 'meaning' of a piece of music, but that meaning is not an all-at-once phenomenon. In fact, it takes as much time to reconstitute the 'meaning' of a piece of music as it did the first time one experienced it. One must play it or listen to it again. Here is how Schutz described the experience of music from the point of view of the listener or performer:

> A piece of music [is] . . . a meaningful arrangement of tones in inner time. . . . The flux of tones unrolling in inner time . . . evokes in the stream of consciousness participating in it an interplay of recollections, retentions, protentions, and anticipations which interrelate the successive elements.[43]

These recollections, retentions, and so on are not the private memories that individuals bring to their experiences, nor are they conceptual matters. (The *Moonlight Sonata* does not have to remind us of moonlight to draw forth the recollections of which Schutz wrote.) Instead, such recollections are internal to the music. He continued:

> The composer, by the specific means of his art, has arranged it in such a way that the consciousness of the beholder is led to refer what he actually hears to what he anticipates will follow and also to what he has just been hearing and what he has heard ever since this piece of music began.[44]

Listening to music differs from reading philosophy in this regard. When one reads, one also participates in the author's presentation of thought, step by step, line by line. Once presented, however, the meaning of a philosophical passage can be grasped monothetically. This is not just because it involves words—poetry, despite its words, resembles music more than philosophy. As Schutz put it, "I can tell in one or two sentences the story of the Ancient Mariner . . . [but] in so far as it is poetry, I can only bring it before my mind by reciting or reading it from beginning to end."[45]

Interestingly, the recitation can even be in one's imagination: Schutz cited Brahms's famous remark: "If I want to listen to a fine performance of 'Don Giovanni,' I light a good cigar and stretch out on my sofa."[46] Brahms could replay the opera internally, but he could not do so all at once; he, like the rest of us, had to experience it in time.

It seems to me that rituals, like theater and music, are polythetic because they have to be experienced. Their existence as a series of temporal actions is central to their being. Unlike philosophy, ritual ideas *do* depend on the particular words, gestures, pauses, songs, and other events used to express them. They depend on those words, gestures, etc. being carried out, ordered, in whatever circumstances are deemed to be appropriate by the intended participants. Rituals are experienced in time by all of their participants: performers and 'audience' alike. In Schutz's view, this creates a sense of co-presence, in which participants of all kinds occupy the same or overlapping experiential spaces. (We will return to this peculiar kind of sociality at the end of this chapter.)

In short, rituals happen in particular places, they involve particular people, and they consist of a particular sequence of steps, one after another, that give them beginnings, middles, and ends. People experience them together, which involves more than just conceptual thinking.

Other things share these characteristics: a piece of theater typically begins when the curtain rises, the stage lights come up, or an actor makes a sound or gesture; musical performances begin by breaking silence and end by releasing themselves into it again. Even John Cage's famous composition *4'33"* is structured so that the audience attends to ambient sounds for its three separate movements of thirty seconds, two minutes and twenty-three seconds, and one minute, forty seconds. (The only oddity about this piece is that the musicians hold their instruments, but do not play them.)

What is involved in experiencing rituals, music, and theater in the flow of time? These events all manipulate participants' stream of attention. As action unfolds, one's senses are pulled first in one direction, then in another. One's awareness moves from one element to the next. A typical Catholic Mass, for example, begins with an opening procession set to music, ritual intonations, raisings and lowerings of holy objects, etc. Each draws attention to itself, then that attention is passed to another element. The better one knows the ritual, the more details one sees, because one is better able to enter into the flow of the event. Different rituals, like different pieces of music, combine these elements in disparate ways, but all focus their participants' sensory awareness in a deliberate progression.

How does such attention work, in practice? Psychologist Susan Blackmore noted that attention is central to human consciousness, because the human brain constructs 'experience' actively, not passively. Experience is not a matter of external reality drawing pictures on the senses. Instead, the brain constructs models of reality based on sensory input, resulting in the experience we perceive. Blackmore used the extremely focused attention found in deep meditation (among other places) as an easy-to-grasp example of how different states of attention produce different subjective experiences.[47]

Compare these two experiences. The first is Blackmore's description of the self in an ordinary state of consciousness; the second is her description of the self in meditation:

> [In ordinary consciousness,] my model of reality consists of self and the world—well divided from each other. "I" consist of a stable body image with arms and legs, a model of myself as someone working, a lot of

modeling of the substance of what I am writing. "I" have plans for future actions (I must tidy up) and wishes that things were different (I wish I could concentrate harder). . . . The world around consists of the room, the sounds outside; the birds (Oh there are some birds singing. Don't they sound nice? I wonder what sort of birds they are. . . .); children [playing] (I wish they'd be quiet), the radio (I hate the noise).

Now see her meditating:

I am still. The birds are singing outside, there are sounds of children playing a long way away, and a distant radio. The muddle on my desk and the room full of things are filled with stillness. There is me sitting. The sounds are full of silence. I hear a woodlouse crawl across the floor.[48]

The contrast is striking—and is a direct result of the individuals' different mode of attention. Though less extreme, religious rituals can also focus attention to provide a different self-experience than our ordinary life. Given the proper balance between familiarity and tedium, one might expect a lessened inner dialogue, a different focus on externals, perhaps even a different sense of one's personal boundaries. These are precisely the traits that psychologist Mihaly Czikszentmihalyi identified as typifying "flow": a state of consciousness that most often occurs when there is an exact balance between a person's skills and the activity that she or he is pursuing. Mountain climbers, chess champions, and dancers, among others, can pour themselves fully into their activities when they have enough skill to avoid anxiety but not so much skill that their minds wander. At this peak point, Czikszentmihalyi showed, the discursive ego shrinks or vanishes. In flow, one no longer experiences life through the veil of a chattering, self-conscious 'I'. Instead, one is drawn out of oneself, able to pay full attention to one's surroundings. The 'I' disappears and one experiences a different kind of selfhood. One feels different and more whole.[49]

Though rituals are not usually this intense, it is clear that focusing attention can affect people's "moods and motivations." This is not, as Bell claimed, because rituals separate and then symbolically reunite thought and action; instead, rituals guide the flow of participants' subjective experience—the whole package of thought, emotion, and sensation that occurs to during ritual—along specific paths. Ritual, theater, and music work when they guide this experience effectively. They pick people up in one place and, by structuring their inner experiences, set them down in another. Time and its role in structuring human experience are the crucial missing concepts that deserve elaboration.

Restoring the World

It should be clear how this approach can help us understand Navajo ritual. We first have to take seriously the Navajo notion that the point of rituals is to reestablish the world's original perfection. Like music, world re-creation cannot be done monothetically. It can only be done physically, visually, aurally, in the same way that it was done in the beginning. Long-life Boy and Happiness Girl—thought and speech—planned the new world, then brought it into being by painting sand and singing in the first hogan. *Hataɫii* do so in the present age. They use the same tools, thought and speech, that did the original deed. Order and harmony arise as the ritual participants reproduce the original act in its minute detail.

If we put ourselves in the place of the patient for whose benefit the ritual is performed, we can see this quite clearly. For a ceremony to occur, something must be out of order. An individual or family must identify an illness, an impending or recently completed journey, or other crisis as disrupting the harmony that should exist. Arranging for the ritual proclaims this crisis, calling forth aid from family and friends. The patient becomes the center of supportive attention.

The early stages of the ritual mark this as well. The patient is painted and sung over, his or her trouble is identified, and preliminary rites mimic the release from evil the ceremony is designed to achieve. In the company of others, the patient is purified by emetic, washing, and sweat. Socially and psychologically, the patient is placed at the center: the ideal spot from which to see creation unfold. The patient is even placed in the center physically: of the sand painting, the high point of the ceremony.

The painting ritual unites the person being cured with the world's creators or with a heroic adventurer who brought some culture element such as agriculture or hunting into the Navajo world. The patient walks onto the painting and sits amidst the holy people that it represents. In Gill's words, "In this way the person is identified with the very forces of the universe. He or she becomes one with the sources of life."[50] Repetitive prayers reinforce this union. Rather than magically compelling the Holy People to aid the patient, they identify the two. 'Now this is happening, now this . . . ' The patient is rooted in the present, with the Holy People.

Such rituals are not magic. Magic would separate patient and Holy People: 'me' here compelling 'them' there. Instead, the patient becomes a Holy Person and experiences the truth of the myths: that the natural and supernatural are not two worlds, but one. As Gill wrote:

> The sand-painting event accomplishes a recreation of the person and the universe. The world which may have seemed at odds with itself, experienced in the person as physical or mental suffering, is unified and reintegrated in the sand-painting rite, where it is acknowledged that the whole drama of the universe is repeated in the human being.[51]

To the Navajo, ritual healing is not just a conceptual act. Conceptual knowing is not enough. Navajo religion works by experience, not by philosophy. Like music, the point of these rituals is to shape the participants' inner time, and thereby to reorient them to the world.

That is one core lesson that I wish us to take from this exercise: that rituals shape human experience in time. We can understand them only if we understand their experiential nature. Navajo rituals make this abundantly clear. Were rituals merely symbolic, then what would be the point of holding a ritual that lasts nine nights and days? Clearly, something experiential is going on.

The second core lesson is an outgrowth of Navajo religious philosophy. The traditional Navajo worldview sees suffering as the result of disorder; rituals re-create order, setting the world aright again. Is this just true of Navajo rituals? I do not think so. In the next chapter, we'll see what this lesson, when combined with the first, can teach us about religious rituals in our own society.

Catholic Worker Soup Kitchen. Photo by J. Spickard, 2005.

8

Navajo Ritual Applied

World-Healing at the Catholic Worker

The previous chapter developed a theory of ritual experience, based on the way that Navajo rituals unfold in time. For the Navajo, those rituals re-create the world as it was in the beginning: balanced and perfect. They do so by shaping people's experiences. Participants emerge from the rituals with a sense of wholeness and reconnection. The rituals do indeed cure sickness, banish enemy ghosts, and restore the world to *hózhǫ*. This does not mean that everyone who is sung over returns to physical health. The Navajo recognize that all people die. The point is to be restored to *hózhǫ* in their subjective experience.

It would not be very helpful to my project if only Navajo rituals were able to create the universal beauty, harmony, and happiness that Navajos describe as *'sǫ 'áh naaghái bik'eh*.[1] Fortunately, other rituals can do so, too. As an illustration, I shall describe the weekly house Masses held by a Catholic Worker community at their home in the Boyle Heights section of East Los Angeles. Over some thirteen years of part-time participant-observation in this community, I came to see how these Masses restore the community's balance. Catholic Workers have set themselves a difficult task: living out the Gospel in a society in which the rich and privileged control the economy, the government, and the Catholic Church.[2] Their weekly rituals help restore their sense of hope and rightness. They remind them of who they are.

My interaction with the community began in 1991 as part of a study of religious social activists. It continued until 2005 as a long-term ethnographic project and as a field trip venue for students in my university courses on homelessness and on the sociology of religion. Somewhere during that time, attendance became personal, not professional, though I am Quaker and decidedly not Catholic.[3] Sometime during that time I also realized that the weekly house Masses had much in common with Navajo rituals.

The Catholic Worker movement is well known. Founded in New York in the 1930s by Dorothy Day and Peter Maurin as a Catholic response to the Depression, the movement combines a relatively orthodox Catholic theology with pacifism, communal living, service to the poor, and a radical orientation to social justice. Groups of Workers live together, dedicating their lives to voluntary poverty, social action, and a life (to use the words of one of the Los Angeles group's members) "of which Jesus would approve." Theirs is not the worldly kingdom, to which most Workers think that the Church as a whole has sunk. They live the Peaceable Kingdom in the here and now, in solidarity with "our friends on the streets." To quote another member of the Los Angeles commune, "We feed the hungry, nurse the sick, clothe the naked, and bring hope to the hopeless. Above all, we try to love them."[4]

Through a loose network in dozens of cities nationwide, Catholic Workers aid homeless people, neither as missionaries nor as rescuers but as friends and witnesses to their plight. The members of the Los Angeles commune run a soup kitchen and free clinic, pass out blankets and clothing, and invite some homeless people to live in their large, rambling house in one of L.A.'s poorest neighborhoods. They have run an AIDS hospice for those with nowhere else to turn. With other activists, they secured port-a-potties for the Skid Row homeless by staging a sit-in that blocked the entrance to the men's restroom at the Los Angeles City Hall. (Creative direct action is a hallmark of their work.)

Along this line, Workers routinely protest war by picketing the Los Angeles Federal Building and by trespassing at various nuclear and missile test sites. In the early 1990s, they occupied the tower of the about-to-be-demolished St. Vibiana's Cathedral, protesting the archbishop's decision to build an extravagant new structure instead of spending more on the poor.[5] Visitors to the commune are frequently introduced by their arrest records: 'So-and-so spent six months in jail for protesting at the School of the Americas and was later arrested in a Plowshares action.'[6] Such acts of civil disobedience are not taken lightly, but the Workers believe that Jesus and 'Saint Dorothy' would approve.

Actually, Dorothy Day might not, though she was famously reported to say, "Our problems stem from our acceptance of this filthy, rotten system."[7] Yet the movement has changed a bit over the years. As one member of the Los Angeles community put it:

Dorothy used to say that she would shut down her operation the moment the archbishop told her to. If the archbishop here wanted us to shut down, we'd invite him to talk about it at our favorite Mexican restaurant—and he should bring his credit card.

Following in Day's tradition, the L.A. Workers publish *The Catholic Agitator*, a monthly eight-page broadsheet of religious reflection on contemporary social issues. An excellent example of radical Catholicism, the *Agitator* once proclaimed the Worker mission with these words:

> We feed the hungry, clothe the naked, comfort the afflicted, afflict the comfortable, and speak truth to power not because we think that the world will suddenly be converted to peace and compassion, but because we will die [spiritually] if we do not practice what we believe.[8]

A quotation from Mohandas Gandhi that graced the door of the soup kitchen refrigerator declared, "Anyone who thinks that religion is not political understands neither religion nor politics." This aptly sums up Catholic Worker philosophy.

It is one thing to set forth one's views discursively; it is quite another to maintain a commitment to a way of being so at odds with the surrounding world. Intellectuals may respond more to the former, and the Los Angeles commune contains at least one first-rate intellectual. Yet most people need a deeper source of reinforcement, in a set of experiences that help renew their sense of the rightness of what they are doing and of the appropriateness of the identity that they have chosen. During my fieldwork, house Masses filled that need. Specifically, the *experience* of this particular ritual restored a polythetic sense of 'rightness' to the world. Although it was not their only ritual, the Workers' Wednesday evening Masses both restated the group's commitments and provided an experience that reinforced their chosen identity.[9]

The Ritual

Throughout my fieldwork, Workers and their friends gathered at their communal house early on Wednesday evening to celebrate Mass. After a longish service, described below, the group of fifteen to thirty shared a potluck supper. Then several Workers took huge pots of soup into Los Angeles's "Skid Row" area to share with the homeless. They passed out soup, bread, and water to as many as 250 residents of the street and of the few SRO hotels that remained after L.A.'s urban renewal. Workers set up their tables outside the rows of cardboard condominiums that dotted the area, serving until the food was gone. End-of-the-month lines were typically longest, because welfare and general assistance checks had run out. There were almost always plenty who needed the food.[10]

When I began my visits in the early 1990s, Wednesday was also the day of the Workers' Federal Building protest, so some who attended the evening's service might have spent the day in jail. If there happened to be a priest at the protest, they would invite him to serve as celebrant that evening. If not, and if none of the local priests was available, a member of the community would serve. If male, the service would follow roughly standard lines, skirting the edge of canon law without falling over it. Female celebrants often took more liberties with the ritual form.

In structure, these Masses generally followed the Catholic norm. After opening prayers and a song there were two or three readings, usually from Scripture but occasionally from other sources. The celebrant then reflected on these readings, but unlike a regular parish Mass, his or her 'homily' lasted at most a minute or two. It was followed by a period of silence into which anyone could speak. These being Catholics rather than Quakers, there was much more speaking than silence; the period often lasted twenty minutes or more. Typically, there were many comments about problems in society and problems with the political and Church establishments. Though not uniformly dark, and by no means hopeless, these statements reinforced the Workers' sense of being part of a small, faithful remnant in a world that has lost touch with God's will.

This group homily often showed a balance between comments framed as 'questions' and comments framed as 'answers'. For example, a November 2001 evening's readings were from newspaper accounts of families' reflections on losing relatives in a major plane crash. This was followed by a participant's reflection on losing his wife during the Gulf War, wondering about the relationship between personal and social tragedy. The next speaker described delivering babies that morning, and how one always has to balance death with new life. Others echoed these themes, enriching them with stories and grieving for those they had lost.

Times of social crisis seemed to give people more to say: the comments during the 1992 Los Angeles riots were particularly lengthy, as
were those in the aftermath of the terrorist attacks of September 2001.
Even in ordinary times, they were seldom shallow. Symbolically and actually, such a group homily reinforced the Workers' egalitarian views.

The typical service then proceeded with more songs and prayers, including a call for prayer requests from the participants. These were also
given plenty of time, ranging from personal prayers to prayers for "our
friends on the street," for "all those in prison," for specific prisoners of
conscience, and for the softening of national and Church leaders' hearts.

Then came a call for "the passing of peace." Though an ordinary
Catholic service would see people shake hands with their neighbors or
at most give a short hug and the words "Peace be with you," the Worker
service always stopped to give each person in the room a chance to
hug everyone else. Everyone who could stand stood and circulated to
others. The celebrant left the head table and joined the milling throng
of huggers, as each wished "peace" to all. It took at least ten minutes
before all the hugging was done, sometimes more. When everyone was
finally seated again, the Eucharistic or neo-Eucharistic portion of the
service began.

This part of the service followed one of two patterns: a standard
Catholic liturgy done by priests or by male members of the Worker community, and a more diverse style led by women.

Priests, of course, followed the standard liturgy, though with home-
baked bread rather than wafers for the Host. Seated behind a table
rather than standing, they blessed the bread and wine, then passed them
around the room, so each communicant took her or his own portion
without priestly mediation. Especially towards the end of my fieldwork,
portions of the blessing were said by all, reinforcing the rather un-
Catholic notion of the priesthood of all believers. Quiet music encouraged reflection, and the period usually ended with a song.

Female celebrants often got more creative. Not only were readings
more eclectic, but the residual hierarchy between celebrant and con-
gregant was practically erased. Specifically, women often gave participants even greater ritual roles. One asked each to take a flower from
the bouquet on the ceremonial table. Another asked them to feed bread
and wine to each other. A third opened time for personal testimonies of

celebration. The results were still recognizably Catholic, but even more non-hierarchical. This is not surprising for a group that saw itself as a prophetic remnant within a priestly Church—and also saw such priestliness as a fall from God's intent.

The ceremony was not yet over. At this point, one of the Workers brought out a large pot of soup, which he set on the celebration table. Celebrant and participants held out their hands in blessing, while an participant (never the celebrant) intoned a ritual blessing modeled on the blessing of the Host. The soup was removed, a few announcements were made, and the room was reconfigured for a potluck supper at which the soup played a key part. Among those announcements was always a call for "Who's doing soup?"—that is, who wanted to take soup, bread, and water to the streets. There were usually lots of volunteers.

Through the end of 2002, "doing soup" was an integral part of the evening's activities; it was done occasionally thereafter, though no longer so integrally. After supper, eight to ten Workers and friends climbed into an aged van for the short drive to the Catholic Worker soup kitchen—known as "the hippie kitchen" to the residents of L.A.'s Skid Row. There they picked up two more huge pots of soup, plus bread, water, paper bowls, plastic spoons, hot sauce, salt, and so on. They drove to a distribution point on one of the nearby streets, where a line of homeless people had already formed. The Workers set up their wares in the parking lane on overturned milk crates. Anyone could have soup, bread, and water. People could go through the line as many times as they wanted until the food was gone. There were no required prayers or "nose dives,"[11] no required thanks, not even a requirement that eaters be homeless. I have seen drug dealers, prostitutes, and businessmen take a bowl and chat with both Workers and homeless people. The meal was completely free, no strings attached, given with face-to-face humanity, one person to another.

Of course, Skid Row was not exactly the gentlest place on earth, particularly at the height of the crack epidemic. Several of the Workers were good at crowd control, especially one gray-haired former nun who was renowned for breaking up fights. Yet there are not many fights at the Wednesday night soup line; I, in fact, never saw one in thirteen years of visits. Even on the night of the 1992 Los Angeles riots, the atmosphere was tense, but not dangerous. After all, the homeless and the Catholic Workers are neighbors, and one does not hurt a long-term neighbor who brings much-needed food to one's 'dwelling' (the street). My middle-class students, who had previously checked the locks on their cars when driving through the area, found themselves relaxing and bantering with street residents. Some later described the experience as life changing.

When the soup was gone, Workers returned to their Skid Row kitchen, cleaned up, and went back home. The evening was over—typically, three to three-and-a-half hours after it started.

Symbols

Like all rituals, this one was full of symbols. We can skip those found in every Catholic Mass, such as the Elevation of the Host, the symbolism of bread and wine, and so on. (Catholic Workers, like most Catholics and unlike many Protestants, consciously highlight these things.)

There are several points, however, at which Worker ritual symbolized the difference that Workers feel between themselves and the Church at large. The first of these is obvious, but not often openly marked: Wednesday evening Masses took place in the Catholic Worker house, not in a church, and the celebrant was either a member of the community or a priest specifically invited to lead the service. That is, the Worker community provided the frame of reference for the service, to which the Church-at-large was at best a visitor. Workers and their friends gathered to celebrate together, not in opposition to the Church but neither in bondage to it. They saw themselves as carrying out the mission that God set for the faithful, and they often prayed that the institutional Church will see the error of its ways.

This sense of the primacy of the community of believers was high-lighted by specific points in the service that assigned tasks traditionally done by priests to everyone present. The first of these was the joint homily. In a 'normal' Catholic service, interpreting scripture is the priest's prerogative; Catholic Workers allowed everyone's voice to be heard. This symbolically put participants and celebrants on the same level, a quite radical notion for traditional Catholicism. The similar openness to prayer requests was partly a function of the small size of the group, but it symbolically emphasized the role of the congregation and deem-phasized that of the priest or celebrant. So did the long "Peace be with you" hugs.[12]

More significant, however, was the joint recitation of parts of the Eucharistic blessing—an aspect of Wednesday Masses even more common toward the end of my fieldwork. Having congregants jointly deliver parts of the blessing specifically asked them to play a priestly role. If it takes a 'priest' to say these words, then congregants became the 'priest' collectively. Jointly blessing the soup followed the same symbolism, especially when a member of the congregation said the blessing, not the celebrant. The celebrant participated on exactly equal terms with the 'lay' people: as one member of a collective priesthood.

This was not the end, however, because "doing soup" carried the most interesting symbolism of all. Seen as part of the liturgy rather than as an after-hours addendum, "doing soup" transformed the entire service into a symbolic double Mass. In a traditional Mass, the priest blesses the bread and wine, eats and drinks, then distributes the ritual meal to the multitudes. The first Worker Mass roughly followed this pattern, though with the weakened role-divide between celebrant and congregants just mentioned. The second Mass began with the congregants' communal blessing of the soup; this was a clear priestly act and was highly marked in the evening ritual. After this blessing, all present ate it as part of the potluck supper. Then members of the community (as 'priests') took it out to the streets and distributed it to all comers.

Not having been raised Catholic, it took me some time to notice the dual nature of this ritual. No Workers had remarked on it in my hearing, and I had been told that serving soup in the streets had begun as a temporary measure, after the original "hippie kitchen" was destroyed in the 1987 Whittier earthquake. When I noticed the symbolism, I was at first unsure whether it was conscious. Some direct questioning told me that it is, at least for the core participants. One even described the event as "priest duty." After 2002, when shifts in the ritual pattern made "doing soup" less central to the evening's activities, most Workers still saw serving soup as a sacred as well as a charitable act. How better to bless the poor than to give them Mass, in the form of nourishing food, in their own living room (the streets)?

In this light, it made sense that rich and poor were both welcome at the soup line, that there were no restrictions or requirements, even of prayers, and that Workers saw themselves as equals to those to whom they provided food and drink. Worker theology roughly follows the theology of liberation, in which Christ is believed to have come for everyone, but especially for the poor. In Worker theology, Jesus does not ask after one's reputation in the world, nor does he call his followers to solve people's problems effectively. Instead, he asks that his followers love people and devote their efforts to helping them. Soup and water are his body and blood, which, given with love, feed the multitudes.

It is helpful here to remember the general Catholic belief in transubstantiation: the real presence of Christ in the sacrament. For many Catholics, the Mass is not just symbolic. It involves the physical incorporation of God. One consumes the Divine Presence, which helps suffuse one's life with holiness and gives one a greater ability to carry out God's work in the world. The Catholic Worker double ritual not only imbued Workers with God's charism but also passed it, through soup, bread, and water, to homeless street people. They, too, became God's instruments, affirming life and peace in a situation too often dominated by the opposite. The relative peacefulness of the Wednesday night soup line is thus expected, not a surprise.

Anthony Stevens-Arroyo noted that similar practices were common in early Christianity. In the early church, he wrote,

> the practice of breaking the host at the conclusion of the Mass for distribution to those unable to attend the ritual was connected to a sharing of free-will offerings to be given to those in need. Thus, in addition to the carrying of the consecrated bread to others, non-consecrated food was shared.[13]

Gradually, the Church dropped the public distribution of consecrated bread in favor of the secular distribution of charity. The Workers' sacramental blessing of soup thus restored a literal holiness to this charity that the recent Church has foregone.

As I have indicated, however, this pattern changed. Starting in 2002, Bible study played a larger role in Worker spiritual life than it did formerly, and Wednesday evening homilies began to spend as much time interpreting the Bible as they did talking about the world's condition. Fewer Workers "did soup," making the double-Mass image relevant only to a minority. Both my symbolic and my experiential analysis, therefore, apply only to the ritual as it was practiced through the end of 2002. (Change affects ritual life as much as it does the rest of religion.)

Experience

I have exposed at least part of the 'meaning' of Catholic Worker house Masses by explaining their symbolism. These Masses expressed Worker egalitarianism, their belief in the priesthood of all the faithful, and their unity with the poor. They expressed the notion that God is present in the lives of the people. They affirmed that God can alter those lives by direct action, using the faithful as God's hands and feet. These symbolic expressions reinforced core Worker beliefs and lend great meaning to the Wednesday evening services.

Such symbolism does not, however, encompass everything that we can say about such rites. I described the difference between monothetic and polythetic phenomena in the previous chapter. Symbols are monothetic—i.e., they are concepts that can be grasped all at once. The ideas that I just listed are so graspable: they are thoughts that shape our sense of the universe and orient our actions. Rituals, however, are more than thoughts; they are polythetic. Like music, they can be fully taken in only by experience, by living one's way through them. Just as one does not exhaust the 'meaning' of a Beethoven sonata by naming its musical references, its chord structure, its orchestration, and the mental associations that it generates, so one does not exhaust a ritual by interpreting its symbols. Living through it, experiencing it unfolding in time does something more than just orient one's intellect toward a particular view of the world.

There are several levels to this experiencing, of which I wish here to focus on two: the role of attention in experiencing rituals and the role of this experience in renewing a sense of purpose to one's life as a social activist.

In the previous chapter, I described the phenomenon of attention, citing the work of psychologists Mihaly Czikszentmihalyi and Susan Blackmore. Czikszentmihalyi wrote that when one is totally focused on a task that exactly matches one's skills, subjective experience changes so that the sense of 'I' disappears. Blackmore traced such experiences to brain-states that do not construct a separate 'I'. For both, different states of attention create different experiences.

Rituals do the same. By manipulating attention, rituals can alter the way that people feel about themselves, about their lives, and about their fellow worshippers.[14] This is precisely what I found in my visits to the Catholic Worker community: for me, for my Worker informants, and for those that I brought with me as guests (and subsequently interviewed about their reactions).

Over the years that I attended Wednesday evening services, I brought several score of visitors. Often students, sometimes colleagues and friends, these visitors have run the gamut from the religiously illiterate to the intensely Catholic, and from the moderately conservative to the politically left-wing. As might be expected, they had varied reactions to the evening ritual, on both religious and political grounds. The most interesting, for present purposes, were the reactions of experienced Catholics who were open to Worker politics but who were not familiar with Worker-style participatory Catholicism.

Almost invariably, these visitors felt drawn into the Worker ritual. The form was familiar and they knew the lines, both those that they were used to saying and those usually said by the priest that the Workers assigned to the congregants. In Czikszentmihalyi's terms, they were not anxious, but neither were they bored: Worker house Masses were unpredictable enough and called for enough participation to make rote recital unlikely.

Several of these visitors reported to me precisely the diminution of internal chitchat that Czikszentmihalyi termed "flow". Without experiencing full-blown flow, they reported finding themselves unusually focused, carried by the ritual to an inner state beyond what they ordinarily experience in church. Specifically, they reported feeling themselves to be part of a collective, centered on those co-present, but extending into the wider world. Through the ritual, but particularly through its participatory transformations, they reported feeling themselves "more Catholic" than usual, more open to new theological insights, and more connected to "God's mission," however they interpreted it. They were moreover clear that it was not just the Worker ideas that did this, but their experience of these ideas in ritual. That is, Wednesday evening Mass worked for them on the level of feeling as well as on the level of symbolism. Its effectiveness also drew on their being able to attend to it in a way that did not usually happen in their home parishes.

Experienced meditators also responded in an interesting way. As Blackmore wrote, meditators are used to focusing their attention to experience altered states of consciousness. Though not always familiar with Catholic ritual, these visitors reported a particular attraction to three parts of the first (in-house) Mass: the group homily, the group prayer requests (including the group hug following immediately after), and the passing of bread and wine. Though the last is meditative in any Catholic context, the first two also elicited the kind of heightened attention at which meditators are skilled. Here are the words of a Quaker visitor:

> I found the group homily both familiar and strange. We Quakers are used to listening deeply to one another and to speaking from silence. These Catholics don't leave much silence, but their words seem to come from a very deep place. I felt myself following along with complete attention, but also felt that we were doing this together, not separately. Each of us had a part of what needed to be said, and if we listened carefully and spoke when needed, it would all come out.

The same visitor reported that his state of attention continued through the rest of the service, lessening only when the room was rearranged for potluck. Later on, he spoke of a similar sense in the soup line.

> This wasn't the same kind of state—what I supposed the Catholics would call a state of prayer. But there was a centeredness to it, a distinct feeling that we were all in this together: us, the street people, everyone. It's hard to specify, because it was beyond thought. But the feeling was very strong.

Clearly, a more-focused-than-usual attention figured in this visitor's experience. Though not universal, such reports recurred often enough to force me to conclude that the actual experience of the ritual was as important as its symbolic messages. Not that they could be separated; instead, they complemented each other, each contributing to the ritual as a whole.

Restoration

So much for our first core lesson from Navajo ritual: that rituals shape human experience in time. Catholic Worker house Masses, like the Navajo chants, had many symbolic elements but they also shaped their participants' experiences—and in ways that the standard sociological treatments of ritual do not fathom.

What about the second lesson? We previously saw how Navajo healing rituals re-create the world's original perfection for their participants. Focusing particularly on the Blessingway, we saw how ritual participants, led by a *Hataɬii*, reenact the story of world-creation in such a way as to set the actual world right again.

Given that the Catholic Workers are not Navajos, how is Navajo theology relevant to the Wednesday evening Mass described above? Two main connections stand out.

First, both Catholic and Navajo theology share a belief in ritual effectiveness. For Catholics, as for Navajos, ritual speech actually makes changes in the world. In Catholic theology, the best-known change is in the Mass itself: ritual language creates the real body and blood of Christ in the sacramental bread and wine. Eating that bread and wine (or soup and water) connects one to the Body of Christ. Specifically, Catholics formally believe that it actually *restores* that connection, enabling one to do God's work in the world. In this view, the ritual importance of Wednesday evening Mass is that it actually transforms the communicants, both those in the Worker house and those in the street.

Yet Navajo theology also leads us beyond the level of belief, by telling us to take seriously the structure of a ritual's experience, not just the structure of its symbolism. What do we find if we track Wednesday evening Mass as an experience, to which its participants devote the heightened attention that I outlined above?

Imagine attending the service as a member or friend of the Worker community, supportive of the group's religious and political aims. Like most Masses, the ritual begins with prayers and readings that recall to one the Catholic tradition and especially its social teachings. One listens to the familiar words and ideas, each with an undertone emphasizing the Worker's social mission. Were the Mass less participatory, one might daydream (as one often does in church). Yet here one cannot just sit back and observe, for the Worker service demands a more active role. This is especially true of the group homily. There one listens with increased attention, seeking whether and when to speak; as a result, one registers the words more deeply than one otherwise might. Listening carefully, those words form a pattern.

Both here and in the prayer requests, most Wednesday evening Masses describe a world gone wrong. Wars bring death to the world's people; the rich triumph and the poor suffer; Church leaders support the political and social Establishment, forgetting that Jesus was an outcast who brought hope to prostitutes, criminals, and the poor. One hears of misplaced priorities, of suffering innocents, of good deeds firmly punished.

One does not just hear of these things conceptually, as information. The unfolding of the group homily, its personalism, and its focusing of attention lead one to experience this world in the same way that one experiences a world when listening to poetry. Words embedded in time draw one in. Given the content of a typical Worker group homily, one focuses on a world out of joint, a world in which the innocent suffer great wrongs, a world that imprisons the righteous along with the guilty, in which wealth too often stands above the law. This is not an evil world, for that is not the Worker message. Yet it is definitely a world that needs repair. Both homily and prayer requests follow this vein—a vein that draws participants into a dark space. Not hopeless, but not yet hearing of hope, the Mass to this point is a downward movement.

Next comes the 'passing of the peace'—the ten-plus-minute milling "Peace be with you" that amounts to an extended group hug. Yes, this symbolizes the participants' commitment to each other and to the path of peace in a world that too often sees peace as weakness. However, such symbolism could be grasped in the first minute; why not stop there, and dispense with the other nine? In fact, the ritual pulls one beyond symbolism, as the extended greeting goes beyond the symbolic 'peace' found in most Catholic parishes. Each participant hears the others' personal best wishes; each one looks into the others' eyes. The structure of the moment encourages each to experience the others as similar refugees from the strife-torn world that has just been imaginatively entered. "We are Catholic Workers . . . committed to the creation of a new social order within the shell of the old."[15] Experience shifts at this point in the service, from an attention to the overwhelming problems of the world to an attention to the possibility of another way of being—a possibility for which the group is both the model and a means. Experientially speaking, the service here changes direction, from a downward move to the beginning of an upward climb into a new world.

The next step in this shift is the Eucharist. First comes the familiar blessing of the bread and wine, undertaken (in part) not just by the celebrant but by everyone. The ritual words tell a story of sacrifice and nurturance. Hearing them with attention reminds one that one is not alone, that Jesus sacrificed himself to save the world from just those social ills of which one has been so recently reminded. Coming just after the reinforcement of the sense of community, this connects one with the group, as does having the community play (in part) the role of priest. Each Worker is reminded of the collective mission. For Catholic Workers, as for Catholics in general, redemption is communal, not individual. The story of the Mass is the story of a community relying on God for sustenance, which becomes (through God's strength) able to carry forth God's work in the world.

Let me pause for a moment to trace the parallel with the Navajo Blessingway. That ritual likewise tells a story that is modeled in action. The Mass imitates Jesus' Last Supper, as Blessingway imitates Long-life Boy and Laughing Girl's creation of a harmonious universe. In each case, the participants identify themselves with characters in the story: Catholic Workers with the Disciples and Navajo with the universe that is being talked into being. That is to say, both rituals work in the same way, symbolically.

Yet both rituals also have a structure and a rhythm that guide their participants from one point in the story to the next, and that identify participants with the story's characters more than just symbolically. Each ritual also takes the form of a series of steps in time. Each step focuses the participants' attention on one ritual element before moving on to the next. Neither ritual can be grasped all at once; instead each consists of 'This, then this, then this . . .': a series of stepwise associations that lead participants forward on the sensory, emotional, and cognitive levels. The ritual experience is structured on all those levels.

Blessingway restores health by restoring the universe to its original harmonious state, in exactly the way that this was done at the world's beginning. The Catholic Worker house Mass restores the relationship between God and the community by leading participants through sorrow, depression, and doubt to a reminder that there are others who also seek peace in the world, to a connection with a greater force that is also working for good in the universe. Entered into with attention, this Mass channels the participants' senses, emotions, and thoughts toward a renewed sense of hope. That hope is both communal and priestly, welcoming the entire Worker community to become the body of Christ in a world needing redemption.

Then, of course, things really get interesting. The indoor Mass ends, participants bless the communal soup, eat it, and get ready to take it out into the streets. Where parishioners typically disperse after an ordinary Mass, each returning to home and private life, Catholic Workers bond together after their Mass for ritual public service. Eight or ten Workers and friends crowd into a run-down van, laughing and joking, enjoying each other's company and the moment. Compared to earlier in the evening, few comments focus on politics or social problems, and those that do are expressed in a lighthearted vein. People talk about what they are doing with their lives, on meaningfulness, on what they have rather than on what they lack. In short, the experience is as 'up' as the group homily was 'down'.

On arriving at the Skid Row kitchen, Workers collect the soup and its accoutrements, load them into the van, then either ride or walk to the distribution site. Here, again, they laugh and joke with street residents, many of whom are as thankful for someone to talk with as they are for the soup they bring. My students often found these interactions the most memorable of the evening. They were not generally surprised by the humanity of the street people. Instead, they more often expressed surprise at their own humanity in responding to them. "I never knew I'd laugh so much with a homeless person," one student visitor reported to her classmates. "I thought I'd be too scared."

Scared they are not, at least in part because the in-house part of the ritual has given them an experience of moving from negativity and despair to a sense of community and hope. The street portion of the ritual continues this, giving them an experience of being part of not just the Worker community, but of the street community of which the Workers are a part. As one of the Workers put it to me, "Our helping hand works because we're not rich tourists; we live here. We're just as dependent on donations as are the street people, and we're just as much a part of the community."

The street portion of the ritual carries the community feeling into one of Los Angeles's worst areas. Participants experience themselves as being part of something larger, set in a framework of hope. If the street portion of the ritual came first, participants would almost certainly emerge discouraged about the possibility of doing anything to help the homeless. Experiencing a sense of the community overcoming despair in the in-house Mass sets one up to experience the street 'Mass' as a hopeful and positive act.

Soup served and cleaned up, the mood becomes inward as the Workers pile into the van to return home. There is usually much less talking, as if people need more space from one another—and not just because of the hour, which is not really very late. My students invariably reported needing time to think over what had happened; meditators occasionally reported finding themselves in a state similar to a very light trance. Almost no one found themselves buried in analytic thought. Instead, visitors recalled scenes from the evening, replaying them in their memories, feeling again the feelings that the ritual had aroused. Unlike my students' visits over the years to other churches, I never had a student react negatively to this event. I am convinced that the ritual experience had a great deal to do with this result.

Understanding Ritual

The study of ritual has been something of a stepchild in mainstream sociology of religion. Few scholars attend to it. Even fewer treat it as central to what goes on in religious places. At best, they do so cursorily, saying, in effect, "Yes, we all know that rituals happen, but let's talk about the other stuff."

The situation is somewhat better in anthropology and in religious studies. There, however, the analysis has emphasized ritual symbolism, usually to the exclusion of other matters. It has, in effect, treated rituals as enacted ideas. The fact that those ideas unfold in time and are thus simultaneously thought and experienced has apparently escaped attention. Though there is nothing wrong with such symbolic analysis, it is only one facet of a larger picture.

In this chapter, I have tried to show how the Navajo notion that ritual actively re-creates the world encourages us to see rituals' experiential structure as central to religion and as a key part of their effectiveness. Catholic Worker house Masses clearly embody symbolism, but that symbolism does not exhaust their importance. Rituals are polythetic, not monothetic. They have to be experienced to be known. The ways that the Worker double-Mass structured its participants' attention was central to its impact. The way that it let them re-experience hope in the midst of a difficult world says a lot about how this religious community works. Catholic Worker activists are not just secular activists with odd religious ideas. They are, as they happily tell people, thoroughly Catholic. Ritual matters to how they make this possible.

The 'meaning' of a religious ritual is thus not only cognitive, but also experiential. That is the first lesson we take from the Navajo. A close attention to ritual experience—alongside the analysis of symbols—can tell us much about the religion and about the communities that perform them.

The second lesson is equally important. Though it is quite likely that not all religious rituals re-create a world in the experience of their participants, some of them clearly do. Navajo rituals gave us a framework for seeing this. My analysis of Catholic Worker ritual shows in detail how this works in a contemporary Christian setting. I invite other scholars to expand this analysis to other groups. I shall be interested to hear what they find.

Navajo religion suggests that ritual is important, and that all ritual involves the co-experiencing of structured time. It guides individual attention along common pathways, leading (at least in the Navajo and Catholic Worker cases) to the creation of community. The details and indeed the theological intent of Navajo and Catholic rituals may differ, yet both guide their participants toward an experienced re-creation of their world. Both move from private sorrows to communal solidarity.

Rituals are deeper than just their cognitive contents, in that they weave both ideas and experiences into a nearly seamless whole. Rituals do not just guide our thoughts; they guide our moment-to-moment attention. This has effects. Perhaps we need to take traditional Navajo thinking seriously in its claim that ritual reshapes the world.

A Methodological Postscript

I have focused the foregoing analysis on the Catholic Worker house Masses as they were practiced from the early 1990s until late 2002. I note this for two reasons. First, I wish to avoid the inaccurate timelessness of traditional ethnographic writing, with its false assumption of an unchanging 'ethnographic present'. Just as rituals structure time, so, too, do they exist in time; like all time-bound things, they can shift, either subtly or in high degree. No matter how stable, one should never assume that a community's spiritual life is unvarying. Ethnographers must therefore be careful with their language, so as not to portray their 'natives' as leading static lives.[16]

In point of fact, both I and my informants perceived a subtle shift in the pattern of Wednesday evening Masses beginning in late 2002. A long-term leader returned from a jail sentence with a desire for more group Bible study and with a seeming need to preach. His influence shifted the group service, though subtly. When I last visited, homilies were still communal, but more centered on Bible texts than before. Fewer participants spoke, and those who did often taught more than conversed. The blessing of the bread and wine was significantly less marked when no priest was present. "Doing soup" was done only by a minority, and ultimately dropped, partly in response to police harassment. My informants tell me that the Wednesday Mass still renews Catholic Worker life, but it now does so in a slightly different mode.

This does not undercut this chapter's analysis, but it does bound it. The fact that changes in a community's life affect its rituals does not undercut the importance of the experiential dimension. Just as reflexive ethnographers have had to relocate their analyses in history,[17] so sociologists must remember that religion is not static. We have to pay attention both to people's narratives and to their subjective experiences. We have to recognize that both can shift.

This leaves standing the basic point of this chapter: to see what intellectual tools a close attention to Navajo religion can give us. These tools can help us illuminate religion in other places.

Elgin Marbles (North Frieze). Photo by Yair Haklai, 2009 (Creative Commons BY-SA 3.0).

9

Are We Stealing the Elgin Marbles?

China. North Africa. Navajo country. Each has a different historical-cultural tradition and each provides different tools for the sociology of religions. There are other places we could visit, had we the time and had I the skill to guide us. For example: the Nigerian sociologist Akinsola Akiwowo explored indigenous Yoruba concepts that he hoped could contribute to a new African sociology. Others joined his conversation, though only M. W. Paye sought to extend it to the sociology of religion. Otto Maduro similarly applied the Nahuatl concept of *texcoatlaxope* to understand what he called "latina/o religious agency," both in colonial times and in the present. Roberto Rodriquez explored "maíz-based knowledge" as a way of understanding resistance to oppression on the part of Mexican and Mexican American peoples. If I knew enough about these traditions, I might be able to use them to help us understand even more aspects of religious life that Western sociology has overlooked. Yet I cannot. Three new traditions are enough for any scholar. I am sure that there are ideas from other cultures and civilizations that can expand Western sociology's view of the world. I shall not be the one to find them.[1]

I can, however, address an issue that I have so far ignored. It is not about Confucianism's relational sense of the sacred, nor about *al 'aṣabiyyah*, nor about the Navajo approach to ritual. Nor is it about the specific ways that I have used these ideas to help us understand religions that are closer to home. Nor is it about this book's root idea: that different historical-cultural traditions see certain aspects of religion more clearly than they see others.

This issue confronts any attempt to use non-Western people's cultural resources to improve a discipline that has contributed to Western societies' dominance of the world order. The problem is both political and ethical. As scholars dedicated to expanding human knowledge, we cannot ignore the context in which that knowledge is generated. Nor can we ignore how it is put to use. We need to bring our current historical-cultural context into the conversation.

It is a commonplace to say that we live in a globalized world. That globalization, however, is not just a matter of the technology that lets us telephone friends across multiple time zones or the trade networks that bring bananas, coffee, and tea to our breakfast tables. It is the fact that our current global system is shaped by power relations, specifically by centuries of Euro-American colonialism. Simply put, Europe and North America, plus Japan, Australia, and a few others, have much more influence than do other places. This makes every intellectual act different than would be the case if these particular power relations did not exist. This book cannot help being shaped by such inequalities.

In this chapter, we will explore some consequences of the fact that contemporary intellectual life is embedded in a world order that revolves around the West. We will begin with the issue of cultural appropriation. By what right do powerful people such as ourselves take resources, artifacts, and ideas from those less powerful than they, using them to their benefit, not to the benefit of their creators? We will then briefly explore some aspects of post-colonial theory—a movement among non-Western intellectuals that pushes back against the ways that Western ideas have been used to maintain Western political and economic domination. Some of these scholars criticize all efforts to use any society's concepts beyond its own borders. They think that these efforts are inherently imperialist, whether or not they are so intended. We need to take this idea seriously, as it challenges this book's entire project.

Finally, we will compare this book's intent to Raewyn Connell's effort to develop what she calls "Southern theory." As was noted at the end of Chapter One, Southern theory is an attempt to bring non-Western voices into the sociological canon; it particularly focuses on non-Western ways of understanding Western hegemony. Both of our projects put non-Western intellectual resources to sociological use. What do these projects have to say to one another?

In short, it is important to locate this book in relationship to the grossly unequal political and economic order in which we currently live. I have repeatedly argued that different historical-cultural contexts lead us to see the world in fundamentally different ways. How is this book's own proposed way of seeing located in our current historical-cultural situation?

You see, we sociologists of religion are no longer living in 19th-century France, even though we still too often see the world through its lenses. Nor are we living in ancient China, in 14th-century North Africa, or in Navajo country. We are living at the end of a colonial era, which is becoming a global one, and we are just beginning to be able to see past that colonial horizon. Among other things, this book is an attempt to envision what lies beyond.

Cultural Appropriation

What exactly is 'cultural appropriation'? We will start with an archetypal case: the early-19th-century 'purchase' of the Parthenon sculptures by Thomas Bruce, the 7th Earl of Elgin. Originally a frieze and ornamental statuary in the Temple to Athena in Athens, Greece, the 'Elgin Marbles' are now in a special gallery in London's British Museum. There's a story about how they got there.

Lord Elgin was the British ambassador to the Ottoman Empire at the turn of the 19th century. At that time, the Ottomans ruled Athens and most of Greece, which they had conquered in 1458. Like many educated Englishmen, Elgin admired Greece as the cradle of Western civilization. He particularly admired ancient sculpture. The Parthenon had been a Greek temple, then a Christian church, then a mosque, and finally a warehouse for storing gunpowder. In 1801 it stood in ruins, having been blown up during the 1687 Venetian siege. Roof gone, marble strewn everywhere, more than half its original sculptures were missing. Elgin feared that the rest would be lost to posterity, so he arranged to have them removed and sent to London. He was not the first to try to take them. The Venetian siege commander looted the temple, destroying some of the most important statues in the process. Elgin was doing the same thing, just more peacefully and with Ottoman cooperation.

The Greeks were not happy with this, but there was little they could do at the time. Two decades later, they won their independence after a joint British, French, and Russian fleet defeated the Ottomans at the battle of Navarino. Various Greek governments have since tried to get the sculptures returned, with the most recent campaign starting in the 1980s. The British have so far refused. The sculptures are, write museum officials, "a part of the world's shared heritage and transcend political boundaries." The museum points out that nearly half the extent Parthenon sculptures remain in Greece.

> The Trustees are convinced that the current division allows different and complementary stories to be told about the surviving sculptures, highlighting their significance within world culture and affirming the place of Ancient Greece among the great cultures of the world.[2]

Elgin claimed to have obtained Ottoman permission for the sculptures' removal. He must have had some local cooperation, as the Ottomans used the Parthenon and the surrounding Acropolis as a fort. One does not just waltz into a military camp and start carting off artwork. Moreover, the excavations took place over eleven years, from 1801 through 1812. Clearly, local officials knew what was going on. Elgin did not, however, have the written authorizations with him when he testified before the House of Commons about his right of ownership.[3] He had left the documents in Athens, he said, with the Ottoman authorities. The British government nearly refused to buy the sculptures, but the last-minute arrival of an Italian translation of the missing document convinced them otherwise. The Marbles have been on public display ever since.

The Greeks are not impressed. The Greek government has argued that the Ottomans, as an invading power, had no right to sell off a Greek heritage. The British had no right to buy it. Even if the Italian document was not a forgery, it spoke, as did Elgin himself, primarily of drawing and copying the sculptures rather than removing them; only two passages mentioned "taking away any pieces of stone." In short, the Greeks accuse Elgin of having bribed Turkish officials and the British of having received stolen loot. They want the sculptures back.[4]

There is more to the story, but these basics will do. The Greeks were as powerless to stop the sculptures' removal then as they are powerless to force their return today. Had Elgin happened along two decades later, or the Greek independence revolt happened two decades earlier, the sculptures would still be in Athens. This is clearly a case in which power mattered.[5]

Cultural appropriation is not always so grand. Popular culture is full of cases. Here are three, taken nearly at random from recent news stories.

Number One: Aaminah Shakur is a Native American woman *doula* (lay birth attendant) who wrote a web article about White American birth counselors appropriating, then selling non-Western birthing practices as their own 'discoveries'. She noted that these White women lead workshops

> with exotic-sounding names like "Mexican Rebozo Use" and "African Belly Binding" to get their fellow white ladies interested. I am not suggesting that white women should not practice belly support/binding and babywearing. . . . What I am uncomfortable with is white women who write articles in which they say they "discovered" these techniques and speak as authorities without ever giving credit to the history and cultural truth of these techniques. Giving credit means much more than using a "foreign" word and pretty "ethnic" print on your website and flyers. It also means . . . a proper understanding of the history and cultural significance of such practices in non-white communities.[6]

Shakur pointed out that in the U.S. today, only White women have enough social power to use 'traditional' birthing practices. They can afford $200 baby wraps, $300 baby carriers, and to have their births at home (home births are typically not covered by insurance). Women of color who use home births, baby wrapping, and so on as part of their cultural heritage are at high risk of being labeled 'bad parents' and having their children taken away from them.[7] Power determines who gets to use which 'natural' birthing techniques and who gets to claim to own them. Shakur argues that this cultural appropriation supports White hegemony. She wants it to stop.

Number Two: ethnic food trucks have become quite common in many American cities. In 2012, a controversy arose in Washington, D.C., about food truck workers who were required to dress up in fake mustaches and turbans and speak to customers in fake South Asian accents while selling them a mashup of Indian/Pakistani and Ethiopian cuisine. Two local activists started a petition against the truck owners, complaining that they were engaged in cultural stereotyping and mockery. *Washington Post* reporter Tim Carmen quoted a Columbia University scholar as saying, "It is harkening back to a colonial period when it was okay to exoticize" other cultures. Is it, Carmen asked, the minstrel-show quality that people find offensive? Or is it the appropriation of non-Western foods by Western entrepreneurs?[8]

The U.S. has a long tradition of domesticating ethnic foods for White consumption. Pizza Hut and Taco Bell are among the most anglified, but there are many others. McDonald's now sells tortilla wraps, and salsa has passed ketchup as the most popular American condiment. Ethnic food seems to be just another commodity. Is this innocent? Or does it let powerful White Americans feel good about their cosmopolitan tastes while they remain oblivious to the relative powerlessness of their ethnic neighbors?

For White Americans, 'ethnic food' symbolizes food from far away, mainly from poorer places. It has to be cheap; no one thinks of French cooking as 'ethnic'. It has to be from other countries; no one stands in line to eat scrapple.[9] Ethnic food means folk fare, at once ordinary and exotic. By appropriating that fare, professional-class White Americans position themselves as consumers of world culture, but they also position themselves above that culture. Not only do they have wide choice ('Which food truck will we visit today?') but they get to engage in what amounts to cheap tourism. Symbolically, the world is theirs for the eating. This is a position of power.

Revolutionaries recognize this. When asked in the 1980s if the Miskito people would accept special status as a Nicaraguan ethnic group, Miskito spokesman Brooklyn Rivera replied, "Ethnic groups run restaurants. We are a people. We have an army. We want self-determination." *Cultural Survival Quarterly*, which picked up this quote from a Karen National Union bulletin, gets right to the underlying problem: "States define nation peoples as 'ethnic groups' and 'minorities' as a tactic to annex their identities in order to incorporate their lands and resources."[10] This is out-and-out colonial appropriation. Dressing your food truck workers as mock South Asians recreates this appropriation in cultural form.

Number Three: the Harlem Shake. In early 2013, Jaimie Utt posted an article attacking a series of dance videos claiming to depict the "Harlem Shake." The videos "begin with a masked individual dancing alone in a group before suddenly cutting to a wild dance party featuring the entire group."

> Though you wouldn't know it from the [videos], the actual dance known as the Harlem Shake is not where one shakes around as if she or he is

having a seizure while humping things and wearing a silly costume. It is part of the rich tradition of dance and the arts in Harlem. Dating back to 1981 and drawing upon an Ethiopian dance called the Eskista, the Harlem Shake has long been a staple of hip-hop dance in this predominantly African American section of New York.[11]

Utt's objection was not that the videos are performed by White people, though he notes that they originated in and are spread through White-dominated friendship networks. His problem was that this is yet another White appropriation of an African American art form. Jazz is one example, though not an unambiguous one. Originally an amalgam of southern Black folk music, African rhythms, and American pop, it has spread worldwide, shifting and changing as it absorbed various musical traditions and styles. The appropriation came in early on, when African American performers were locked out of the mainstream music industry. Whites like Benny Goodman, Tommy Dorsey, and others headed jazz bands; Blacks were only gradually admitted as sidemen before reclaiming a spot in what had by then become an international musical movement.[12]

Rock 'n' roll is a clearer case. Also a Black musical genre, it was famously marketed to Whites as a music epitomizing teen rebellion.

"It started out as rhythm and blues," says Little Richard, the flamboyant rock pioneer who saw such tumultuous songs of his as Tutti Frutti and Long Tall Sally taken to the charts in white-bread "cover" versions by the likes of Pat Boone. "There wasn't nobody playing it at the time but black people—myself, Fats Domino, Chuck Berry. White kids started paying more attention to this music, white girls were going over to this music, they needed somebody to come in there—like Elvis."[13]

Elvis was key. Despite the myth, Sam Phillips, the man who 'discovered' him, probably never said: "If I could find a white man who had the Negro sound and the Negro feel, I could make a billion dollars."[14] Yet Elvis did take the rhythm-and-blues sound into the White mainstream, mixed with his own take on working-class country pop. He did not make the cultural appropriation; music industry executives did that. Later integration does not change the fact that most people now think of rock 'n' roll as a White art form.

The power, here, did not rest with the musicians. It rested with a White-dominated music industry and a White-dominated music market. Breaking into that market was a matter of hard work and chance. Having one's own art form appropriated by others did not improve one's odds of success. As Utt put it,

> The reason that White cultural appropriation is so insidious is that it is not an intentionally racist, but it plays into a system of racism where White people believe that everything is ours, everything is in-bounds to us, so we can take whatever we want, and in doing so, divorce it from its history and meaning.[15]

There are other examples, some of them perhaps more egregious than these. We could talk about White New Age entrepreneurs appropriating and marketing Native American religious practices to rich White folks: 'Spirit Journeys', 'Shamanic Immersions', and 'Spiritual Warrior' retreats. We could explore the world of fake Aboriginal art. We could examine White entrepreneurs selling 'genuine' Native American woven rugs that are actually made by child labor in India. We could look at chain stores like Cost Plus World Market that sell 'traditional' furniture and crafts from around the world to middle-class Americans, pocketing most of the profits. Each of these cases involves powerful people capitalizing on weaker people's religions, crafts, or decorative styles. Imagine a world in which Euro-American Christians were an oppressed minority, reduced to selling hand-made crosses as jewelry to rich Muslims, and you'll see the problem.[16]

Not every borrowing is a cultural appropriation. There's nothing wrong with liking burritos, eating 'Asian fusion' cuisine, or attending a performance of *La Traviata*. Nor do Euro-American men appropriate 16th-century Croatian military 'culture' by wearing neckties. Nor, arguably, are we complaining about the Ghanaian government's appropriation of a Caribbean holiday, Emancipation Day, marketing it as a time for African diaspora tourists to return to 'the homeland' to celebrate their ethnic roots. Though each of these cases exists in the context of national, ethnic, class, gender, and other power differentials, none of them is a matter of a powerful minority appropriating for its own benefit a less powerful group's cultural property.[17] As the Nigerian American writer Jarune Uwujaren put it,

Westerners are used to pressing their own culture onto others and taking what they want in return. We tend to think of this as cultural exchange when really, it's no more an exchange than pressuring your neighbors to adopt your ideals while stealing their family heirlooms. . . . Cultural appropriation is itself a real issue because it demonstrates the imbalance of power that still remains between cultures that have been colonized and the ex-colonizers.[18]

Taking other peoples' resources, practices, and cultural property is not 'exchange' unless those people are equally free to take our own—and if neither taking involves treating the other party to the exchange as somehow less important.

The question is whether this book involves such an unequal taking. Does applying Chinese, Muslim, and Navajo ideas outside their cultural contexts constitute an unwarranted appropriation? If so, then this book's effort is implicitly a colonial one. It appropriates weaker people's ideas and uses them for its own purposes. Such appropriation raises ethical concerns, particularly for a civilization (the West) that prides itself on its support of *liberté, egalité, et fraternité.*

Orientalism

Here is a related concern: one commonly called "Orientalism." This is the condescending attitude, famously decried by Edward Said, of Western scholars toward Middle Eastern, Asian, and North African societies.[19] Said described what he called a pervasive Western approach to these societies that portrayed them as static, tradition-bound, and undeveloped. The West, on the other hand, was seen as dynamic, flexible, and able to harness knowledge to improve social life. According to Said, this view justified colonialism because it put dynamic, knowledgeable people in charge of static, tradition-bound ones. 'Orientalist' scholars generated knowledge that aided colonial rule. This rule, in turn, made Eastern societies more static than they would otherwise have been, precisely because their colonial masters resisted popular change. Said showed how scholars, artists, and literary figures shaped and perpetuated global inequality.

We could focus this discussion on any one of a number of fronts. Anthropologists have been sensitive to this issue at least since the appearance of Eric Wolf's *Europe and the People Without History*. That book exposed the ways that pre-capitalist European expansion transformed the various subject peoples that sent tribute to the colonial powers in silver, cotton, indigo, and slaves. Clifford Geertz's *Works and Lives* described the roles that early anthropologists played in helping colonial authorities rule their new subjects. E. E. Evans-Pritchard's analysis of Nuer political dynamics, for example, made British rule over these stateless people possible—despite the fact the Evans-Pritchard himself did not see that as his chief aim. The backlash has caused an anthropological rethinking of cultural relativism—an idea with a long and complex history.[20]

Alternately, we could follow historian Michael Latham in showing how the specific form of modernization theory that was developed in the United States in the 1950s provided the rationale for President John Kennedy's Alliance for Progress. That program tried to modernize Latin American societies to save them from communism. While it improved education, health, and adult literacy, it also undercut Latin American democracy. By the end of the 1960s thirteen of that region's constitutional governments had been overthrown by military coups. Here, American sociological orthodoxy proposed 'solutions' for Latin American problems that deeply misunderstood the situation and caused considerable harm.[21]

We shall, however, take a different tack. Western intellectual domination has understandably produced a backlash, and the most interesting backlash has appeared under the banner of "post-colonial theory." This movement has been and continues to have considerable influence. It is, at core, an attempt on the part of writers and intellectuals from Europe's former colonies to reclaim, even celebrate, their civilizational identities while criticizing the works of their former conquerors. Authors like Said, Franz Fanon, Albert Memmi, Homi Bhabha, Aimé Césaire, Gayatri Spivak, and Minh-ha Trinh have explored how colonialism has shaped both the colonized and the colonizer. They have deconstructed the ways in which science and literature, in particular, have been used to justify Euro-American hegemony by portraying colonized peoples as intellectually, morally, and spiritually inferior. They have also shown how the colonizers' knowledge—including social scientific knowledge—has served imperial interests, even after the end of formal colonial rule.[22]

Edward Said, for example, showed how European scholars' portrayals of the Middle East and Asia in literature, history, and social science reinforced European colonial control by creating an image of 'the Orient' that both needed and deserved to be ruled by outsiders. To take one of his literary examples,

> Flaubert's encounter with an Egyptian courtesan produced a widely influential model of the Oriental woman; she never spoke of herself, she never represented her emotions, presence, or history. He spoke for and represented her. He was foreign, comparatively wealthy, male, and these were historical facts of domination that allowed him not only to possess Kuchuk Hanem physically but to speak for her and tell his readers in what way she was "typically Oriental."[23]

Said pointed here to a double domination. Not only did the Europeans dominate the Middle East and Asia (and other places) politically and economically; their intellectual products dominated the portrayal of these regions, both for the colonizers but also for the colonized themselves. The former controlled the terms of debate; the latter were forced to express themselves in European terms or remain silent. The title of Gayatri Spivak's famous article, "Can the Subaltern Speak?" asked more than whether colonized peoples are allowed to talk about their condition. She asked about the concepts they have to use, if they want to be treated as legitimate conversation partners. She pointed out that having to use the colonizers' ideas limits what the colonized can say about their own situation. Concepts shape what can be expressed. Having to express oneself in the colonizers' idiom (both linguistic and philosophical) amounts to an intellectual colonialism that maintains existing power relations.[24]

The opening chapters of this book showed how Western Christian ideas have dominated the sociology of religion. This volume's whole project has been to explore what sociology might look like, had it arisen in other cultural settings. Western scholars typically dismiss non-Western ways of thought as unscientific holdovers from an unscientific age, not as insightful tools for understanding core aspects of religions—including our own. The fact that few sociologists have even heard of Confucian relationalism or al 'aṣabiyyah, or have thought through the implications of Navajo ceremonial religion is evidence enough that ideas born from the Euro-American experience have so far been able

to define the field. The parallel fact that contemporary sociology of religion does not emphasize the creation of community as a religious act,
or see the connection between religion and ethnicity as forms of social
solidarity, or understand the restorative power of experienced ritual,
tells us that we have missed much by not listening to colonized voices
on their own terms.

To put this in terms of scholarly privilege: at present, 'we' get to study
'them', using our culturally derived concepts, but 'they' do not get to
study 'us' using their own culturally derived concepts in turn. To quote
Joanne Sharp, the issue is

> understanding the power involved in the *continued* dominance of west-
> ern ways of knowing. Because of the networks of power through which
> western forms of representation of the world circulated, this influenced
> not only how 'they' [colonized peoples] were known by 'us' [the coloniz-
> ers], but also how 'they' were persuaded to know themselves. Western
> ways of knowing—whether this be science, philosophy, literature, or even
> popular Hollywood movies—have become universalized to the extent
> that they are often seen as the only way to know. Other forms of under-
> standing and expression are then marginalised and seen as superstition,
> folklore, or mythology.[25] [emphasis added]

A key point is that intellectuals from the colonies and former colonies were forced to reject their own societies' ways of understanding
the world. In field after field, Chinese, Indian, African, Arab, Native
American, and other forms of knowledge were seen as inferior, less
insightful, and above all 'unscientific'. This was not just in sociology.
To take another field I know reasonably well, American university
courses in historiography typically have students read Thucydides and
not Sima Qian, Tacitus and not Ban Gu, Eusebius and not Kalhana or
al-Tabari, Bede and not Gulbadan, Thomas Macaulay and not Romesh
Dutt, Frederick Jackson Turner and not Eucledes da Cunha.[26] Western
authors are deemed to be able to teach us how history is written; those
from other parts of the world are not. Post-colonial theorists argue that
this is intellectual colonialism. They are right.

This is not to say that the colonial project ignored learning about
subject peoples; quite the opposite. Colonial authorities encouraged

Westerners to study the colonies, but not in order to let them influence Euro-American ways of thinking. Said quoted Lord Curzon, the British viceroy of India from 1899 to 1905, who advocated parliamentary support for such work. Curzon argued that

> our familiarity, not merely with the languages of the people of the East but with their customs, their feelings, their traditions, their history and religion, our capacity to understand what may be called the genius of the East, *is the sole basis upon which we are likely to be able to maintain in the future the position we have won,* and no step that can be taken to strengthen that position can be considered undeserving. [emphasis added]

Curzon practiced what he preached. He wrote two well-received books on Eastern peoples: *Russia in Central Asia* (1889) and *Persia and the Persian Question* (1982). Both aimed to give the British Foreign Office the information it needed to succeed.[27]

Encouraged by the colonial project, Western scholars were presumed to have a better grasp of the rest of the world than that world had of the West. As Said put it,

> Under the general heading of knowledge of the Orient, and within the umbrella of Western hegemony over the Orient during the period from the end of the eighteenth century, there emerged a complex Orient suitable for study in the academy, for display in the museum, for reconstruction in the colonial office, for theoretical illustration in anthropological, biological, linguistic, racial, and historical theses about mankind and the universe, for instances of economic and sociological theories of development, revolution, cultural personality, national or religious character.[28]

This was real knowledge as the Europeans understood that term. 'Superior' European knowledge of this Orient both justified and made plausible European colonial rule.

Against Universalism

From all this, one would expect that post-colonial writers would look favorably on this book's effort. It is, after all, affirming the value of non-Western ideas, not just for understanding religion in non-Western societies but for understanding religion everywhere.

I suspect, however, that I may be criticized by at least some who have written in this vein. Some post-colonial writers censure Western scholarship not just because it has been used to support colonial power, and not just because it has ignored the contributions of people from other parts of the world. They also oppose using one society's ideas to understand another, saying that there are no "irreducible features of human life and experience that exist beyond the constitutive effects of local cultural conditions."[29] Quoting from Bill Ashcroft's summary of this approach:

> Universalism offers a hegemonic view of existence by which the experiences, values, and expectations of a dominant culture are held to be true for all humanity. For this reason, it is a crucial feature of imperial hegemony, because its assumption (or assertion) of a common humanity—its failure to acknowledge or value cultural difference—underlies the promulgation of imperial discourse for the "advancement" or "improvement" of the colonized, goals that thus mask the extensive and multifaceted exploitation of the colony.[30]

Yes, the targets here are those academic disciplines that treat Western ideas as universal and non-Western ideas as parochial. Yet the argument goes farther than that. It rejects *any* attempt to apply ideas across cultural boundaries. It rejects universalism *per se*. I am arguing precisely that the non-Western ideas that we have been exploring are applicable cross-culturally. Logically, the post-colonial critique of universalism must reject my project as well.

To take just one example of this, the late Peter Park joined a frontal assault on sociological universalism as part of a 1988 symposium on "indigenizing sociology" that was sponsored by the International Sociological Association.[31] The whole symposium is worth reading, but Park's critique is particularly acute. He argued that

> sociology conceived of and practised as a universalistic science in the positivist tradition turns people into passive objects suitable for manipulation by centralised bureaucratic apparatuses. Fully indigenous sociology, by

contrast, seeks to restore people as creators of knowledge and agents of social change. This conception of sociology returns science to the people and assists them in bringing about a new world that is as different from post-Renaissance Europe as the latter was from the Middle Ages.[32]

Park argued that the development of universalistic science historically involved two separate intellectual moves. One was the process of "formulating principles at an abstract and general level"; once formulated, such principles were thought to apply to many particular cases. Doing this, however, required a second, more doubtful move. Modern science was only possible by

> exorcising the universe of its animistic forces . . . for the Aristotelian world that had existed until then was full of objects and spirits possessing intentions, sentiments, and vitality.[33]

For example, Aristotle thought that weights fell and hot air rose because they sought their proper levels. Newton's physics replaced this animate 'seeking' with the concept of gravity: an external force in place of an internal compulsion. Denying animism made physics more open to mathematical prediction. This has been one of the hallmarks of universalistic Western science ever since.[34]

Park pointed out that though the natural sciences are arguably not harmed by this intellectual move, the human sciences cannot exorcise 'animism' without seriously misunderstanding their subject matter.

> A universalistic social science would succeed only by exorcising the social world of its *anima* as well, that is by treating social formations, social relations, and human beings as objects devoid of . . . history, teleology, self-reflection, or consciousness.[35]

Yet human societies *are defined* by history, teleology, self-reflection, and consciousness. Eliminating these aspects of social life makes it impossible to understand human beings.

For Park, this meant that any universalistic sociology is ideological at its core. It treats people as moveable counters, ready for manipulation. This ideology makes colonial mastery much easier. Universalistic sociology provides technical solutions derivable from abstractly stated universalistic laws, which are applied by administrators of social policies to 'target populations', without the latter's participation in the policy-making processes. . . . This view of the social world justifies regimentation, management, and moulding—in short, domination of people.

'Indigenising' sociology, on the other hand, "return[s] science to the people from whom it arose." Park's goal was to craft local sociologies that serve the people whom they are trying to understand. He was not interested in greater inclusion, but in what he called "emancipatory sociology." His vision was a close-to-the-ground sociology that eschewed abstract theorizing in favor of solving people's concrete problems.[36]

Park's support of locally grown sociologies is entirely consonant with my wish to use those sociologies to understand aspects of religion that Western sociology has previously ignored. I disagree, however, with his claim that the use of one society's concepts to understand aspects of another society inevitably supports colonial domination. Reducing people to manipulable automata is not a characteristic of sociology that reaches across cultural boundaries; it is characteristic of a poorly thought-out sociology that misunderstands human beings.

To me, the problem is not universalism *per se*, but a false universalism that presumes that ideas arising from one society's historical-cultural situation are 'scientific' and ideas arising from other societies' historical-cultural situations are not. The applicability or inapplicability of ideas across cultural boundaries is an empirical matter. I no more expect Confucian or Navajo concepts to explain everything than I expect Western ones to do so. In fact, exploring the applicability of ideas across boundaries reveals patterns to social life that purely indigenous ideas (Western or otherwise) ignore.

In other words, the present hegemony of Western conceptual tools in sociology is a problem, but a correctable one. Like all sciences, social science works by identifying ways that its reigning concepts fail to grasp reality and finding new concepts that do a better job. For Park's antiuniversalism to hold, he would have to demonstrate that *all* attempts to apply sociological ideas across cultural boundaries produce worse knowledge than do indigenous ideas. The fact that some varieties of 'universal' sociology have both misunderstood human beings and been used to support empire does not mean that all transcultural sociologies must do so.

In fact, neither Ashcroft nor Park really attacks universalism. Take a close look at the language that each of them used above. Though both claimed to target 'universalism', instead, they attacked Western scholars' tendency to treat Western culture as superior to others. Ashcroft wrote that "universalism offers a hegemonic view of existence by which the experiences, values, and expectations of a dominant culture are held to be true for all humanity." Park objected to positivist sociology for "treating social formations, social relations, and human beings as objects devoid of . . . history, teleology, self-reflection, or consciousness." Both statements criticize 'universalism' for imposing particular Western ideas on everyone. Both imply that these ideas misunderstand non-Western people's realities.[37]

I agree with this last assessment, but I would further argue that standard Western sociology does not just misunderstand non-Western peoples; it misunderstands Western peoples as well. The previous chapters have shown several aspects of religion that non-Western ideas grasp more clearly than do Western ones. The whole point of this book is that history and culture shape what we see. Accepting this does not mean that social scientific knowledge cannot reach across these historical-cultural boundaries. It actually means that it *must* do so, if it is to understand the world thoroughly. Further, it must do so in multiple directions. No one or two societies' ideas capture social life *in toto*.

In short, Park's anti-universalist argument is like a call for banning cucumbers because someone once used a cucumber as a blunt weapon. His post-colonial project depends for its rhetorical force on the Enlightenment idea that all people and societies are equal (at least metaphysically); thus all have equal rights to their place in the intellectual sun. I agree, but I want to use that equality to correct sociology's previous shortsightedness. I do not think this calls for the abandonment of universal sociology altogether.

Southern Theory

Raewyn Connell shares many of the post-colonial thinkers' concerns. Her writings show that Western theories (she uses the term "Northern") claim a privileged place in the sociological canon.[38] She argues that they arise out of specific Western concerns, which include the maintenance of Euro-American political and intellectual hegemony. She argues that these theories' claim to universality diverts attention from many important aspects of social life. In short, she, like I, thinks that sociological theories wear blinders. She grounds sociology in colonial power relations, while I ground it in the 19th-century European historical-cultural context, of which those power relations were one part. She looks to other historical-cultural contexts for alternate points of view. I do, too.

In *Southern Theory*, Connell demonstrated the Western canon's limits by analyzing three contemporary sociological theories. She first faulted James Coleman's *Foundations of Social Theory* for its claim that society is the sum of countless interactions between featureless self-interested individuals.[39] Not only is this ahistorical; it also imagines people as genderless, raceless, bodiless players in some imaginary game. The problem, she pointed out, is that the game is real and that it is made up of players who very much have bodies, genders, and races and moreover are either given or denied resources because of them. In her words,

> Coleman ignores the whole historical experience of empire and global domination. He never mentions colonies. He treats slavery briefly, in terms of the intellectual problem it creates for an exchange theory of society. . . . *Foundations* misses or misrepresents vast tracts of human history, and ignores the social experience of the majority world now.[40]

Connell's second target was Anthony Giddens's *The Constitution of Society*.[41] That book outlined an approach to social life that takes individual agency and social structure equally seriously. Neither is independent; each builds on the other. Giddens developed this into an extremely abstract framework for understanding all societies at all levels of complexity. Agents know their social surroundings and act on the basis of social conventions; this knowledge and these actions create the very structures that channel their lives and choices. Giddens thus avoided the problems of Parsonian sociology, with its over-socialized "judgmental dopes" unable to do more than act out the rules society has given them.[42] He also avoided the inability of micro-interactionists to comprehend social structures.[43]

The problem, wrote Connell, is that the result is

> so generalized that it covers every episode in the history of the world, yet says almost nothing about them. . . . The relationship that *Constitution* does not theorise is colonisation; the structuring principle it does not explicitly name is imperialism; and the type of society that never enters its classifications is the colony.[44]

This ignores the actual world we live in, in her (and my) view.

> Giddens sees modernity as an endogenous change within Europe (or "the West"), producing a pattern which is *afterwards* exported to the rest of the world. . . . Other social orders are passing away not because Europeans with guns came and shattered them but because modernity is irresistible.[45] [emphasis in the original]

Though she did not mention Said's critique of Orientalism in this passage, I think it is fair to say that Connell would see Giddens approach as equally presenting a false image of 'the Orient'—or the global South, to use her preferred term.

Connell's third target was Pierre Bourdieu's *Logic of Practice*.[46] That book also attempted to grasp the universal patterns of structure and agency. Unlike Coleman's agents, Bourdieu's agents act in a world that is already formed by structures. Those structures shape the agents' *habitus*, or internalized principles of action. Those agents maneuver, wrote Connell, "always within the limits set by the *habitus*. Thus Bourdieu's theory of practice becomes, systematically, a theory of social reproduction."[47] He illustrated this with long examples from his fieldwork in Algeria, among Berber-speaking farming communities in Kabylia.

The problem, Connell wrote, was that his Kabylia was idealized, static, and culturally homogenous—in short, Orientalized. This was quite unlike the actual Kabylia at the time of his research. In fact, Algeria was then in the middle of a vicious anti-colonial war. Bourdieu himself was forced to leave the country under the threat of violence. He wrote of this elsewhere, but not in the *Logic*. This was, Connell argued, because Bourdieu's conception of theory . . . makes the anti-colonial struggle irrelevant. To arrive at "something like a subject," the European conceptual framing is significant. . . . Bourdieu's own project of creating a universally applicable toolkit gave him no reason to seek out colonial voices, because it made irrelevant the specific history of the societies through which the tools are illustrated. Nor did the toolkit require him to address a liberation struggle as a social process.[48]

For Connell, Bourdieu's approach privileges the experiences and intellectuals of the North and erases the experiences and intellectuals of the South. She criticized Northern theory's claim to universality, its tendency to place itself at the world's center, its exclusion of Southern voices and its erasure of Southern events. It treats the global South as *terra nullius*: unoccupied land.

To put this in the terms that have been used in this book's previous chapters, the sociologists whom Connell criticized tacitly assume that the sociological ideas that arise out of the West's history and culture can be applied to the rest of the world, unproblematically. Other voices can be ignored because they have nothing sociologically significant to add. In contrast, both I and Connell think that those other voices matter. They have insights, drawn from their own historical-cultural traditions. Those insights have their own universal value. They can teach us a lot about the world that we share.

Moreover, Connell and I agree that our contemporary world is shaped by several hundred years of colonialism and that it continues to be a radically unequal place. This is no longer the 19th-century world of Said's Orientalists, nor of the Ultramontane Catholicism that shaped sociology's beginnings. Nor is it even the mid-20th-century world of the modernization theorists, the Cold War, and the armed anti-colonial struggle. It does, however, bear the scars of all these events. Those events continue to have consequences.

Where Connell and I differ is on how to respond to this situation. Connell wrote *Southern Theory* to explore the work of a series of intellectuals from the global South, among them Paulin Hountondji, Ali Shariati, Veena Das, Ashis Nandy and Raúl Prebisch.[49] Each provided a critique of colonial power relations from the point of view of the colonized, not the colonizers. Connell introduced her readers to African,

Iranian, Latin American, and Indian thinkers, plus others, showing how each revealed aspects of global inequality that Northern thinkers miss. This is, ironically, an attempt to focus Southern theory on the problem that Connell has decided is the world's most significant issue: colonial and neo-colonial power relations.

Connell's project is a worthy one, but I am taking a slightly different approach. I have chosen in this book to cast a narrower net—focusing just on the sociology of religion—in order to cast a wider one. By sticking with religion, I can show in some detail how both individual writers (Ibn Khaldūn) and cultural traditions (Confucian and Navajo) illuminate aspects of religious life that Western (Northern) sociology ignores. Their ability to see these aspects is grounded in their historical-cultural situations just as our *inability* to see them is grounded in ours. *That is this book's central argument.* Every society's history both limits and enhances its vision. Every society's culture shapes what it can and cannot see. We can learn to improve our ideas only by listening to those whose ways of seeing are the products of different histories and cultures than our own. We can, in turn, speak to them about what our history and culture let us see clearly. No society can legitimately claim that it alone understands the whole of social life, nor can it claim that other societies' visions are false or irrelevant.

I agree with Connell that colonial power relations are part of our history and culture, and that they shape what we in the West understand about the world. They are not the whole of our history, but they do radically affect the present. Connell is also right that much Euro-American sociology does not attend to this fact, and that much of what passes for high theory is unable to grasp the forces that have structured the world we live in.

What Connell misses, however, is that she, I, and other contemporary sociologists are also shaped by our historical-cultural situation. That situation is crucially different from the one that faced sociology's founders because we live in a different world than they. We are, for better as well as for worse, much more connected globally. We are much more apt to interact with people from around the world. Advanced communications technologies, cheap air travel, and global job markets connect people at the top and middle of the economic pyramid. Worldwide flows of refugees, political and economic, connect people at the middle and the bottom. Such transnational connection is one aspect of our world; continued Western political, economic, and intellectual dominance is another. It is no wonder that Connell's sociological project arose in our era, rather than fifty or a hundred years ago.

With this history, we are forced to see different things than did the sociologists who founded our discipline. We also see different things than did the sociologists of my parents' generation. That's what happens when the world changes.

Thinking from Our Own Historical-Cultural Situation

It is time to return to the issues raised at the beginning of this chapter. Does this book's effort amount to an unfair cultural appropriation, in which I, a relatively powerful Western, White, heterosexual, male scholar go shopping among the world's intellectual goods, bringing home those that I think might best decorate my walls? Am I a latter-day Orientalist, claiming to know the 'natives" philosophies better than they do themselves—and in the process generating 'universal' knowledge that silences those natives' voices? Does this book's focus on religion rather than on colonial and neo-colonial power relations amount to an erasure of the structural inequalities that rend our contemporary world? For me, the answer to all three questions is clearly "no," but that's not a sufficient defense. What convincing reasons can I give?

The first is the seriousness with which I have treated each of these issues over the last several pages. I have dismissed none of them, nor have I claimed their irrelevance. I have, in fact, pointed out that they all result from a world in which some people have power and others do not. That happens to be the world we live in, so we have to take these arguments seriously. Taking them seriously does not, however, mean that they apply to every project that crosses cultural boundaries.

Cultural appropriation is the copying of other people's practices, either in order to profit from them (by selling baby wraps, classes on baby-binding, or what have you) or in order to make fun of their former owners (fake South Asian mustaches and accents). Describing the importance and usefulness of ideas that originated in other historical-cultural traditions, while clearly locating them in their cultural milieux, on the other hand, honors those ideas' creators. It shows their universal relevance.

Edward Said criticized Orientalism for its portrayal of non-Western societies as static, tradition-bound, and undeveloped. He criticized dividing "the West and the Rest" (to use an oft-repeated phrase),[50] especially while essentializing the differences between them. What he did *not* do was criticize the study of non-Western civilizations, particularly when that study was designed to undercut the essentialism that Orientalists practiced. He thus supported the work of the scholars who wrote for the *Review of Middle East Studies*, because they were applying the critical tools that showed the importance of race, class, and empire in shaping the 'Oriental' world.[51] Here, too, using non-Western ideas with respect and care is quite the opposite of the Orientalism that Said decried.

Finally, the fact that colonial and neo-colonial power relations still shape our world does not mean that they are the only topic worth studying. One way to overcome colonialism's legacy is by showing the worth of non-Western ideas. Connell does this, and so do I.

Yet there is a second, stronger argument ready to hand. That stems from the facts that, first, our intellectual lives are shaped by our historical-cultural situations, and second, that our situation has changed over my lifetime. When I grew up it was almost impossible to imagine that the West was not special and that the rest of the world might not need more than just our charity and guidance. That is no longer the only option. Western efforts to improve the world have an obviously checkered career: aid in some places, disaster in others. For every Green Revolution there is a Vietnam War. For every anti-smallpox campaign there is an invasion of Iraq. We Americans, particularly, have had a hard time recognizing our country's complicity in such matters, but a significant portion of our population now recognizes the problem.

Not everyone does so. Some people find it easier to ignore inequalities than do others. In our world, only men have the privilege of imagining that they lack gender. Only Whites have the privilege of imagining that they lack race. Only heterosexuals have the privilege of ignoring peoples' varied and complex sexualities. Only those living in the heart of the Empire can imagine that all peoples have equal access to the world's wealth—or can imagine, to use Thomas Friedman's rather ideological phrase, that the world is 'flat'.[52] The world is in fact gendered, raced, sexed, and hilly. Opportunity is decidedly not available to everyone. Power divides us wherever we turn.

Yet this, too, shows the importance of historical-cultural context to the ways that people see the world. People at the margins cannot ignore inequalities, and those who listen to them can learn to see them as well. Certain learnings come more easily to those whose social location is far from the center. As bell hooks wrote about growing up on the wrong side of the racial tracks in rural Kentucky,

> Living as we did—in the edge—we . . . focused our attention at the center as well as on the margin and we understood both. . . . Our survival depended on an ongoing public awareness of the separation between margin and center and an ongoing private acknowledgement that we were a necessary vital part of the whole.[53]

I did not grow up on the wrong side of the tracks. I did, however, grow up on the edge of an African American neighborhood and attended its schools at a time of reasonable interracial peace. Even as a kid, I had a pretty good sense of what my Black friends had to put up with. This taught me that the current social system does not benefit everyone. Then, in 1968, I was in Berlin at the time of the *Studentenbewegung*, in Paris just after the May student/worker strike, and in Prague three weeks before the Soviet invasion. I returned to the U.S. two days before the police riot at the Chicago Democratic National Convention. Martin King and Robert Kennedy were murdered while I was overseas. I joined Vietnam War protests when I returned. All of this changed my way of thinking. I like to joke that I have two undergraduate degrees: one in intellectual history from a rather famous university, the other in "willfully and maliciously blocking a public street or sidewalk" from that university town's police department.[54]

With this history and my experiences since, I cannot unsee a world in which arbitrary authorities misuse power, in which powerful nations seek to control weaker ones, in which wealthy people suppress the poor, and in which racism and sexism are so endemic as to be invisible. Nor can I forget the long history of colonial conquest that put Europe and America at the top of the international heap. To take just a single case: the thousand people who were living and picking trash in the Managua, Nicaragua, city dump the last time I visited that country are there as a direct result of the U.S. government policies that brought down the

1980s Sandinista regime and imposed neo-liberal austerity on its successors. My students cried after visiting a program for street children there. So did I.[55]

Such experiences are common among my generation of scholars. They have changed the way we see the world, in large part by forcing us to question the adequacy of our previous ways of thinking.

This is why I take the three critiques outlined in this chapter so seriously. It is also why I think we can do better. Our historical-cultural situation includes not just lingering colonial power relations but also independence movements. It includes not just gender oppression but also second-wave feminism. In includes not just racism but the American Civil Rights Movement, the American Indian Movement, the struggle against South African apartheid, Black Lives Matter, and other fights against racism. It includes numerous anti-war movements, anti-nuclear movements, anti-sweatshop movements, and—more positively—environmental movements, peace movements, labor movements, and movements for the reconciliation of peoples. These have all shaped contemporary scholarship. They have also brought people together across national and cultural boundaries. We have more resources than before for understanding other societies and cultures respectfully.

Learning about other ways of seeing the world, then using them to enhance our own visions, is neither cultural appropriation nor Orientalism. Nor does it involve forgetting the inequities that still haunt our world.

It is not the equivalent of stealing the Elgin marbles. It is trying to create a better world.

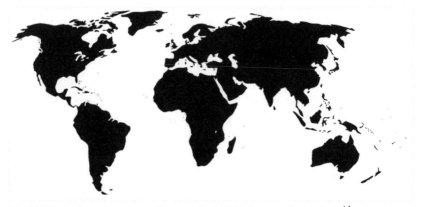

World Map without Antarctica. Drawing by E_Pluribus_Anthony chris 論, 2010.

Postscript

Living in a Global World

If this book accomplishes nothing else, I hope it shows that context matters. The social world in which we live shapes us, including scholars, no matter how much we wish this were not the case. Sociology was shaped by the context of its birth, especially by its self-image as a progressive science set against what it saw as its chief opponent: reactionary, authoritarian religion. It also developed in a colonial age, one whose self-justificatory ideology arrayed societies along a continuum from 'traditional' to 'modern'. Europe and America were (supposedly) at the progressive end of the scale, while the colonies and neo-colonies were (supposedly) stuck in backwardness. Euro-Americans thought that the colonized had much to learn from us but that we had next to nothing to learn from them. The sociology of religion was typical in failing to see that its core concepts grew out of the peculiarities of the Euro-American experience. Its concepts illuminated much but they hid much as well. I have written this book to show what we might be able to understand better, were we to see things from other societies' points of view.

I have focused on the sociology of religion because that is the field I know best. Having spent much of my adult life studying religions, I can command more striking examples and more detailed analyses on this topic than on any other. This helps me communicate my points more effectively. Other scholars are welcome to produce their own analyses in their own areas. The point is the same: sociology (and other social sciences) have assumed that Euro-American concepts can show us everything we need to know about the social world. This is simply not true.

The time has come, however, to imagine what a more equal world might look like. Despite its continued inequities, our global world demands nothing less. In my experience, three things are crucial if we are to transcend the long colonial era.

- First, we have to see that there is a problem; I hope, by now, that you do, too.
- Second, we have to be able to imagine a better world society than the one we have. The Book of Proverbs says, "Where there is no vision, the people perish"; this is as true today as it was in King Solomon's time.[1] Without vision, we lose hope and give up on the possibility of change.
- Third—and this is beyond the scope of this volume—we have to create the *We* that can make that imagined society real.

All three steps are important: we have to realize that we are not doing things right, we have to see that things could be different, and we have to unite to create the world we hope to become. We are all in this together. No group can do it alone.

Feminist scholars have long noted that you cannot "just add women and stir" when your previous ideas have been constructed from a male point of view.[2] Stirring does not free you from the same old concepts that failed you before. Real inclusion goes farther than that. Treating women as people changes everything; so does seeing our own social world through other societies' eyes. Both force us to recognize new possibilities. Even if we do not embrace everything that other traditions might want to teach us, taking them seriously will move scholarship forward.

This book is one step in this process of reconceptualization. It is not a sufficient step, but I hope that it has accomplished two tasks. Its narrower task has been to expand the sociology of religion's conceptual toolkit, so that we can understand more aspects of religious life. What can the sociology of religion better understand, when it abandons its default view and treats the insights of all peoples as potential resources? I have noted this aim repeatedly, so I shall say no more about it here.

The second task is an outgrowth of the first. What happens to us, as scholars, when we expand our ways of thinking? Specifically, what happens when we realize that our previous ways of thinking have limited our vision? The sociology of religion has for too long seen the world through Western Christian lenses. Realizing the worth of other conceptual starting points has both intellectual and psychological consequences. In the scheme of things, the latter are perhaps as important as the intellectual realizations on which I have focused so far.

To reprise the litany at the end of the last chapter: male, White, heterosexual, Euro-American—and Christian-descended—sociologists have for a long time thought that their ways of seeing religions were accurate, objective, and true. Now we know they are partial and that there are other ideas that illuminate aspects of religious life that the established ideas do not. Might this not recommend some humility? Might such sociologists now decide to seek out other unaccustomed ideas, so as to avoid repeating past mistakes? I hope so.

Although less personally intense, this parallels the aftermath of successful psychotherapy. Once someone has become aware of her or his previously unconscious patterns, and has brought them into the daylight, two things happen. First, one becomes humbler, more aware of the need to remove the beam from one's own eye than the mote from someone else's. Second, one tries not to repeat the patterns that caused trouble in the first place. One learns to check oneself, to make sure that one has listened well, that one is not belittling others, that one is not reacting automatically. Patterns are hard to break and breaking them is especially hard for those of us who are used to having social power.

For us, developing a world-conscious sociology of religion will take considerable care. bell hooks was right that living on the edge reminds one constantly that there are many different ways of seeing the world.[3] We who are used to living at the center can more easily forget that those at the margins can see things that we miss.

Now, however, we can choose to embrace our global world's intellectual opportunities. We can ask whether everyone with insights is at the table. We can ask if we are listening carefully to others and treating them as equals, so their wisdom can advance the world's knowledge. If these happen, then our fields will progress. If not, we will continue to impose our own historical-cultural visions on others and fail to learn what others' visions might teach us. We will miss a major part of the whole.

They say that raising a child takes a village. Doing good scholarship takes an entire world.

I can make this a bit more concrete by borrowing a story from Paul Lichterman, who wrote an award-winning book about what it takes for churches to reach across racial divides and work with people unlike themselves.[4]

In *Elusive Togetherness*, Lichterman recounted the efforts of White churches in a Wisconsin city to partner with African American churches to improve their community. Many churches tried doing so, but those few who succeeded had to confront their own failings and had to learn to treat their desired conversation partners as equals. The White church members had to recognize their racism and classism. Only after they had acknowledged their 'sinfulness' were they able to interact with the members of the Black churches with whom they wished to connect.

The successful churches were mostly Christian Evangelical. Part of their success stemmed from the fact that the Black Protestants with whom they wished to partner were similarly Evangelical in their theology. More important, in Lichterman's view, was the White Evangelicals' willingness to engage in serious self-reflection. When pushed to it, they examined their own motives for seeking to work with others and found that they had seen themselves as givers rather than as partners. They had been practicing *noblesse oblige*. They rethought, prayed, and realized that they needed the partnership for themselves, not just for the good of those whom they had thought of as less fortunate. They wanted to be "brothers and sisters in Christ." This is a different task than being charitable donors. They decided that being brothers and sisters was far more important than mere giving.

Absorbing this message reinvigorated the White churches. It let them became real partners with the African Americans. Both sides began to listen to each other and to treat each other as equals; they gradually learned how to be parts of the same community.

Though this example comes from religion, not scholarship, it exactly exemplifies my point. Privileged people can progress only after they have realized, then overcome, their own unacknowledged sense of superiority. To overcome the scars of colonialism and shape a truly global world, those of us who are used to having social and intellectual advantage need to take off our unconscious blinders. We need to be vigilant, lest those blinders return. Only then can we work together with those who have other insights that we need.

We sociologists of religion need to be open to the insights of other peoples who have different ways of understanding religious life. We need to listen to the early Confucians, whose sense of the sacred importance of relationships opens our eyes to those who maintain those relationships in our own churches, mosques, and synagogues. We need to seek out the insights of other civilizational geniuses, such as Ibn Khaldūn, who teaches us that race and religion have a lot in common; we need to examine how they operate in particular cases. We also need to listen carefully to the insights of people whom we have been taught to regard as 'primitive'; in the case of the Navajo, their understanding of ritual is superior to our own.

These are just three of many possibilities. As we become committed to overcoming sociology's dependence on the Euro-American ways of seeing, I hope we will explore many more. In doing so, we will shift the world's intellectual power relations. Euro-American sociology will become an equal partner to others.

This will take time and considerable effort. In the present world, the old ways of thinking still dominate intellectually. Sociology is still largely trying to impose Western ideas on others. We have, however, come far enough that we can begin to imagine what a more inclusive world would be like. I hope that others will do for their fields what I have tried to do for the sociology of religion. I will be fascinated to see what they find.

NOTES

INTRODUCTION

1 McGuire (2008).

2 The polling data in this paragraph come from the 1998, 2000, 2002, 2010, and 2012 General Social Surveys. I have used the 2010 and 2012 surveys for most items and the older data for questions that were not asked recently. These data are available through the UC Berkeley Survey Data Archive website (http://sda.berkeley.edu/archive.htm).

3 Source: World Values Survey, 2005–2007; the 1995–1997 WVS found similar numbers. You can find this data at the World Values Survey website (www.worldvaluessurvey.org).

4 See McGuire (2008, ch. 2); Wallace (2004).

5 Episcopal Church in America (1928; 1979).

6 I timed it. This is the average over the six services that I attended during my short research project.

7 The same priest also revealed to me a wish that is perhaps common to many clergy. "We sometimes fantasize," he said, "about treating our congregations like baseball teams that can trade players. 'Mrs. Jones, you're going to be going to church at St. Mark's from now on; I've traded you for Mr. Smith and two parishioners to be named later.'"

8 *Cursillo* (Spanish for 'little course') is a spiritual renewal event built around a three-day retreat. It was begun as a Catholic renewal movement in Spain in the 1940s, but has since spread to other denominations in the U.S., where it focuses on developing lay Christian leadership. *Taizé* services are contemplative Masses done in the style of the ecumenical Christian community in Taizé, France.

9 Fowler (1981).

10 Meredith McGuire and I explored this problem for understanding radical Catholic identity in McGuire and Spickard (2003).

11 McGuire (2008); Roof (1999); Beaudoin (1998); Ammerman (1996); Bellah et al. (1985)—but see Pearce and Littlejohn (1997, 75–76). Increased religious individualism is but one of several answers to the question "What is happening to religion?" See J. Spickard (2006b) for an outline of this answer, plus another four.

12 Luckmann (1967, 98–99).

13 Said (1978).

14 Cronin (2002).

15 For overviews of post-colonial theory, see Ashcroft, Griffiths, and Tiffin (1995; 1998; 2002); Barker, Hulme, and Iverson (1994); Young (2001).

16 See, for example, *Cultural Studies Review* 15(2), the September 2009 special issue on "Critical Indigenous Theory."

17 E.g., Smith (2001).

18 Robinson (2002).

CHAPTER 1. SOCIOLOGY'S DEFAULT VIEW OF RELIGION

1 Herberg (1955). Figures come from the 2012 General Social Survey, available online at the UC Berkeley Survey Data Archive (http://sda.berkeley.edu/archive. htm). On the veracity of polling data, see Hadaway et al. (1993).

2 See especially Chaves (2011); Putnam and Campbell (2010).

3 See Kuhn (1970) for a detailed analysis of the role that textbooks play in reflecting and establishing consensus in the natural sciences. See Manza, Sauder, and Wright (2010) for an updated discussion.

4 At this writing, there are three major texts with the title *The Essentials of Sociology* and one titled *Sociology: The Essentials*. Each covers the same material, each is close to five hundred pages long, and each provides a (supposedly) cheaper alternative to the longer hardbound comprehensive texts.

5 Why this common chapter structure? There's an interesting loop, here. Textbooks are written to support existing courses—especially the three-hundred- to five-hundred-student courses introductory taught at big state universities. That's an attractive market and publishers want sales. They thus design texts to fit the course as it exists, with fifteen or sixteen chapters matching the typical fifteen- or sixteen-week semester. Courses, however, are also structured around textbooks! University professors do not get much status from teaching introductory sociology. It thus pays to go with the texts available rather than inventing anything new. It's no wonder that today's texts are structured very much like those of the 1970s.

6 This is a bit shorter than the chapter on the family and about the same size as the chapter on education. For comparison, the chapters on race and gender average 6% and 5% of the total, respectively, while stratification (other than race and gender) averages 9%.

7 Meredith McGuire's (2002) specialty text on the sociology of religion provides the most nuanced view of this typology. See her chapter "The Dynamics of Religious Collectivities."

8 Lutz and Collins (1993) showed how *National Geographic* similarly uses photographs of rituals to create a sense of the 'exotic other'.

9 Unfortunately, not much has changed in the twenty years since I first reviewed such comprehensive textbooks for an international journal that wanted to know how American sociology students learn (J. Spickard 1994). Many of the textbooks are the same, though in new editions. Three of the current top-selling texts were then in the top four: Kornblum (2011), Macionis (2011), and Schaeffer (2011)—now in their 9th, 14th, and 11th editions, respectively. Henslin (2011) (11th), Gid-

dens et al. (2011) (8th), Brinkerhoff, Ortega, and Weitz (2013) (8th), and a new text
by Ritzer (2013) all treat religion similarly.

10 The three older American texts are Roberts and Yamane (2011); Johnstone (2015);
McGuire (2002). The two newer ones are Christiano, Swatos, and Kivisto (2008);
Emerson, Mirola, and Monahan (2010). The two European texts are G. Davie
(2013); Repstad and Furseth (2013).

11 See Finke and Stark (2005); Stark and Finke (2000); Iannaccone (1988; 1994);
Stark and Bainbridge (1985).

12 Stark and Finke (2000) contains the most explicit statement of these propositions.

13 The book has had two major editions: 1992 and 2005.

14 See, for example, Kelley (1972); Roof and McKinney (1987).

15 For my critique, see J. Spickard (1998a; 2006b; 2007). For a different approach, see
Bruce (1993; 1999; 2002). On the 'religiosity' of the Middle Ages, see Stark (1999,
255ff); but cf. McGuire (2008, ch. 2). The church pew research is reported in Finke
and Stark (1986).

16 See Yang's (2012) useful distinction between "Red Market," "Grey Market," and
"Black Market" religion in China.

17 Wilson (1982, 11–12).

18 Warner (1993). Parsons (1960a; 1967; 1969). Berger (1970). Berger (1999) has since
rejected his earlier view.

19 For a more nuanced distinction between American and European religion, see
Berger, Davie, and Fokas (2008).

20 See Douglas (1970). For some attempts to define religion using beliefs, see Spiro
(1966); Stark and Bainbridge (1985).

21 On Navajo religion, see Wyman (1950; 1983); Gill (1987); Chapter Seven of this
volume. On Sheilaism, see Bellah et al. (1985, 221); Chapter Four of this volume.

22 On women's religion, see Bynum (1986); Daly (1978). For contemporary examples,
see Winter, Lummis, and Stokes (1994); J. Davie (1995); McGuire (2002, ch. 4).

23 Douglas (1968; 1970); J. Spickard (1992); (1994); McGuire (1994).

24 Asad (1993b; 2003); Chidester (1996); Masuzawa (2005); Beyer (2006). Vásquez
(2013). Simpson (1990, 371).

25 Greil and Bromley (2003); J. Spickard (2003); McGuire (2003); Beyer (2003).

26 Bender (2003; 2010); Levitt (2001; 2007); Adogame (2013).

27 Bender et al. (2013).

28 Bender et al. (2013, 2).

29 Bender et al. (2013, 5).

30 Bender et al. (2013, 5).

31 Bender et al. (2013, 8).

32 Smilde and May (2010). J. Spickard (2012a). Bender et al. (2013, 13).

33 No edited volume can present a coherent view, but this one does not produce any
sustained positive program. Some contributors focus on the micro-interactional
construction of religious selves. Others focus on religious discourse. Others produce historical and transnational comparisons. All, however, generalize European

and American insights, albeit different ones than do the theorists they criticize. It strikes me that this is just a gentler form of intellectual colonialism.

34 McGuire (2008); Ammerman (2013); Hall (1997); Orsi (2005).

35 McGuire (2008). The quote is on page 17. The names are pseudonyms.

36 The market model and secularization theory are two others. See J. Spickard (2006a; 2006b).

37 Tönnies (1887); de Tocqueville (1835; 1840).

38 See Neitz (2000; 2002; 2004; 2011).

39 See Ezzy (2014).

40 Neitz (2000).

41 Neitz (2000, 370).

42 See especially Neitz (2002).

43 Connell (2007). Cf. Chakrabarty (2000); Spivak (1996).

44 The Arabic name is *ad-Dawlat al-Islamiyya fi'l-'Iraq wa'sh-Sham*. This makes "ISIS" "Islamic State in Iraq and ash-Sham"; *Sham* refers to all the lands of the north that were conquered by the 7th- and 8th-century Muslim armies: from Jerusalem through present-day Syria and Lebanon to southern Turkey. This matches the other English acronym, "ISIL", for "Islamic State in Iraq and the Levant". The Levant is the historic name given to the lands of the eastern Mediterranean, from Turkey to Egypt and east to the border with Iran. See Tharoor (2014); Guthrie (2015).

CHAPTER 2. THE DEFAULT VIEW'S HISTORICAL-CULTURAL ORIGINS

1 For a detailed history of Greek religious practices, see Burkert (1985).

2 McGuire (2008, ch. 2) nicely summarizes this history. For greater detail, see Muir (1997); Scribner (1993); Luria (1991); Martin (1993).

3 Quoted by Ginzburg (1983, 120).

4 McGuire (2008, 27).

5 Frazer (1890) claimed magic is manipulative where religion is not. Durkheim (1912) saw religion as social and beneficial where magic is individual and selfish. Anthropologist E.E. Evans-Pritchard (1937; 1956) pointed out the cultural insularity of this distinction this long ago.

6 Scribner (1987; 1990; 1993); Luria (1989; 1991).

7 McGuire (2008, 37).

8 Besides McGuire's (2008) book on popular religion, see also her 1988 book on ritual healing.

9 Vásquez (2013). The quotes are from pages 26 and 24.

10 Comte popularized the word "sociology," though he did not invent it. The term was first used by the French essayist Emmanuel Sieyès in an unpublished 1780 manuscript. See Fauré and Guilhaumou (2006).

11 Durkheim (1972, 71).

12 Vásquez (2013, 24–25).

13 For details, see Tallet (1991, 1–17).

14 Furet (1995); Hasquin (2003).

15 Peter Berger, Grace Davie, and Effie Fokas (2008) have produced an excellent analysis of the differences between the American and French systems of church/state separation.

16 France restored diplomatic relations with the Vatican in 1921; French participation in appointing bishops was restored with the Briand-Ceretti Pact. See Gildea (2010, ch. 12).

17 The full title of the 1859 edition was *On the Origin of Species by Means of Natural Selection, or the Preservation of Favoured Races in the Struggle for Life*. Later editions shortened the title to the one we now know.

18 Gray (1860); Bowler (2003, 202ff); Hodge (1874).

19 Gould (1977, 20ff); see also Gould (1997b). Van Wyhe (2007, 183).

20 Darwin (1871, 609).

21 Orr (1910). The entire set of essays can usually be found on the Internet.

22 Wright (1913); Orr (1910).

23 Orr addressed the evolution of human beings towards the end of his essay. He was perfectly willing to accept this, but he saw it as "creation from within," not a solely natural process. Throughout, he set scientific findings within a theistic context.

24 Orr was careful to say that most scientists of his time were Christians, not atheists. Ecklund (2010) has recently shown that about half of American elite scientists are personally religious today.

25 Fletcher (2013).

26 Comte's (1853) work is most accessible through Harriet Martineau's abridgement. Durkheim's *Division of Labor* (1893) has never been out of print. See the last pages of Weber's *Protestant Ethic* (1920a) for his elegy to vanishing religion.

27 Vásquez (2013, 27).

28 Vásquez (2013, 28).

29 Vásquez (2013, 29).

30 Bourdieu (1997, 132).

31 Asad (1993a, 207).

32 See Nisbet (1967; 1978). Here I draw from, but revise, Anthony Giddens's (1976) critique of three myths of sociology's origins.

33 Nisbet (1978, 105).

34 Nisbet (1978, 105–106).

35 Nisbet (1978, 106).

36 Nisbet (1978, 108).

37 Nisbet (1978, 109).

38 Nisbet (1978, 110).

39 Burke (1790).

40 Aron (1965, 260).

41 Giddens (1976, 710–711).

42 Giddens (1976, 711–712).

43 Durkheim (1912).

44 See Durkheim (1912, 39–44). He followed Johann Kern (*History of Buddhism in India*) in regarding "Northern Buddism" as "less advanced." See page 48.

45 Quotes are from Durkheim (1912, 39).

46 Durkheim (1912, 60). He specifically cited Hubert and Mauss's (1902) study of magic in drawing this conclusion. Cf. Frazer (1890); Malinowski (1948).

47 Durkheim (1912, 56).

48 Durkheim (1912, 56).

49 Durkheim (1912 [French-language edition] 65, [English-language edition] 62).

50 Durkheim (1912, 86ff, 102ff).

51 Durkheim (1912, 464).

52 Spencer (1879–1893). Durkheim wrote about the division of labor in society in his 1893 book of that name (Durkheim 1893).

53 Durkheim (1912, 62).

54 Durkheim (1912, 475).

55 Both his *Division of Labor in Society* (1893) and *Suicide* (1897) voice this theme.

56 Douglas (1975, xi–xii).

57 Swatos and Kivisto (1991). The quote is on page 347.

58 Weber (1946; 1922b; 1925, 458ff).

59 Weber (1920b).

60 Weber (1922a, 21–22; 1922c); Drysdale (1996).

61 See Richard Sennet's (2007) insightful analysis of the connection between the growth of bureaucracy and the Prussian military state. Both organizations applied rationality to leadership, with world-shaking results.

62 On traditional action: Weber (1922a, 26). On China: Weber (1920b, 107–170).

63 See Kalberg (1996). "Iron cage" is Talcott Parsons's felicitous mistranslation of "*stahlhartes Gehäuse.*"

64 Weber (1920a, 181). His next sentence, though unrelated to our topic, was prescient: "Perhaps it will so determine them until the last ton of fossilized coal is burnt."

65 Shils (1981, 8–10). Shils cited his own failure to notice this in his earlier joint article with Talcott Parsons (Parsons and Shils 1951). His 1981 book is partly an attempt to amend his previous views.

66 Niebuhr (1963). See Hoedemaker (1970); Malloy (1977); Gardner (1979; 1983). Weber outlined his action-schema in Weber (1922a, 21ff).

67 Niebuhr (1963, 67).

68 Augustine clearly modeled his narrative on the Bible's story of Jesus in the Garden of Gethsemene, who also surrendered his will as his disciples slept.

69 Cf. Weber (1917–19, 278–282, 292ff).

70 O'Dea (1961).

71 For some interesting alternate perspectives, see MacIntyre (1984); Rosemont (1991a); An-Na'im (1992).

72 Comte (1853); Durkheim and Mauss (1902); Weber (1958).

CHAPTER 3. TO CHINA

1 Now called Shàntóu, this city sits at the eastern end of Guangdong Province. My grandfather was first stationed in Chaozhou, then at Kityang (now Jieyang), about thirty-five miles west of Swatow. American (Northern) Baptist missionary records say that my grandfather's wife died from appendicitis. They do not mention the child ("'Death of Mrs. Adkins'" 1908, 269).

2 Davidman (2000).

3 She did talk to my younger brother, so I have one anecdote that gives me a sense of who he was. As a small child, my mother had just learned that there are different kinds of Baptists—American Baptists, Southern Baptists, National Baptists, and so on. She asked him, "What kind of Baptists are we?" According to the story, he looked at her over his reading glasses and, perhaps with a wry smile, said, "Cranky Baptists." This may be apocryphal, yet it shows both my mother's attitude toward organized religion and her love of him.

4 As I describe later in this chapter, there have been several different varieties of Confucianism. For this book's purposes, what Bryan Van Norden (2003) calls "a thin description" will do. This emphasizes what these varieties have in common, not what separates them.

5 On preschoolers, see Tobin, Wu, and Davidson (1989). On learning styles, see Willis and Hodson (2013). Buzzfeed.com has based much of its business plan on providing quizzes and other Facebook entertainment.

6 I base these contrasting introductions on a pair by Henry Rosemont (1991a, 71–73).

7 On human rights as a quasi-religion, see J. Spickard (1999a; 2002). Chang argued that East Asian philosophy does not think that people are rights-bearing individual. In part because of his influence, the drafters deliberately left out any founding principles because they could not agree on what those might be. For accounts of the Declaration's origin, see Humphrey (1984); J. Spickard (1999b).

8 As I do not read any variety of Chinese and am not an expert on Chinese philosophy, I base my account on the work of those who do and are. For more on the Confucian approach to the self, see Rosemont (1991a; 1991b); Ames (1991; 1994); Hall and Ames (1998a, 23–43); Fingarette (1991); Jiang (2006).

9 This is, of course, an infinite task. I cannot list everyone who has influenced me— not all my teachers, nor all my students, nor all my colleagues and certainly not all my friends. If any of you are reading this, I thank you for what you have contributed to my life.

10 I report a better alternative a few pages hence.

11 Rosemont (1991a, 71–73).

12 Pan (1990); Lakos (2010).

13 Latourette (1964, 537).

14 Keightley (2004). Keightley (1999) calls the Shang "China's first historical dynasty." See also Keightley (1990).

15 On *Dia de los Muertos*, see McGuire (2008, 58–60). Lakos (2010) quotes Hsu (1971, 158) on page 27. Overmyer (1986, 11–12).

16 Lakos (2010, 31).

17 Lakos (2010, 28). The first quote in this passage is from Freedman (1979, 275); the second is from Baker (1979, 86).

18 Addison (1924, 498).

19 Lakos (2010, 33ff); Overmyer (1986, 14). Overmyer's comment is on page 15.

20 See Lakos (2010, 32).

21 Yang (1964, xxxix).

22 'Ancestor worship' is found in some of the other East Asian countries besides China, with the same relational overtones. See Hamabata (1990, 70ff) for a detailed description of a Japanese family's *obon* ceremony.

23 Lakos (2010, 6–7).

24 Zhou political control lasted only until 771, a period generally referred to as the Western Zhou. The empire then broke into several states, though the Zhou continued to have formal ritual status until overthrown by the short-lived Qin (Chin) dynasty.

25 Hsün Tzu (1963, 41): "The Regulations of a King."

26 Nuyen (2013).

27 Chan (1963, 62).

28 Rosemont (1991b, 98).

29 Cheng (1979, 4).

30 Schwartz (1985, 52–53).

31 Readers who are new to Chinese philosophy may find this section a bit technical, particularly toward the end. Specialists, on the other hand, will find it too brief. I have tried to show enough details to satisfy the latter without losing the former.

32 Fairbank and Goldman (2006, 29); Ho (1976).

33 Lakos (2010, 13–14).

34 Ho (1976, 550); see also Ho (1965). The quotations are from *The Analects*.

35 Indeed, Pan Jianxiong (1990) wrote that Confucius actually invented very little. Instead, he merely regularized elements of traditional Chinese thinking, even while giving that thinking a more this-worldly gloss than was originally the case.

36 Yao (2000, 17). Lakos (2010, 8) must have been referring to the religious parallel in writing, "Confucianism is a generic Western term that has no corresponding term in the Chinese languages."

37 Mencius was perhaps a more orthodox Confucian than was Hsün Tzu. Ho wrote that the later synthesized Confucius's teachings with Legalism, which had been the chief opposing school.

38 Yao (2000); the two quotes are from pages 26 and 34. The quote from *The Analects* Book 3 is on page 32.

39 Pan (1990).

40 Arbuckle (1995).

41 See Ebrey (1991).

42 Beyer (2006, 224–41). The quotes are from pages 230 and 237. Anna Sun (2013) has recently traced this history from a different angle. She argues that post-Mao China has reopened the question of whether Confucianism should be called a religion. This time, the outcome may be different than it was before.

43 Sun (2013). See Yang et al. (2007).

44 See, *inter alia*, Tu (1979; 1984a; 1984b); Hall and Ames (1987; 1995; 1998a; 1998b); Rosemont (1991a; 2015).

45 Rosemont (1991a, 60).

46 Hall and Ames (1998a, 23–43).

47 Hall and Ames (1998a, 26–27).

48 Hall and Ames (1998a, 43).

49 Hall and Ames titled their 1987 book *Thinking Through Confucius* and their 1998 book (which contains their essay on the focus-field self) *Thinking from the Han*. They clearly see this model of the self as more than narrowly Confucian.

50 Van Norden (2003, 100). He cites similar distinctions by Martha Nussbaum, Gilbert Ryle, and others.

51 An eclectic 2nd-century BCE philosophical text compiled under the patronage of Liu An.

52 Lakos (2010, 84).

53 Chow (1994, 56).

54 *Analects* Book 3, #3. The translation is from Lakos (2010, 83), though he attributes it to Book 13, #18. Cf. the translation at *Chinese Text Project* (http://ctext.org): "If a man be without the virtues proper to humanity, what has he to do with the rites of propriety?"

55 Lakos (2010, 85).

56 Hsün Tzu, Lilun L417. Quoted by Lakos (2010, 88).

57 *Analects* Book 12, #1. Translation at *Chinese Text Project* (http://ctext.org).

58 Chan (1967, 367).

59 Dennerline (1988, 9).

60 Ho (1976, 550).

61 Lakos (2010, 3).

62 Fingarette (1972, 77–78). My bow to Fingarette is undertaken in true Confucian fashion, as a bow to one of my graduate school mentors, Robert Bellah. Though I have chosen a different route for engaging Confucian thinking than did he, I would be remiss if I failed to mention the writer whom he found so moving and insightful.

63 *Analects* Book 4, #25. Quoted by Fingarette (1972, 77).

64 On Chinese Christianity, particularly under Communism, see Yang (2012). On popular religion, see, *inter alia*, McGuire (2008). The phrase 'sociology of religion with Chinese characteristics' recalls the phrase used in the Chinese Communist government's efforts to remodel international human rights law to fit its image of Chinese tradition. See Chan (2013).

65 De Bary (1995). It is as intellectually dangerous to posit a fundamental split between the Chinese past and present as it is to attempt to read current Chinese

politics as merely the newest manifestation of the old dynastic system. One is reminded of Zhou Enlai's 1968 comment on being asked what he thought of the enduring effects of the French Revolution: "It has not been long enough yet to tell." (In fact, he was probably referring to the student-led 'revolution' going on in France at the time, but that is not how it was played in the press.)

CHAPTER 4. CHINA APPLIED

1 See especially Warner and Wittner (1998); Ebaugh and Chafez (2000).
2 I have written about Quaker worship practices in J. Spickard (2004).
3 On Quaker decision-making, see Sheeran (1983).
4 Stookey (1996, 147), quoted in Guthrie (1996).
5 Sack (2000, 7).
6 The Midwestern list comes from Sack and from my in-laws' memories. The Southern list comes from Foreman (2008). You can find Blair Hobbs's "Shout Hallelujah Potato Salad" recipe at www.myrecipes.com.
7 The quote is from Sack (2000, 65). See Holifield (1994).
8 Sack (2000, 65).
9 Sack (2000, 73, 75, 76, 77).
10 Sack (2000, 74, 88). Sack's quotes come from old church bulletins.
11 Sack (2000, 89).
12 Dodson and Gilkes (1995).
13 Dodson and Gilkes (1995, 521).
14 Dodson and Gilkes (1995, 520).
15 Dodson and Gilkes (1995, 530), citing Williams (1974, 118).
16 Dodson and Gilkes (1995, 531–532).
17 Dodson and Gilkes (1995); Gilkes (2000). See also Peter Goldsmith's (1989) ethnography of African American churches on the Georgia coast. He provided rich detail about the ways that food and food rituals are central to church and to community life.
18 See the New Hope website at www.newhopebc-sac.org/ministries/kitchen-ministry.
19 Flores (1994; 1995).
20 Flores (1994, 171).
21 Díaz-Stevens (1994, 26).
22 Flores (1994, 175).
23 Flores (1994, 176).
24 Flores (1994, 177).
25 Davidman (2007, 58–59) similarly described family food rituals among unsynagogued Jews.
26 Gilkes (2000, 43).
27 Bureau of Labor Statistics (2014, tables 2 and 7).
28 Sack (2000, 91).
29 Sack (2000, 90–91).
30 Marler (2008).

31 Marler (2008, 23).
32 Marler presented evidence that this process affected Evangelicals and Catholics as well, albeit more slowly.
33 O'Brien (2012). See Lim and Putnam (2010).
34 Estimates vary, but the officially reported sex ratio for zero-to-four-year-olds in China in 2012 was 118 males for every 100 females (National Bureau of Statistics of China 2013: table 3–10). This is considerably greater than the natural sex ratio for that age. Amartya Sen (1990) estimated that after twenty years of China's 'one-child-per-family' policy, China had about fifty million fewer women than it should have had, if nature had taken its course.
35 Bellah et al. (1985, 221).
36 Bellah (1986).
37 I say "probably" because almost everyone I have met has some sort of social ties; I have to allow for the possibility that she might have none.
38 Stout (1988, 197).
39 Heelas and Woodhead (2005); see Heelas (1992; 1996).
40 Heelas (2006, 47).
41 Voas and Bruce (2007). The quote is Heelas's summary of their findings (Heelas 2006, 50). Heelas responded to both issues in his 2009 article.
42 Heelas (2009, 761).
43 See, *inter alia*, Heelas (2008; 2009; 2012); Woodhead (2008a; 2008b; 2009; 2010; 2011a; 2011b).
44 Martikainen and Gauthier (2012); Gauthier and Martikainen (2013); Campbell (2012); Cheong et al. (2012).
45 J. Spickard (2012b). Cf. J. Spickard (2012a).
46 Ezzy (2014).
47 Both this quote and the one in the previous paragraph are from Ezzy (2014, 149).
48 O'Dea (1961).
49 J. Spickard (1998b).
50 Noddings (1984).

CHAPTER 5. TO NORTH AFRICA

1 This name takes some attention. Walī al-Dīn is an honorific, meaning "Guardian of the Religion." Al-Tūnisī and al-Haḍramī, respectively, refer to his origins in Tunis and his family's origins in southern Arabia. Ibn Khaldūn—the name by which he is most often known—is his immediate ancestors' clan, which had been prominent in Moorish Spain. Ibn Muḥammad means "son of Muhammad," his father. His given name was 'Abd ar-Raḥmān. I have not been able to trace the origin of the name Abū Zayd. See Rosenthal (1958, xxxxviii); Alatas (2011, 12).
2 Syed Farid Alatas has done more than anyone to explore Ibn Khaldūn's relevance for sociology, particularly the sociology of state formation (Alatas 2006a; 2006b; 2007; 2010; 2011; 2013; 2014). My own 2001 article takes a somewhat narrower tack. See also Lawrence (1984).

3 On the Black Death, see Benedictow (2005). For a short overview of the 13th century, see Franklin (1982). For a readable history of Europe's collapse, see Tuchman (1978).

4 The best source for this family history in English is Franz Rosenthal's (1958) "Translator's Introduction" to the *Muqaddimah*.

5 This is Rosenthal's (1958, xlvii) suggestion, and it seems reasonable.

6 Rosenthal (1958, xxxvi–lxv).

7 Rosenthal (1958, liii).

8 Quoted by Alatas (2011, 14), who provides the Arabic words for "surface," "inner meaning," and the two descriptions that Ibn Khaldūn used for his project.

9 Rosenthal (1958, lv) pointed out that Ibn Khaldūn was on much firmer ground when describing the history of Moorish Spain and North Africa than he was when he described the Muslim east and earlier eras. For the former, he could draw on his own detailed experience and on local records. For the latter, he relied on other historians whose work was not always very precise.

10 Frank Lechner (1994) used the phrase "tribes and cities" with explicit reference to Ibn Khaldūn. Roy Woodbridge (2004) used these terms in the title of his treatise on contemporary international conflict. Benjamin Barber used a similar construction in his *Jihad vs. McWorld* (1995). The contrast underlies much of Robert Kaplan's writing on world conflict (e.g., 1990; 1997; 2000).

11 Ibn Khaldūn (1377–1399, 257–258).

12 Ibn Khaldūn (1377–1399, 257).

13 See Weber (1922c, 90): "An ideal type is formed by the one-sided accentuation of one or more points of view and by the synthesis of a great many diffuse, discrete, more or less present and occasionally absent concrete individual phenomena, which are arranged according to those one-sidedly emphasized viewpoints into a unified analytical construct." Cf. McIntosh (1977).

14 Ibn Khaldūn (1377–1399, 282–283).

15 Ibn Khaldūn (1377–1399, 252–253).

16 Pipes (1981, 79–82). Pipes noted that Egypt's leader was responding to the success of the French national army. He hoped that citizen-soldiers would fight better than mercenaries. Barber (1995).

17 Ibn Khaldūn (1377–1399, 264).

18 E.g., Al-Jabri (1983).

19 Ibn Khaldūn (1377–1399, 286–287).

20 Pipes (1981, 82ff) saw this as one of two drawbacks with using soldiers from economically marginal areas. The other is their tendency to become unruly if they are not continually rewarded. These are opposites, he wrote—solving one problem makes the other worse.

21 Ibn Khaldūn (1377–1399, 264–265).

22 See P. Spickard and Fong (1995).

23 For insights into this controversy, see Reitveld (2014).

24 See Omi and Winant (1994); P. Spickard (2004; 2013).

25 Cose (1993). The Gates incident was covered by newspapers all over the world.

26 See Thye and Lawler (2002). Michael Hannan (1979) used the first edge-focused theory. Michael Hechter (1975) used the second. Cf. Nielsen (1985).

27 He referred to them as simply 'Arabs' in these passages, but the context makes it clear that these are the same tribes that he previously called 'Bedouins'. Ibn Khaldūn (1377–1399, 251–252).

28 Ibn Khaldūn (1377–1399, 302–303).

29 Ibn Khaldūn (1377–1399, 303–304). The translator has added various words in this and the following passages to clarify the meaning.

30 Ibn Khaldūn (1377–1399, 304–306). See also pages 319–327.

31 Ibn Khaldūn (1377–1399, 284–285)

32 Ibn Khaldūn (1377–1399, 313–327).

33 Ibn Khaldūn (1377–1399, 320–321).

34 For more details on Ibn Khaldūn's analysis of religion, see Ibn Khaldūn (1377–1399, 327–356, 372–385).

35 Durkheim (1893). Soyer and Gilbert (2012) compare Ibn Khaldūn with Durkheim, though on a different basis than I do here. They also compare his theories with Auguste Comte's.

36 Maine (1861).

37 Durkheim argued that this is a matter of balance. All societies have both kinds of law, but he argued that simpler societies are dominated by penal law and complex societies are dominated by contract law. This echoes Maine's description of the shift from 'status' to 'contract', but only Durkheim used this to examine the nature of various societies' social bonds.

38 Durkheim (1897).

39 Durkheim (1912, 464).

40 There are other classical theorists who would make interesting comparisons. Ferdinand Tönnies (1887) is one, for his Gemeinshaften, like Khaldūn's tribes, are tied together by feelings. For Khaldūn, however, these feelings arise from the rigors of a harsh life, not just from a face-to-face society. Similarly Khaldūn shared Marx's emphasis on the primary role of economics in society, along with some technical economic concepts (see Soofi 1995, 390ff). For Khaldūn, however, the mode and means of production work on a society's group-feeling, not just on its class structure. His overriding concern for the forms of social solidarity led him to ask Durkheimian rather than Tönniesian or Marxist questions.

41 Especially Du Bois (1903). See Zuckerman (2004).

42 Jacobson (1998); P. Spickard (2007).

43 Herberg (1955).

44 On the Mainline, see Roof and McKinney (1987); Putnam and Campbell (2010). On Catholic dissatisfaction, see Greeley, McCready, and McCourt (1976, esp. the discussion on pages 135ff); Greeley (2005). Intermarriages began to rise about 1970 and have increased steadily since then. According to a 2013 Pew Research Center study, more than half of American Jews married after 1995 have married

non-Jews (35ff). On the rise of Evangelicalism, see Smith (1998); Miller (1999); Miller and Yamamori (2007); Putnam and Campbell (2010); Marti and Ganiel (2014). Rodney Stark and William Sims Bainbridge described the west coast of the United State as the "Unchurched Belt." For some early numbers, see Stark (1987).

45 Morris (2009, 254).

46 Morris (2009, 276). He also suggests a possible personal agenda: Khaldūn started his autobiography by suggesting that "the political failures and retreat of his own father and grandfather, after centuries of familial prestige and public renown . . . [can be] traced to the influence of a leading Sufi preacher of Tunis."

47 Morris (2009, 280).

CHAPTER 6. IBN KHALDŪN APPLIED

1 Bax (1990, 66).

2 Bax (1990, 66).

3 Bax (1990, 66–67, 73, fn1); Markle and McCrea (1994, 197).

4 Bax (1990); Berryman (2001); Mestrovic (1991, 136–162).

5 Sells (2003, 319).

6 For a history of the wars, see, *inter alia*, Silber and Little (1994); Cigar (1995); Tindemans et al. (1996); West (1996). See also Ignatieff (1993; 1995).

7 Sells (2003, 309).

8 Anderson (1991). See Borofsky (2000).

9 Simic (2009). On the memorial, see Ignatieff (1993, 19–56).

10 Sekulic, Massey, and Hodson (1994).

11 Dimitrovova (2001).

12 Sells (2003, 319, 317–318).

13 Carmichael (2006, 283–285). The International Criminal Tribunal for the former Yugoslavia (ICTY) considers "ethnic cleansing" a crime against humanity, one not as severe as "genocide." A few Bosnian Serbs were convicted of "genocide," Croats of at most "ethnic cleansing," and Bosnian Muslims of "breaches of the Geneva Conventions." See the ICTY website at www.icty.org. Deaths among each group were in reverse proportion to the gravity of the charges brought against its members.

14 See Wuthnow (2006, ch, 5); McGuire (2008).

15 Silber and Little (1994).

16 Giddens (1976); Parsons (1960b); Inkeles and Smith (1974); Rostow (1971).

17 On differentiation, see Dobbelaere (2002); Wilson (1966); but cf. Casanova (1994). On the consequences of pluralism, see Berger (1967); but cf. Berger (1999). Examples of theories that connect modernization with particular individual characteristics range from Inkeles and Smith (1974) to Giddens (1991). On economic changes, see Chirot (1977); Robertson (1992).

18 See, *inter alia*, Ignatieff (1993); Barber (2001); Lechner (1993); Marty and Appelby (1991; 1997); Kaplan (1993; 2000); Kimmel (1996); but see Simpson (1996),

19 However, Mart Bax (2000, 47) noted that one of the local 'Muslim' clans was of Croat descent, while a rival 'Croat' group had settled there only after World War II—at the instigation of Serbian authorities.

20 Sells (2003, 319) noted the pre-conflict similarity to the pilgrimage literature of another famous Catholic site, Our Lady of Fátima, Portugal.

21 On intra-Catholic conflict, see Bax (1995, 108–114).

22 Bax (1995, 53–65). The quote is from page 60. As Meredith McGuire has noted, eclectic non-church religion is a common pattern (McGuire (2008).

23 Sells (2003).

24 On Milošević, see Silber and Little (1994, 37ff). On Tudjman: "Newsline," Radio Free Europe/Radio Liberty, November 10, 2000 (www.rferl.org), quoting a prosecutor for the Tribunal. The quote is from Smith (2001, 54–55). On 'playing the ethnic card', see Caspersen (2009); Reilly (1998).

25 Sells (2003, 311–312, 316, 310, 317).

26 Sells (2003, 310, n1); Van Metre and Akan (1997). Flottau (2007); Mayr (2009).

27 Bax (1995, 108–114). See the detailed report of the academic investigating committee commissioned by the Vrije Universiteit Amsterdam (Baud, Legêne, and Pels 2013).

28 Sells (2003, 320).

29 Bax (1995, 119–126).

30 For insight into the first Trade Center bombing, see Mark Juergensmeyer's (2003) interview with Sheik Omar Abdel-Rahman about the worldview that produced this bit of religious violence.

31 For details, see Tharoor (2014); Guthrie (2015).

32 Kelley et al. (2015).

33 For some recent thoughtful efforts, see Wilson (2015); Packer (2015); Lilla (2015); Cohen (2015). Cf. Byman (2010); Anti-Defamation League (2013).

34 This is, of course, not an accurate term. Technically, 'Fundamentalism' is a movement in American Evangelical Christianity. The term has, however, been applied by extension to all sorts of resurgent religious movements that advocate a return to religious authority. See, for example, the volumes issued by The Fundamentalism Project, under the editorship of Martin Marty and Scott Appleby (1991; 1992; 1994; 1995; 1997).

35 Almukhtar (2015).

36 Wilson (2015).

37 Gerwehr and Daly (2006).

38 Ibn Khaldūn (1377–1399, 304–306).

39 Roy (2004).

40 Roy (2004, 38).

41 Roy (2004, 52). Muhammed Atta was one of the September 11 hijackers.

42 Roy (2004, 48–49). Cf. Packer (2015).

43 Roy (2004, 53).

44 Juergensmeyer (2003, 248).

CHAPTER 7. TO THE AMERICAN SOUTHWEST

1 *Naabeehó Bináhásdzo* or *Diné Bikéyah*. The first has firm geographic borders, while the second is best translated more vaguely as "Navajoland." The broadest term, *Dinétah*, refers to the traditional Navajo homeland stretching between the four sacred mountains. The present-day Nation occupies the western part of that original heartland.

   Diné means 'people' in the Na-Diné language, a branch of the southern Athabaskan language family. *Naabeehó* comes from the Tewa language, spoken by some of the Navajo Nation's Puebloan neighbors; most linguists trace it to a term for the Navajo's cultivated cornfields. About half of all Navajo speak Na-Diné reasonably well.

   The term "domestic dependent nation" comes from the 1831 U.S. Supreme Court decision in *Cherokee Nation v. Georgia*, in which the Cherokees sued for relief from the state of Georgia's attempt to force them off their lands. The court ruled that they had no standing to sue under the Constitution, as they were not a foreign nation but at best a quasi-sovereign entity. Subsequent statute law places Native American groups under federal control, albeit with certain powers of self-governance. Understandably, not everyone agrees, so the real relationship varies across times and places.

   Employment and other figures come from Kruhly (2012); Landry (2013).

2 The statistical report is by Grammich et al. (2012). The first quote is from Birchfield (n.d.). On the Native American Church, see Aberle (1966). The second quote is from Wyman (1983, 536). For a discussion of such counts, see the 2014 special issue of *Diskus* titled "The Problem of Numbers in the Study of Religion," edited by Bettina Schmidt (2014).

3 Wyman (1983, 536).

4 Wyman (1983, 539ff).

5 Wyman (1983, 536).

6 My description is drawn from Wyman (1983) and Reichard (1950), supplemented by Gill (1987, 19ff). Other good sources on traditional Navajo religion include Csordas (1995; 2000a; 2005); Gill (1979); Haile (1938a); Kluckholn (1944); Lamphere (1969); Witherspoon (1977; 1983).

7 Reichard (1950, xxxv).

8 Wyman (1983). The Red Ant painting is on page 545. The others are on page 553.

9 Reichard (1950, xxxv).

10 Haile (1938b, 207–213).

11 Reichard (1944; 1950); Villaseñor (1966).

12 Reichard (1950, 224).

13 Reichard (1950, 237). Chart I faces page 20.

14 Reichard (1950, xlvii).

15 Lamphere (1969, 303).

16 Gill (1987, 110).

17 The quote is from Gill (1987, 150), referencing Austin (1962). Witherspoon (1983, 575) made this point as well.
18 Gill (1987, 30–32).
19 Gill (1987, 19).
20 I have pulled together this short version from Gill (1983, 503–504; 1987, 19ff) and Witherspoon (1983). For a longer version with analysis, see Wyman (1970).
21 Gill (1987, 29).
22 Witherspoon (1983, 575).
23 Witherspoon (1983, 573).
24 Witherspoon (1983, 575).
25 Gill (1987, 42).
26 Witherspoon (1983, 572, see 570–573)
27 Reichard (1950, 45, 47).
28 Witherspoon (1983, 573).
29 Csordas (2000b, 472).
30 Csordas (1995b); Milne and Howard (2000, 543).
31 Gill (1987, 123).
32 Geertz (1973, 90).
33 See the essays reprinted as chapters 6 and 15 in Geertz (1973). See also Geertz (1960).
34 Turner (1967; 1968; 1969). The quote is from Turner (1967, 28).
35 Douglas (1966); de Heusch (1972); Lévi-Strauss (1981, 671).
36 Deflem (1991, 111), citing Turner (1969, 42–43).
37 Bell (1992).
38 Bell focused on anthropological analysts—from Durkheim and Malinowski to Geertz, Rappaport, Turner, and Tambiah. She left aside various psychoanalytically oriented observers, though they, too, notoriously saw rituals as disguised forms of thought.
39 Bell (1992, 80, 80–81).
40 Bell (1992, 92).
41 See J. Spickard (1993).
42 Schutz (1951).
43 Schutz (1951, 170).
44 Schutz (1951, 170).
45 Schutz (1951, 173n).
46 Schutz (1951,174).
47 Blackmore (1986; 1988). I discuss her work in greater detail in J. Spickard (2004).
48 Blackmore (1986, 73).
49 See Czikszentmihalyi (1975; 1991; 1997); Neitz and J. Spickard (1990).
50 Gill (1987, 55).
51 Gill (1987, 56).

CHAPTER 8. NAVAJO RITUAL APPLIED

1 Witherspoon (1983, 573).

2 This is a strong statement, but a defensible one. It is certainly how the Catholic Workers see the situation. Few serious people would deny that the wealthy have much more economic and political power than do others. The Church, too, often bends to the wishes of the powerful. The Workers focus on that, while recognizing that members of the Church also often stand on the side of the poor. Like some contemporary American Evangelicals, they ask, "What would Jesus do?" They note that he sat down with lepers, tax collectors, and prostitutes, not with bankers.

3 For various reasons, my attendance slowed after 2004, though I still consider myself a fellow traveler. Like Toni Flynn (1989), though with less direct commitment, I still travel along their rim.

4 Among the many books on the Catholic Worker movement, I have found Piehl (1982), Roberts (1984), Murray (1990), and Zwick and Zwick (2005) to be the most useful. Coles (1987) discussed the specific contribution of Dorothy Day to the movement—see also Thorn, Runkel, and Mountin (2001)—while Aronica (1987) reminded us that Day was just a part of that movement, not the whole of it. Ellis (1978) and Flynn (1989) provided personal descriptions of Worker life and mission. Troester (1993) collected reflections and reminiscences of many current and former group members. On the Los Angeles group specifically, see Dietrich (1983; 1993; 2011); and Flynn (1989).

5 See Dietrich (1996). The new cathedral is, by the way, architecturally stunning. It was expensive, however. Local newspaper columnists referred to it as "The Taj Mahoney" or "The Rog Mahal"—jokes on the name of Cardinal Roger Mahoney, the (now-retired) archbishop who instigated its building.

6 The School of the Americas is a now-renamed training school at Fort Benning, Georgia. It was founded to train Latin American military forces in counterinsurgency techniques. Graduates perpetrated some of the worst atrocities of Latin America's various civil wars. A 'Plowshares action' is a means of protesting nuclear-armed missiles, often by beating them with hammers (Isiah 2:4: "They will beat their swords into plowshares and their spears into pruning hooks.") or pouring blood on them. Both forms of protest typically draw long jail terms.

7 Brian Terrell (2012) reported that Day may not have said those particular words, though they appear on a famous poster showing her quiet confrontation with sheriffs in the California grape fields. Biographer Jim Forest did find the word "rotten" in a 1956 column she wrote: "We need to change the system. We need to overthrow, not the government, as the authorities are always accusing the Communists of conspiring to teach to do, but this rotten, decadent, putrid industrial capitalist system which breeds such suffering in the whited sepulcher of New York."

8 *Catholic Agitator*, December 2001. Issues from November 2004 to the present can be found at the Catholic Worker website: http://lacatholicworker.org.

9 I describe the Wednesday evening Mass as it was practiced through the end of 2002. Since then, a shift in the community's spiritual life has subtly but significantly reshaped that event. See the "Methodological Postscript" at the end of this chapter. Note: most Workers were careful to reserve the term "Mass" for those situations in which a priest was officiating, using "ceremony" for other times.

10 There were once nearly nine hundred single-room-occupancy hotels in what used to be the Los Angeles warehouse district; some eighty or so remain, at the time of my fieldwork run by two competing non-profits. No longer flophouses, they provide minimal shelter for those poor people able to afford something more than the streets.

The event that historically most predicts the number of Los Angeles street homeless is not need, but police sweeps. For example: when First Lady Barbara Bush visited Los Angeles's Skid Row in the early 1990s, activists charge that police moved out nearly 80% of the area's usual inhabitants so that she would not see how bad the homeless problem really was. Toward the end of my fieldwork, the Weingart Center (2004) estimated that there were some eighty thousand homeless people in Los Angeles County on any given night. This counted people in shelters, temporary housing, cars, and so on—not just those living on the streets. Recent biennial Continuum of Care homeless counts currently show about forty to fifty thousand. Experts tell me that L.A.'s counting method is among the nation's best. Other counties—including the one containing my university town—use very bad counting techniques; they thus seriously underestimate the homeless problem. See J. Spickard (2016, ch. 14).

11 This term is tramp-culture slang for having to listen to a required prayer before being fed (Spradley 1970).

12 This does not mean that the Catholic Worker community was as theologically eclectic as, say, the Quakers. Joint homilies sometimes hovered around what amounted to a 'party line'—the limited range of theological and political interpretations found in other Worker writings. Symbolically speaking, however, shared homilies emphasize the intellectual importance of each member of the community, regardless of the relative unity of views that in fact prevails. Interestingly, Catholic Charismatic groups are also often open to individual prayer requests, and for similar symbolic reasons. These are, however, typically more tightly controlled than Worker requests, rarely straying from personal calls for converting relatives and friends in need. See Neitz (1987).

13 Anthony Stevens-Arroyo, personal communication, November 9, 2004.

14 It is important to note that this is a physiological, not an intellectual process. Though Wayne Proudfoot (1985) is certainly right that much so-called religious experience is a result of interpretation, the underlying experience itself need not be. See J. Spickard (2004).

15 *Catholic Agitator*, October 2001.

16 See Spickard and Landres (2002).

17 Wolf (1982); Clifford and Marcus (1986); Spickard, Landres, and McGuire (2002).

CHAPTER 9. ARE WE STEALING THE ELGIN MARBLES?

1 On African sociology, see Akiwowo (1983; 1986; 1988; 1999); Makinde (1988); Lawuyi and Taiwo (1990); Payne (1992), among others. On *texcoatlaxope*, see Maduro (1993); see also Maduro (1995; 1999; 2004); Rodriguez (2014).

2 British Museum (n.d.). Cf. Swindale (1997–2012).

3 House of Commons (1816, 32–54).

4 Advocates of returning the sculptures to Greece have posted a translation of the document at www.parthenon.newmentor.net/firman.htm. Swindale (1997–2012). On its possible forgery, see Gibbon (2005, 115).

5 Interestingly, the Greek revolt against Ottoman rule would not likely have succeeded without British help. Lord Byron's death while aiding the Greeks is but the most famous instance. I have already mentioned the battle of Navarino. For more on the controversy, see Beard (2002); Hitchens (1998); St. Clair (1998).

6 Shakur (2014).

7 For a discussion of how race influences judgments about other people's parenting, see Berger, Davie, and Fokas (2008).

8 Carmen (2012).

9 Scrapple is cheap pig trimmings, mixed with cornmeal, served by poor Southern and Mid-Atlantic families. It is jokingly described as meat that was not good enough to include in Spam.

10 The furthest I have been able to trace this quote is to a bulletin of the Karen National Union (1988, 18), a revolutionary group seeking independence for the Karen peoples of eastern Burma. *Cultural Survival Quarterly* (1991) lifted the passage without citation, but added the comment about how states treat minorities.

11 Utt (2013).

12 Hennessey (1994).

13 DeCurtis (2001).

14 Rodman (1996, 31ff).

15 Utt (2013).

16 On 'Spiritual Warrior' retreats, see Taliman (2009). On theft of Aboriginal art designs, see "Aboriginal Art under Fraud Threat" (2003). On child labor in the rug industry, see Navajo Rug Repair (n.d.). In response to such exploitation, a new industry has grown up to channel profits directly to the craft producers. Equal Exchange, Ethical Threads, SERRV International, Ten Thousand Villages, and other companies buy from worker-owned cooperatives, pay higher prices to producers, and (or) reinvest in the communities from which they receive their goods.

17 Hasty (2002).

18 Uwujaren (2013).

19 Said (1978; 1985; 1993a).

20 Wolf (1982). See also Wolf (1998). Geertz (1988). On relativism, see *inter alia* Geertz (1984); Hollis and Lukes (1982); Jarvie (1975a); Scholte (1984).

21 Latham (2000:151–208). Latham also showed how modernization theory provided intellectual support for the Strategic Hamlet program during the Vietnam War. See pages 69–108.

22 Said (1978; 1985; 1993); Fanon (1952; 1961); Memmi (1967); Bhabha (1994); Césaire (1972); Spivak (1999); Trinh (1989). For overviews of post-colonial theory, see Ashcroft, Griffiths, and Tiffin (1995; 1998; 2002); Barker, Hulme, and Iverson (1994); Young (2001).

23 Said (1978, 6).

24 Spivak (1988).

25 Sharp (2009, 110).

26 See P. Spickard, J. Spickard, and Cragg (1998).

27 The quote is taken from a speech Curzon made in September 1909 to the House of Lords (Said 1978, 214). Curzon (1889; 1892).

28 Said (1978, 7–8).

29 Ashcroft, Griffiths, and Tiffin (1998, 235).

30 Ashcroft, Griffiths, and Tiffin (1998, 235).

31 The symposium was organized by Akinsola Akiwowo and contains his own article (1988), Park's (1988), and others by Frederick Gareau (1988), Jan Loubser (1988) and A. Muyiwa Sanda (1988).

32 Park (1988, 161).

33 Park (1988, 161).

34 Never mind that the key terms of Newton's system, including 'mass', 'position', 'time', and 'gravity' were basically undefined. Newton's *Principia* was modeled on Euclid's *Geometry*, and these terms were definitional.

35 Park (1988, 161).

36 Park (1988, 167). See also Park (2006).

37 Ashcroft, Griffiths, and Tiffin (1998, 235); Park (1988, 161).

38 Connell (2007; 2010; 2014). Cf. Connell (1997).

39 Coleman (1990).

40 Connell (2007, 33).

41 Giddens (1984).

42 Wrong (1961); Garfinkel (1967, 68).

43 Alexander et al. (1987). Cf. Archer (1990).

44 Connell (2007, 35, 37).

45 Connell (2007, 38).

46 Bourdieu (1990).

47 Connell (2007, 41).

48 Connell (2007, 43–44).

49 Hountondji (1983); Shariatri (1979); Das (1995); Nandy (2004); Prebisch (1981).

50 E.g., Ferguson (2011); Samuel Huntington (1996, ch. 4) used the phrase as a section title.

51 See Owen (2012).

52 Friedman (2006). Cf. de Blij (2009).

53 hooks (2004, 156).

54 I have no quarrel with that police department; they did their job courteously and well. I have since met authorities with much less integrity, but I learned early not to generalize. There is no point in demonizing people because of the work they do.

55 I include Russia and China as colonial powers. Colonialism is not just a First World or a capitalist phenomenon. The peoples of Siberia, Tibet, and the Silk Road have felt the imperial boot from self-proclaimed communists, too. On Nicaragua: there is lots of literature on the U.S. domination of that country and the incredible damage it has done; see Walker and Wade (2011) for an overview. My students' 2011 visit was hosted by Los Quinchos, a group that provides education and alternatives for Managua's street kids.

POSTSCRIPT

1 Proverbs 29:18, King James Version. Yes, I know that the translation is spotty, but it expresses my point. The New International Version's "Where there is no revelation, people cast off restraint" is far more sectarian and justifies control from the top. That produces quite a different politics than the inclusive equality that I think we need. (Vision apparently affects translators, too.)

2 Harding (1995).

3 hooks (2004, 156).

4 Lichterman (2006).

REFERENCES

PART I. PREVIOUS PUBLICATIONS CONTAINING MATERIAL
RESHAPED FOR THIS VOLUME (USED BY PERMISSION OF THE
COPYRIGHT HOLDERS)

Solo-Authored Works
Spickard, James V. 1991. "Experiencing Religious Rituals: A Schutzian Analysis of Navajo Ceremonies." *Sociological Analysis* (now *Sociology of Religion*) 52(2): 191–204.
———. 1994. "Texts and Contexts: Recent Trends in the Sociology of Religion as Reflected in American Textbooks." *Social Compass: An International Review of Sociology of Religion* 41(3): 313–328.
———. 1998. "Ethnocentrism, Social Theory, and Non-Western Sociologies of Religion: Towards a Confucian Alternative." *International Sociology* 13(2): 173–194.
———. 2000. "Fashioning a Post-Colonial Sociology of Religion." *Tidsskrift for Kirke, Religion og Samfunn* 13(2): 113–127. (Also published as "*Conformando una sociología de la religión postcolonial.*" *Religiones y Sociedad* N°9 [Mayo/Agosto 2000]: 123–140. Translated by Roberto Blancarte.)
———. 2001. "Tribes and Cities: Towards an Islamic Sociology of Religion." *Social Compass: An International Review of Sociology of Religion* 48(1): 103–116.
———. 2003. "Cultural Context and the Definition of Religion: Seeing with Confucian Eyes." *Religion and the Social Order* 10: 189–199.
———. 2004. "Charting the Inward Journey: Applying Blackmore's Model to Meditative Religious Experience." *Archiv für Religionpsychologie* 26: 157–180.
———. 2005. "Ritual, Symbol, and Experience: Understanding Catholic Worker House Masses." *Sociology of Religion* 66(4): 337–358.
———. 2012. "Centered in Time: A Sociological Phenomenology of Religious Rituals." Pp. 154–167 in *Understanding Religious Ritual*, edited by John P. Hoffman. Routledge, 2012.
———. 2013. "Accepting the Post-Colonial Challenge: Theorizing a Khaldūnian Approach to the Marian Apparition at Medjugorje." *Critical Research on Religion* 1(2): 158–176.

Co-Authored Work
McGuire, Meredith B., and James V. Spickard. 2003. "Narratives of Commitment: Social Activism and Radical Catholic Identity." *Temenos: Studies in Comparative Religion* 37–38: 131–150.

PART II. WORKS CITED

Aberle, David F. 1966. *The Peyote Religion among the Navajo*. Publications in Anthropology, vol. 42. New York: Viking Fund.

"Aboriginal Art under Fraud Threat." 2003. *BBC News Online*, Nov. 28. http://news.bbc.co.uk. Retrieved 11/26/2014.

Addison, James Thayer. 1924. "The Modern Chinese Cult of Ancestors." *Journal of Religion* 4(5): 492–503.

Adogame, Afe. 2013. *The African Christian Diaspora: New Currents and Emerging Trends in World Christianity*. London: Bloomsbury.

Akiwowo, Akinsola A. 1983. *Ajobi and Ajogbe: Variations on the Theme of Sociation*. Inaugural Lecture Series 46. Ile-Ife: University of Ife Press.

———. 1986. "Contributions to the Sociology of Knowledge from an African Oral Poetry." *International Sociology* 1(4): 343–358.

———. 1988. "Universalism and Indigenisation in Sociological Theory." *International Sociology* 3(2): 155–160.

———. 1999. "Indigenous Sociologies: Extending the Scope of the Argument." *International Sociology* 14(2): 115–138.

Alatas, Syed Farid. 2006a. "A Khaldūnian Exemplar for a Historical Sociology for the South." *Current Sociology* 54(3): 397–411.

———. 2006b. "Ibn Khaldūn and Contemporary Sociology." *International Sociology* 21(6): 782–795.

———. 2007. "The Historical Sociology of Muslim Societies: Khaldūnian Applications." *International Sociology* 22(3): 267–288.

———. 2010. "Religion and Reform: Two Exemplars for Autonomous Sociology in the Non-Western Context." Pp. 29–39 in *ISA Handbook of Diverse Sociological Traditions*, edited by S. Patel. London and New York: Sage Publications.

———. 2011. "Ibn Khaldūn." Pp. 12–29 in *The Wiley-Blackwell Companion to Major Social Theorists*, edited by G. Ritzer and J. Stepnisky. Oxford and New York: Blackwell.

———. 2013. *Ibn Khaldūn*. Delhi: Oxford University Press.

———. 2014. *Applying Ibn Khaldūn: The Recovery of a Lost Tradition in Sociology*. New York: Routledge.

Al-Jabri, Mohammed. 1983. *Al-Assabiyya and the State: Ibn Khaldūn's Theoretical Perspectives in Arab-Islamic History* [in Arabic]. Beirut: Dar Attalia.

Alexander, Jeffrey C., Bernhard Giesen, Richard Munch, and Neil J. Smelser, eds. 1987. *The Micro-Macro Link*. Berkeley: University of California Press.

Almukhtar, Sarah. 2015. "ISIS Finances Are Strong." *New York Times*, May 19. www.nytimes.com. Retrieved 11/15/2015.

Ames, Roger T. 1991. "Reflections on the Confucian Self: A Response to Fingarette." Pp. 103–114 in *Rules, Rituals, and Responsibility: Essays Dedicated to Herbert Fingarette*, edited by M. I. Bockover. La Salle, IL: Open Court.

———. 1994. "The Focus-Field Self in Classical Confucianism." Pp. 187–214 in *Self as Person in Asian Theory and Practice*, edited by R. T. Ames, W. Dissansayake, and T. P. Kasulis. Albany: State University of New York Press.

Ammerman, Nancy T. 1996. "Organized Religion in a Voluntaristic Society." *Sociology of Religion* 58(3): 203–215.

———. 2013. *Sacred Stories, Spiritual Tribes.* New York: Oxford University Press.

An-Na'im, Abdullahi Ahmed, ed. 1992. *Human Rights in Cross-Cultural Perspectives.* Philadelphia: University of Pennsylvania Press.

Anderson, Benedict. 1991. *Imagined Communities: Reflections on the Origin and Spread of Nationalism.* Rev. ed. London: Verso.

Anti-Defamation League. 2013. "Al Shabaab's American Recruits." www.adl.org. Retrieved 11/15/2015.

Arbuckle, Gary. 1995. "Inevitable Treason: Dong Zhongshu's Theory of Historical Cycles and Early Attempts to Invalidate the Han Mandate." *Journal of the American Oriental Society* 115(4): 585–597.

Archer, Margaret S. 1990. "Human Agency and Social Structure: A Critique of Giddens." Pp. 73–84 in *Anthony Giddens: Consensus and Controversey*, edited by Jon Clark, Celia Modgil, and Sohan Modgil, 73–84. London: Falmer Press.

Aron, Raymond. 1965. *Main Currents in Sociological Thought I: Montesquieu, Comte, Marx, DeTocqueville.* London: Weidenfeld & Nicolson.

Aronica, Michele Teresa. 1987. *Beyond Charismatic Leadership: The New York Catholic Worker Movement.* New Brunswick, NJ: Transaction Publishers.

Asad, Talal. 1993a. *Genealogies of Religion: Discipline and Reasons of Power in Christianity and Islam.* Baltimore: Johns Hopkins University Press.

———. 1993b. "The Construction of Religion as an Anthropological Category." Pp. 27–54 in *Genealogies of Religion: Discipline and Reasons of Power in Christianity and Islam.* Baltimore: Johns Hopkins University Press.

———. 2003. *Formations of the Secular: Christianity, Islam, Modernity.* Stanford, CA: Stanford University Press.

Ashcroft, Bill, Gareth Griffiths, and Helen Tiffin, eds. 1995. *The Post-Colonial Studies Reader.* London: Routledge.

———. 1998. *Key Concepts in Post-Colonial Studies.* London: Routledge.

———. 2002. *The Empire Writes Back: Theory and Practice in Post-Colonial Literatures.* New York: Routledge.

Austin, John L. 1962. *How to Do Things with Words.* Oxford: Clarendon Press.

Baker, Hugh. 1979. *Chinese Family and Kinship.* New York: Columbia University Press.

Barber, Benjamin R. 1995. *Jihad vs. McWorld: How Globalism and Tribalism Are Reshaping the World.* New York: Times Books.

———. 2001. *Jihad vs. McWorld: Terrorism's Challenge to Democracy.* New York: Ballantine Books.

Barker, Francis, Peter Hulme, and Margaret Iverson, eds. 1994. *Colonial Discourse, Postcolonial Theory.* New York: St. Martin's Press.

Baud, Michiel, Susan Legêne, and Peter Pels. 2013. "Circumventing Reality: Report on the Anthropological Work of Professor Emeritus M.M.G. Bax." *Vrije Universiteit Amsterdam*, Sept. 9. www.vu.nl. Retrieved 11/11/2015.

Bax, Mart. 1990. "The Madonna of Medjugorje: Religious Rivalry and the Formation of a Devotional Movement in Yugoslavia." *Anthropological Quarterly* 63(2): 63–75.

———. 1995. *Medjugorje: Religion, Politics, and Violence in Rural Bosnia.* Amsterdam: VU University Press.

———. 2000b. "Holy Mary and Medjugorje's Rocketeers: The Local Logic of an Ethnic Cleansing Process in Bosnia." *Ethnologia Europaea: Journal of European Ethnology* 30(1): 45–58.

Beard, Mary. 2002. *The Parthenon.* Cambridge, MA: Harvard University Press.

Beaudoin, Tom. 1998. *Virtual Faith: The Irreverent Spiritual Quest of Generation X.* San Francisco: Josey-Bass.

Bell, Catherine. 1992. *Ritual Theory, Ritual Practice.* New York: Oxford University Press.

Bellah, Robert N. 1986. "Habits of the Heart: Implications for Religion." St Marks Catholic Church (Isla Vista, CA), Feb. 21. www.robertbellah.com. Retrieved 1/11/2015.

Bellah, Robert N., Richard Madsen, William M. Sullivan, Ann Swidler, and Steven M. Tipton. 1985. *Habits of the Heart: Individualism and Commitment in American Life.* Berkeley: University of California Press.

Bender, Courtney. 2003. *Heaven's Kitchen: Living Religion at God's Love We Deliver.* Chicago: University of Chicago Press.

———. 2010. *The New Metaphysicals: Spirituality and the American Religious Imagination.* Chicago: University of Chicago Press.

Bender, Courtney, Wendy Cadge, Peggy Levitt, and David Smilde, eds. 2013. *Religion on the Edge: De-Centering and Re-Centering the Sociology of Religion.* New York: Oxford University Press.

Benedictow, Ole J. 2005. "The Black Death: The Greatest Catastrophe Ever." *History Today* 55(3): 42–49.

Berger, Lawrence M., Marla McDaniel, and Christina Paxson. 2006. "How Does Race Influence Judgments about Parenting?" *Focus* 24(2): 24–30.

Berger, Peter L. 1967. *The Sacred Canopy: Elements of a Sociological Theory of Religion.* Garden City, NY: Doubleday.

———. 1970. *A Rumor of Angels: Modern Society and the Rediscovery of the Supernatural.* Garden City, NY: Anchor/Doubleday.

———, ed. 1999. *The Desecularization of the World: Resurgent Religion and World Politics.* Grand Rapids, MI: William B. Eerdmans.

Berger, Peter L., Grace Davie, and Effie Fokas. 2008. *Religious America, Secular Europe?: A Theme and Variations.* London and New York: Ashgate.

Berryman, Edward. 2001. "Medjugorje's Living Icons: Making Spirit Matter (for Sociology)." *Social Compass* 48(4): 593–610.

Beyer, Peter F. 2003. "Defining Religion in Cross-National Perspective: Identity and Difference in Official Conceptions." Pp. 163–188 in *Defining Religion: Investigating the Boundaries between Sacred and Secular*, edited by Arthur L. Greil and David G. Bromley. Religion and the Social Order, vol. 10. Bingley: Emerald Group.

————. 2006. *Religions in Global Society*. New York: Routledge.

Bhabha, Homi K. 1994. *The Location of Culture*. London: Routledge.

Birchfield, D. L. n.d. "Navajos." *Countries and Their Cultures*. www.everyculture.com. Retrieved 10/5/2014.

Blackmore, Susan J. 1986. "Who Am I? Changing Models of Reality in Meditation." Pp. 71–85 in *Beyond Therapy: The Impact of Eastern Religions on Psychological Theory and Practice*, edited by G. Claxton. London: Wisdom Publications.

————. 1988. "A Theory of Lucid Dreams and OBEs." Pp. 373–387 in *Conscious Mind, Sleeping Brain: Perspectives on Lucid Dreaming*, edited by J. Glackenbach and S. La Berge. New York: Plenum Press.

Borofsky, Robert. 2000. "To Laugh or to Cry?" *Anthropology News* 41(2): 9–10.

Bourdieu, Pierre. 1990. *The Logic of Practice*. Translated by Richard Nice. Stanford, CA: Stanford University Press.

————. 1997. *Pascalian Meditations*. Stanford, CA: Stanford University Press.

Bowler, Peter J. 2003. *Evolution: The History of an Idea*. 3d ed. Berkeley: University of California Press.

British Museum. n.d. *The Parthenon Sculptures*. Trustees of the British Museum. www.britishmuseum.org. Retrieved 11/22/2014.

Brinkerhoff, David B., Suzanne T. Ortega, and Rose Weitz. 2013. *Essentials of Sociology*. 9th ed. Stamford, CT: Cengage.

Bruce, Steve. 1993. "Religion and Rational Choice: A Critique of Economic Explanations of Religious Behavior." *Sociology of Religion* 54(2): 193–205.

————. 1999. *Choice and Religion: A Critique of Rational Choice*. Oxford: Oxford University Press.

————. 2002. *God Is Dead: Secularization in the West*. Oxford: Blackwell.

Bureau of Labor Statistics. 2014. "Women in the Labor Force: A Databook" (BLS Reports: Report 1049). www.bls.gov. Retrieved 1/1/2015.

Burke, Edmund. 1790. *Reflections on the Revolution in France*. London: Penguin Classics, 1986.

Burkert, Walter. 1985. *Greek Religion*. Cambridge, MA: Harvard University Press.

Byman, Daniel L. 2010. "Al Qaeda's M&A Strategy." *Foreign Policy*, Dec. 7. www.foreignpolicy.com. Retrieved 3/1/2016.

Bynum, Caroline Walker. 1986. ". . . 'And Woman His Humanity': Female Imagery in the Religious Writing of the Later Middle Ages." Pp. 257–288 in *Gender and Religion: On the Complexity of Symbols*, edited by Caroline Walker Bynum, Stevan Harrell, and Paula Richman, 257–88. Boston: Beacon Press.

Campbell, Heidi A., ed. 2012. *Digital Religion: Understanding Religious Practice in New Media Worlds*. New York: Routledge.

Carmen, Tim. 2012. "Fojol Bros. Food Trucks Criticized for Stereotyping." *Washington Post*, May 18. www.washingtonpost.com. Retrieved 11/22/2014.

Carmichael, Cathie. 2006. "Violence and Ethnic Boundary Maintenance in Bosnia in the 1990s." *Journal of Genocide Research* 8(3): 283–293.

Casanova, José. 1994. *Public Religions in the Modern World.* Chicago: University of Chicago Press.

Caspersen, Nina. 2009. *Contested Nationalism: Serb Elite Rivalry in Croatia and Bosnia in the 1990s.* Oxford: Berghahn Books.

Catholic Agitator. Los Angeles Catholic Worker. Issue archive posted at http://lacatholicworker.org.

Césaire, Aimé. 1972. *Discourse on Colonialism.* Translated by Joan Pinkham. New York: Monthly Review Press.

Chakrabarty, Dipesh. 2000. *Provincializing Europe: Postcolonial Thought and Historical Difference.* Princeton, NJ: Princeton University Press.

Chan, Phil C. W. 2013. "Human Rights and Democracy with Chinese Characteristics?" *Human Rights Law Review* 13(4): 645–689.

Chan, Wing-tsit, ed. and trans. 1963. *A Source Book in Chinese Philosophy.* Princeton, NJ: Princeton University Press.

———, ed. and trans. 1967. *Reflections on Things at Hand: The Neo-Confucian Anthology.* Compiled by Chu His and Lu Tsu-ch'ien. New York: Columbia University Press.

Chaves, Mark. 2011. *American Religion: Contemporary Trends.* Princeton, NJ: Princeton University Press.

Cheng, Chung-ying. 1979. "Human Rights in Chinese History and Chinese Philosophy." *Comparative Civilizations Review* 1: 1–19.

Cheong, Pauline Hope, Peter Fischer-Nielsen, Stefan Gelfgren, and Charles Ess, eds. 2012. *Digital Religion, Social Media and Culture: Perspectives, Practices and Futures.* New York: Peter Lang.

Chidester, David. 1996. *Savage Systems: Colonialism and Comparative Religion in Southern Africa.* Charlottesville: University Press of Virginia.

Chirot, Daniel. 1977. *Social Change in the Twentieth Century.* New York: Harcourt Brace Jovanovich.

Christiano, Kevin J., William H. Swatos, Jr., and Peter Kivisto. 2008. *Sociology of Religion: Contemporary Developments.* Lanham, MD: Rowman & Littlefield.

Chow, Kai-wing. 1994. *The Rise of Confucian Ritualism in Late Imperial China: Ethics, Classics, and Lineage Discourse.* Stanford, CA: Stanford University Press.

Cigar, Norman. 1995. *Genocide in Bosnia: The Policy of 'Ethnic Cleansing' in Eastern Europe.* College Station: Texas A&M University Press.

Clifford, James, and George E. Marcus, eds. 1986. *Writing Culture: The Poetics and Politics of Ethnography.* Berkeley: University of California Press.

Coleman, James S. 1990. *The Foundations of Social Theory.* Cambridge, MA: Harvard University Press.

Coles, Robert. 1987. *Dorothy Day: A Radical Devotion.* Reading, MA: Addison-Wesley.

Cohen, Roger. 2015. "Why ISIS Trumps Freedom." *New York Times,* Aug. 13. www.nytimes.com. Retrieved 11/15/2015.

Comte, Auguste. 1853. *The Positive Philosophy of Auguste Comte*. Edited and translated by Harriet Martineau. London: Chapman.

Connell, Raewyn. 1997. "Why Is Classical Theory Classical?" *American Journal of Sociology* 102(6): 1511–1557.

———. 2007. *Southern Theory: The Global Dynamics of Knowledge in Social Science*. Cambridge, UK: Polity Press.

———. 2010. "Learning from Each Other: Sociology on a World Scale." Pp. 40–51 in *The ISA Handbook of Diverse Sociological Traditions*, edited by Sujata Patel. London: Sage Publications.

———. 2014. "Rethinking Gender from the South." *Feminist Studies* 40(3): 518–539.

Cose, Ellis. 1993. *Rage of a Privileged Class: Why Are Middle-Class Blacks Angry?* New York: HarperCollins.

Cronin, Michael. 2002. "The Empire Talks Back: Orality, Heteronomy and the Cultural Turn in Interpreting." Pp. 45–62 in *Translation and Power*, edited by Edwin Gentzler and Maria Tymoczko, 45–62. Boston: University of Massachusetts Press.

Csordas, Thomas J. 1995. "Words from the Holy People: A Case Study in Cultural Phenomenology." Pp. 269–290 in *Embodiment and Experience: The Existential Ground of Culture and Self*, edited by T. J. Csordas. Cambridge, MA: Cambridge University Press.

———, ed. 2000a. Thematic issue on ritual healing in Navajo society. *Medical Anthropology Quarterly* 14(4).

———. 2000b. "The Navajo Healing Project." *Medical Anthropology Quarterly*, n.s., 14(4): 463–475.

———. 2005. "Gender and Healing in Navajo Society." Pp. 291–304 in *Religion and Healing in America*, edited by L. L. Barnes and S. S. Sered. Oxford and New York: Oxford University Press.

Cultural Survival Quarterly. 1991. "The State of the Nation: Indigenous Nations Struggle to Be Heard over the Din of State Policies." *Cultural Survival Quarterly* 15(4). www.culturalsurvival.org. Retrieved 11/22/2014.

Curzon, George Nathaniel. 1889. *Russia in Central Asia*. London: Frank Cass & Co. Ltd.

———. 1892. *Persia and the Persian Question*. London: Longmans, Green, and Co.

Czikszentmihalyi, Mihaly. 1975. *Beyond Boredom and Anxiety*. San Francisco: Josey-Bass.

———. 1991. *Flow: The Psychology of Optimal Experience*. San Francisco: HarperCollins.

———. 1997. *Finding Flow: The Psychology of Engagement with Everyday Life*. New York: Basic Books.

Daly, Mary. *Gyn/Ecology: The Meta-Ethics of Radical Feminism*. Boston: Beacon Press, 1978.

Darwin, Charles. 1871. *The Descent of Man and Selection in Relation to Sex*. New York: Appleton and Co..

Das, Veena. 1995. *Critical Events: An Anthropological Perspective on India*. New Delhi: Oxford University Press.

Davidman, Lynn. 2000. *Motherloss*. Berkeley: University of California Press.

———. 2007. "The New Voluntarism and the Case of Unsyngogued Jews." Pp. 51–67 in *Everyday Religion: Observing Modern Religious Lives*, edited by N. T. Ammerman. New York: Oxford University Press.

Davie, Grace. 2013. *Sociology of Religion: A Critical Agenda*. 2d ed. London: Sage Publications.

Davie, Jodie Shapiro. 1995. *Women in the Presence: Constructing Community and Seeking Spirituality in Mainline Protestantism*. Philadelphia: University of Pennsylvania Press.

"'Death of Mrs. Adkins.'" 1908. *Baptist Missionary Magazine*: 269.

de Bary, Wm. Theodore. 1995. "The New Confucianism in Beijing." *American Scholar* 64(2, Spring): 175–189.

de Blij, Harm. 2009. *The Power of Place: Geography, Destiny, and Globalization's Rough Landscape*. New York: Oxford University Press.

DeCurtis, Anthony. 2001. "Is Rock 'n' Roll a White Man's Game?" *Time*, June 24. http://content.time.com. Retrieved 11/23/2014.

Deflem, Mathieu. 1991. "Ritual, Anti-Structure, and Religion: A Discussion of Victor Turner's Processual Symbolic Analysis." *Journal for the Scientific Study of Religion* 30(1): 1–25.

de Heusch, Luc. 1972. *The Drunken King or The Origin of the State*. Translated by R. Willis. Bloomington, IN: Indiana University Press, 1982.

Dennerline, Jerry. 1988. *Qian Mu and the World of the Seven Mansions*. New Haven: Yale University Press.

de Tocqueville, Alexis. 1835. *Democracy in America*. Vol I. Translated by Henry Reeve. New York: Schocken Books, 1961.

———. 1840. *Democracy in America*. Vol II. Translated by Henry Reeve. New York: Schocken Books, 1961.

Díaz-Stevens, Ana María. 1994. "Analyzing Popular Religiosity for Socio-Religious Meaning." Pp. 17–36 in *An Enduring Flame: Studies of Latino Popular Religiosity*, edited by A. M. Stevens-Arroyo and Ana María Díaz-Stevens. New York: Bildner Center for Western Hemisphere Studies/ PARAL.

Dietrich, Jeff. 1983. *Reluctant Resister*. Greensboro, NC: Unicorn Press.

———. 1993. "Authentic Alternatives Have Always Been Pretty Rare." *National Catholic Reporter*, May 21: 11.

———. 1996. "Scaling Cathedral Walls to Preach Gospel." *National Catholic Reporter*, Sept. 13: 15.

———. 2011. *Broken and Shared: Food, Dignity, and the Poor on Los Angeles' Skid Row*. Los Angeles: Marymount Institute Press.

Dimitrovova, Bohdana. 2001. "Bosniak or Muslim? Dilemma of One Nation with Two Names." *Southeast European Politics* 2(2): 94–108.

Dobbelaere, Karel. 2002. *Secularization: An Analysis at Three Levels*. Brussels: Peter Lang.

Dodson, Jualynne E., and Cheryl Townsend Gilkes. 1995. "'There's Nothing Like Church Food': Food and the U.S. Afro-Christian Tradition: Re-Membering Community and Feeding the Embodied S/spirit(s)." *Journal of the American Academy of Religion* 63(3): 519–538.

Douglas, Mary. 1966. *Purity and Danger: An Analysis of Concepts of Pollution and Taboo.* New York: Praeger.

———. 1968. "The Contempt of Ritual, Parts I & II." *New Blackfriars* 49 (June/July).

———. 1970. *Natural Symbols: Explorations in Cosmology.* London: Barrie & Rockliff.

———. 1975. *Implicit Meanings: Essays in Anthropology.* London: Routledge & Kegan Paul.

Drysdale, John. 1996. "How Are Social-Scientific Concepts Formed? A Reconstruction of Max Weber's Theory of Concept Formation." *Sociological Theory* 14(1): 71–88.

Du Bois, W.E.B. 1903. *The Souls of Black Folk.* Chicago: A.C. McClurg.

Durkheim, Émile. 1893. *The Division of Labor in Society.* Translated by George Simpson. New York: Free Press, 1964.

———. 1897. *Suicide: A Study in Sociology.* Translated by J. A. Spaulding and G. Simpson. Edited by G. Simpson. New York: Free Press, 1951.

———. 1912. *The Elementary Forms of the Religious Life.* Translated by Joseph Ward Swain. New York: Collier Books, 1961. Originally published as *Les formes élémentaires de la vie religieuse: Le système totémique en Australie.* French-language edition referenced: Paris: Quadrige/Presses Universitaires de France, 1994.

———. 1972. *Selected Writings.* Edited by Anthony Giddens. Cambridge, UK: Cambridge University Press.

Durkheim, Émile, and Marcel Mauss. 1902. *Primitive Classifications.* Translated by Rodney Needham. Chicago: University of Chicago Press, 1963.

Ebaugh, Helen Rose, and Janet Chafetz, eds. 2000. *Religion and the New Immigrants: Continuities and Adaptations in Immigrant Congregations.* Abridged student ed. Walnut Creek, CA: Altamira Press.

Ebrey, Patricia. 1991. *Chu Hsi's Family Rituals.* Princeton, NJ: Princeton University Press.

Ecklund, Elaine Howard. 2010. *Science vs. Religion: What Scientists Really Think.* New York: Oxford University Press.

Ellis, Marc. 1978. *A Year at the Catholic Worker.* New York: Paulist Press.

Emerson, Michael, William Mirola, and Susan C. Monahan. 2010. *Religion Matters: What Sociology Teaches Us about Religion in Our World.* New York: Routledge.

Episcopal Church in America. 1928. *The Book of Common Prayer.* New York: Oxford University Press.

———. 1979. *The Book of Common Prayer.* New York: Church Publishing.

Evans-Pritchard, Edward E. 1937. *Magic, Witchcraft and Oracles among the Azande.* Oxford: Oxford University Press.

———. *Nuer Religion.* 1956. New York: Oxford University Press.

Ezzy, Douglas. 2014. *Sex, Death, and Witchcraft: A Contemporary Pagan Festival.* London and New York: Bloomsbury Press.

Fairbank, John King, and Merle Goldman. 2006. *China: A New History.* 2d ed. Cambridge, MA: Belknap Press.

Fanon, Frantz. 1952. *Black Skin, White Masks*. Translated by Charles Lam Markmann. New York: Grove Press, 1967.

———. 1961. *The Wretched of the Earth*. Translated by Constance Farrington. New York: Ballentine Books, 1963.

Fauré, Christine, and Jacques Guilhaumou. 2006. "Sieyès et le non-dit de la sociologie: du mot à la chose." *Revue d'Histoire Des Sciences Humaines* 15.

Ferguson, Niall. 2011. *Civilization: The West and the Rest*. London and New York: Penguin Books, Ltd.

Fingarette, Herbert. 1972. *Confucius: The Secular as Sacred*. New York: Harper & Row.

———. 1991. "Comment and Response." Pp. 169–220 in *Rules, Rituals, and Responsibility: Essays Dedicated to Herbert Fingarette*, edited by M. I. Bockover. La Salle, IL: Open Court.

Finke, Roger, and Rodney Stark. 1986. "Turning Pews into People: Estimating 19th-Century Church Membership." *Journal for the Scientific Study of Religion* 25 (2): 180–192.

———, eds. 2005. *The Churching of America, 1776–2005: Winners and Losers in Our Religious Economy*. Revised ed. New Brunswick, NJ: Rutgers University Press.

Fletcher, Joshua. 2013. "Textbook Hearing Draws Evolution Supporters, Detractors." *San Antonio Express-News*, Sept. 18. www.mysanantonio.com. Retrieved 3/1/2016.

Flores, Richard R. 1994. "Para el Niño Dios: Sociability and Commemorative Sentiment in Popular Religious Practice." Pp. 171–190 in *An Enduring Flame: Studies on Latino Popular Religiosity*, edited by A. M. Stevens-Arroyo and A. M. Díaz-Stevens. New York: Bildner Center for Western Hemispheric Studies.

———. 1995. *Los Pastores: History and Performance in the Mexican Shepherd's Play of South Texas*. Washington, DC: Smithsonian Institution Press.

Flottau, Renate. 2007. "Balkan Mujahedeens: Fundamentalist Islam Finds Fertile Ground in Bosnia." *Der Spiegel Online*, Nov. 9. www.spiegel.de. Retrieved 10/7/2009.

Flynn, Toni. 1989. *Finding My Way: A Journey along the Rim of the Catholic Worker Movement*. Los Osos, CA: Sand River Press.

Foreman, Mary. 2008. "Recipes for Potlucks, Church Socials, Picnics, Reunions, and Other Gatherings." *Deep South Dish: Food, Family, Memories*. www.deepsouthdish.com. Retrieved 12/20/2014.

Fowler, James W. 1981. *Stages of Faith: The Psychology of Human Development*. New York: Harper & Row.

Franklin, James. 1982. "The Renaissance Myth." *Quadrant* 26(11): 51–60.

Frazer, James. 1890. *The Golden Bough: A Study in Comparative Religion*. London: Macmillan.

Freedman, Maurice. 1979. *The Study of Chinese Society*. Stanford, CA: Stanford University Press.

Friedman, Thomas L. 2006. *The World Is Flat: A Brief History of the Twenty-First Century*. Expanded and updated ed. New York: Farrar, Strauss, and Giroux.

Furet, François. 1995. *Revolutionary France, 1770–1880*. New York: Wiley Blackwell.

Gardner, E. Clinton. 1983. "Character, Virtue and Responsiblity in Theological Ethics." *Encounter* 44: 315–339.

———. 1979a. "Niebuhr's Ethic of Responsibility: A Unified Interpretation." *St. Luke Journal of Theology* 23(4): 265–283.

Gareau, Frederick H. 1988. "Another Type of Third World Dependency: The Social Sciences." *International Sociology* 3(2): 171–178.

Garfinkel, Harold. 1967. *Studies in Ethnomethodology.* Englewood Cliffs, NJ: Prentice-Hall.

Gauthier, François, and Tuomas Martikainen, eds. 2013. *Religion in Consumer Society: Brands, Consumers, and Markets.* London: Ashgate.

Geertz, Clifford. 1960. *The Religion of Java.* Glencoe, IL: Free Press.

———. 1973. *The Interpretation of Cultures: Selected Essays.* New York: Basic Books.

———. 1984. "Distinguished Lecture: Anti Anti-Relativism." *American Anthropologist* 86(2): 263–278.

———. 1988. *Works and Lives: The Anthropologist as Author.* Stanford, CA: Stanford University Press.

Gerwehr, Scott, and Sara Daly. 2006. "Al-Qaida: Terrorist Selection and Recruitment." Pp. 73–89 in *The McGraw-Hill Homeland Security Handbook,* edited by D. Kamien. New York: McGraw-Hill.

Gibbon, Kate. 2005. *Who Owns the Past? Cultural Policy, Cultural Property, and the Law.* New Brunswick, NJ: Rutgers University Press.

Giddens, Anthony. 1976. "Classical Social Theory and the Origins of Modern Sociology." *American Journal of Sociology* 81 (4): 703–729.

———. 1984. *The Constitution of Society: Outline of a Theory of Structuration.* Cambridge, UK: Polity Press.

———. 1991. *Modernity and Self-Identity: Self and Society in the Late Modern Age.* Stanford, CA: Stanford University Press.

Giddens, Anthony, Mitchell Duneier, Richard P. Appelbaum, and Deborah Carr. 2011. *Introduction to Sociology.* 8th ed. New York: W.W. Norton & Company.

Gildea, Robert. 2010. *Children of the Revolution: The French, 1799–1914.* London and New York: Allen Lane/Penguin.

Gilkes, Cheryl Townsend. 2000. *If It Wasn't for the Women . . . : Black Women's Experience and Womanist Culture in Church and Community.* Maryknoll, NY: Orbis Books.

Gill, Sam D. 1979. *Songs of Life: An Introduction to Navajo Religious Culture.* Leiden: E.J. Brill.

———. 1983. "Navajo Views of Their Origin." Pp. 502–505 in *Southwest: Volume 10 of the Handbook of American Indians,* edited by A. Ortiz. Washington, DC: Smithsonian Institution Press.

———. 1987. *Native American Religious Action: A Performance Approach to Religion.* Columbia: University of South Carolina Press.

Ginzburg, Carlo. 1983. *The Night Battles: Witchcraft and Agrarian Cults in the Sixteenth and Seventeenth Centuries.* Translated by John Tedeschi and A Tedeschi. Baltimore: Johns Hopkins University Press.

Goldsmith, Peter. 1989. *When I Rise Cryin' Holy: African-American Denominationalism on the Georgia Coast.* New York: AMS Press.

Gould, Stephen Jay. 1977. *Ever Since Darwin.* London: Penguin.

———. 1997. "Non-Overlapping Magesteria." *Natural History,* March: 16–22.

Grammich, Clifford, Kirk Hadaway, Richard Houseal, Dale E. Jones, Alexei Krindatch, Richie Stanley, and Richard H. Taylor. 2012. *2010 U.S. Religion Census: Religious Congregations & Membership Study.* Association of Statisticians of American Religious Bodies.

Gray, Asa. 1860. "Natural Selection Not Inconsistent with Natural Theology." *Atlantic Monthly,* July, August, and October: 109–116, 229–235, 406–425.

Greeley, Andrew M. 2005. *The Catholic Revolution: New Wine, Old Wineskins, and the Second Vatican Council.* Berkeley: University of California Press.

Greeley, Andrew M., William C. McCready, and Kathleen McCourt. 1976. *Catholic Schools in a Declining Church.* Kansas City, KS: Andrews and McMeel.

Greil, Arthur L., and David G. Bromley, eds. 2003. *Defining Religion: Investigating the Boundaries between the Sacred and the Secular.* Religion and the Social Order, vol. 10. Bingley: Emerald Group.

Guthrie, Alice. 2015. "Decoding Daesh: Why Is the New Name for ISIS So Hard to Understand?" *Free Word Centre Blog,* Feb. 19. www.freewordcentre.com. Retrieved 11/30/2015.

Guthrie, Clifton F. 1996. "Why a Sanctoral Cycle? Or Are We Ready for a Methodist Hagiography?" *Doxology: Journal of the Order of Saint Luke* 13. www.materialreligion.org. Retrieved 12/19/2014.

Hadaway, C. Kirk, Penny Long Marler, and Mark Chaves. 1993. "What the Polls Don't Show: A Closer Look at US Church Attendance." *American Sociological Review* 56: 741–752.

Haile, Berard. 1938a. "Navajo Chantways and Ceremonials." *American Anthropologist* 40(4): 639–652.

———. 1938b. *Origin Legend of the Navajo Enemy Way: Text and Translation.* Publications in Anthropology, vol. 17. New Haven, CT: Yale University Press.

Hall, David D., ed. 1997. *Lived Religion: Toward a History of Practice.* Princeton, NJ: Princeton University Press.

Hall, David L. and Roger T. Ames. 1987. *Thinking Through Confucius.* Albany: State University of New York Press.

———. 1995. *Anticipating China: Thinking Through the Narratives of Chinese and Western Culture.* Albany: State University of New York Press.

———. 1998a. *Thinking from the Han: Self, Truth, and Transcendence in Chinese and Western Culture.* Albany: State University of New York Press.

———. 1998b. "Chinese Philosophy." *Routledge Encyclopedia of Philosophy.* www.rep.routledge.com. Retrieved 8/12/2014.

Hamabata, Mathews Masayuku. 1990. *Crested Kimono: Power and Love in the Japanese Business Family.* Ithaca, NY: Cornell University Press.

Hannan, Michael T. 1979. "The Dynamics of Ethnic Boundaries in Modern States." Pp. 253–275 in *National Development and the World System*, edited by J. W. Meyer and M. T. Hannan. Chicago: University of Chicago Press.

Harding, Sandra G. 1995. "Just Add Women and Stir?" Pp. 295–307 in *Missing Links: Gender Equity in Science and Technology Development*, edited by Gender Working Group. Ottawa: International Development Research Centre.

Hasquin, Hervé. 2003. "La Loi Du Sacrilège dans la France de la Restauration (1825)." *Problèmes d'Histoire des Religions* 13: 127–142.

Hasty, Jennifer. 2002. "Rites of Passage, Routes of Redemption: Emancipation Tourism and the Wealth of Culture." *Africa Today* 49(3): 47–76.

Hechter, Michael. 1975. *Internal Colonialism: The Celtic Fringe in British National Development*. Berkeley: University of California Press.

Heelas, Paul. 1992. "The Sacralization of the Self and New Age Capitalism." Pp. 139–166 in *Social Change in Contemporary Britain*, edited by N. Abercrombie and A. Warde. Cambridge, UK: Polity Press.

———. 1996. *The New Age Movement: The Celebration of the Self and the Sacralization of Modernity*. Oxford: Basil Blackwell.

———. 2006. "Challenging Secularization Theory: The Growth of 'New Age' Spiritualities of Life." *Hedgehog Review*, Spring–Summer: 46–58.

———. 2008. *Spiritualities of Life: New Age Romanticism and Consumptive Capitalism*. Malden, MA: Wiley-Blackwell.

———. 2009. "Spiritualities of Life." Pp. 758–782 in *Oxford Handbook of the Sociology of Religion*, edited by P. B. Clarke. Oxford: Oxford University Press.

———, ed. 2012. *Spirituality in the Modern World. Within Religious Tradition and Beyond*. London: Routledge.

Heelas, Paul, and Linda Woodhead. 2005. *The Spiritual Revolution: Why Religion Is Giving Way to Spirituality*. Oxford: Basil Blackwell.

Hennessey, Thomas J. 1994. *From Jazz to Swing: African-American Jazz Musicians and Their Music, 1890–1935*. Detroit: Wayne State University Press.

Henslin, James M. 2011. *Sociology: A Down to Earth Approach*. 11th ed. Upper Saddle River, NJ: Pearson.

Herberg, Will. 1955. *Protestant, Catholic, Jew: An Essay in American Religious Sociology*. Garden City, NY: Doubleday.

Hitchens, Christopher. 1998. *Imperial Spoils: The Curious Case of the Elgin Marbles*. London: Verso.

Ho, Ping-ti. 1965. "An Historian's View of the Chinese Family System." Pp. 15–30 in *Man and Civilization. The Family's Search for Survival*, edited by S. Farber, P. P. Mustacchi, and R. Wilson. New York: McGraw-Hill.

———. 1976. "The Chinese Civilization: A Search for the Roots of Its Longevity." *Journal of Asian Studies* 35(4): 547–554.

Hodge, Charles. 1874. *What Is Darwinism?* New York: Scribner, Armstrong, and Company.

Hoedemaker, Libertus A. 1970. *The Theology of H. Richard Niebuhr.* New York: Pilgrim Press.

Holifield, E. Brooks. 1994. "Toward a History of American Congregations." Pp. 23–53 in *American Congregations*, vol. 2, *New Perspectives in the Study of Congregations*, edited by J. P. Wind and J. W. Lewis. Chicago: University of California Press.

Hollis, Martin, and Steven Lukes, eds. 1982. *Rationality and Relativism.* Cambridge, MA: MIT Press.

hooks, bell. 2004. "Choosing the Margin as a Space of Radical Openness." Pp. 153–160 in *The Feminist Standpoint Theory Reader: Intellectual and Political Controversies*, edited by Sandra G. Harding. New York: Routledge.

Hountondji, Paulin J. 1983. *African Philosophy: Myth and Reality.* Translated by H. Evans. London.

House of Commons. 1816. *Report of the Select Committee of the House of Commons on the Earl of Elgin's Collection of Sculptured Marbles.* London: John Murray.

Hsu, Francis L. K. 1971. *Under the Ancestors' Shadow: Kinship, Personality, and Social Mobility in China.* Stanford, CA: Stanford University Press.

Hsün Tzu. 1963. *Hsün Tzu: Basic Writings.* Translated by B. Watson. New York: Columbia University Press.

Hubert, Henri, and Marcel Mauss. 1902. "Esquisse d'une théorie générale de la magie." *Année Sociologique VII.*

Humphrey, John P. 1984. *Human Rights and the United Nations: A Great Adventure.* Dobbs Ferry, NY: Transnational Publishers.

Huntington, Samuel P. 1996. *The Clash of Civilizations and the Remaking of World Order.* New York: Simon & Schuster.

Iannaccone, Laurence R. 1988. "A Formal Model of Church and Sect." *American Journal of Sociology* 94(supplement): S241–S268.

———. 1994. "Why Strict Churches Are Strong." *American Journal of Sociology* 99(5): 1180–1211.

Ibn Khaldūn. 1377–1399. *The Muqaddimah: An Introduction to History.* 3 vols. 2d ed. Translated by Franz Rosenthal. Bollingen Series XLIII. Princeton, NJ: Princeton University Press, 1967.

Ignatieff, Michael. 1993. *Blood and Belonging: Journeys into the New Nationalism.* New York: Farrar, Strauss, and Giroux.

———. 1995. "The Politics of Self-Destruction." *New York Review of Books*, Nov. 2: 17–19.

Inkeles, Alex, and David Smith. 1974. *Becoming Modern.* Cambridge, MA: Harvard University Press.

Jacobson, Matthew Frye. 1998. *Whiteness of a Different Color: European Immigrants and the Alchemy of Race.* Cambridge, MA: Harvard University Press.

Jarvie, I. C. 1975. "Cultural Relativism Again." *Philosophy of the Social Sciences* 5: 343–353.

Jiang, Xinyan. 2006. "The Concept of the Relational Self and Its Implications for Education." *Journal of Chinese Philosophy* 33(4): 543–555.

Johnstone, Ronald L. 2015. *Religion in Society: A Sociology of Religion*. 8th ed. New York: Routledge.

Juergensmeyer, Mark. 2003. *Terror in the Mind of God: The Global Rise of Religious Violence*. 3d ed. Berkeley: University of California Press.

Kalberg, Stephen. 1996. "On the Neglect of Weber's Protestant Ethic as a Theoretical Treatise: Demarcating the Parameters of Postwar American Sociological Theory." *Sociological Theory* 14(1): 49–70.

Kaplan, Robert D. 1990. *Soldiers of God: With the Mujahidin in Afghanistan*. Boston: Houghton Mifflin.

———. 1993. *Balkan Ghosts: A Journey through History*. New York: St. Martin's Press.

———. 1997. *The Ends of the Earth: From Togo to Turkmenistan, from Iran to Cambodia, a Journey to the Frontiers of Anarchy*. New York: Vintage Books.

———. 2000. *The Coming Anarchy: Shattering the Dreams of the Post-Cold War*. New York: Vintage Books.

Karen National Union. 1988. "The Third World War." *Karen National Union Bulletin* 15 (March): 18–19. www.ibiblio.org. Retrieved 11/18/2014.

Keightley, David N. 1990. "Early Civilization in China: Reflections on How It Became Chinese." Pp. 15–54 in *Heritage of China: Contemporary Perspectives on Chinese Civilization*, edited by P. S. Ropp. Berkeley: University of California Press.

———. 1999. "The Shang: China's First Historical Dynasty." Pp. 232–291 in *Cambridge History of Ancient China*, edited by M. Loewe and E. L. Shaughnessy. Cambridge, UK: Cambridge University Press.

———. 2004. "The Making of the Ancestors: Late Shang Religion and Its Legacy." Pp. 3–63 in *Chinese Religion and Society: The Transformation of a Field*, edited by J. Lagerwey. Hong Kong: Chinese University Press.

Kelley, Colin P., Shahrzad Mohtadi, Mark A. Cane, Richard Seager, and Yochanan Kushnir. 2015. "Climate Change in the Fertile Crescent and Implications of the Recent Syrian Drought." *Proceedings of the National Academy of Sciences* 112(11): 3241–3246.

Kelley, Dean. 1972. *Why Conservative Churches Are Growing: A Study in Sociology of Religion*. New York: Harper & Row.

Kimmel, Michael S. 1996. "Tradition as Revolt: The Moral and Political Economy of Ethnic Nationalism." *Current Perspectives in Social Theory* 16: 71–98.

Kluckholn, Clyde. 1944. *Navaho Witchcraft*. Cambridge, MA: Peabody Museum.

Kornblum, William. 2011. *Sociology in a Changing World*. 9th ed. Stamford, CT: Cengage.

Kruhly, Madeleine. 2012. "What America Looked Like: The Struggles of the Navajo Nation in 1972." *Atlantic Monthly*, July. www.theatlantic.com. Retrieved 3/1/2016.

Kuhn, Thomas S. 1970. *The Structure of Scientific Revolutions*. 2d ed., enlarged. Chicago: University of Chicago Press.

Lakos, William. 2010. *Chinese Ancestor Worship: A Practice and Ritual Oriented Approach to Understanding Chinese Culture*. Newcastle upon Tyne: Cambridge Scholars Publishing.

Lamphere, Louise. 1969. "Symbolic Elements in Navajo Ritual." *Southwestern Journal of Anthropology* 25(3): 279–305.

Landry, Alyssa. 2013. "Navajo Nation Economic Growth Creating Jobs and True Independence." *Indian Country*, Aug. 8. http://indiancountrytodaymedianetwork.com. Retrieved 10/9/2014.

Latham, Michael E. 2000. *Modernization as Ideology: American Social Science and "Nation-Building" in the Kennedy Era*. Chapel Hill: University of North Carolina Press.

Latourette, Kenneth Scott. 1964. *The Chinese: Their History and Culture*. New York: Macmillan.

Lawrence, Bruce B., ed. 1984. *Ibn Khaldun and Islamic Ideology*. Leiden: E.J. Brill.

Lawuyi, O. B., and Olufemi Taiwo. 1990. "Towards an African Sociological Tradition: A Rejoinder to Akiwowo and Makinde." *International Sociology* 5(1): 57–73.

Lechner, Frank J. 1993. "Global Fundamentalism." Pp. 19–36 in *A Future for Religion? New Paradigms for Social Analysis*, edited by W. H. Swatos, Jr. Newbury Park, CA: Sage Publications.

———. 1994. "Tribes and Cities: Particularism and Universalism as Global Processes." Presented at the Research Committee 16 of the International Sociological Association, XIIIth World Congress of Sociology, July, Bielefeld, Germany.Lévi-Strauss, Claude. 1981. *The Naked Man*. London: Jonathan Cape.

Levitt, Peggy. 2001. *The Transnational Villagers*. Berkeley: University of California Press.

———. 2007. *God Needs No Passport: Immigrants and the Changing American Religious Landscape*. New York: New Press.

Lichterman, Paul. 2006. *Elusive Togetherness: Church Groups Trying to Bridge America's Divisions*. Princeton, NJ: Princeton University Press.

Lilla, Mark. 2015. "Slouching toward Mecca." *New York Review of Books*, Apr. 2. www.nybooks.com. Retrieved 11/15/2015.

Lim, Chaeyoon, and Robert D. Putnam. 2010. "Religion, Social Networks, and Life Satisfaction." *American Sociological Review* 75(6): 914–933.

Loubser, Jan J. 1988. "The Need for the Indigenisation of the Social Sciences." *International Sociology* 3(2): 179–187.

Luckmann, Thomas. 1967. *The Invisible Religion: The Problem of Religion in Modern Society*. New York: Macmillan and Co.

Luria, Keith P. 1989. "The Counter-Reformation and Popular Spirituality." Pp. 93–120 in *Christian Spirituality: Post-Reformation and Modern*, edited by L. Dupré and D. E. Saliers. New York: Crossroad.

———. 1991. *Territories of Grace: Cultural Change in the Seventeenth-Century Diocese of Grenoble*. Berkeley: University of California Press.

Lutz, Catherine A., and Jane L. Collins. 1993. *Reading National Geographic*. Chicago: University of Chicago Press.

MacIntyre, Alasdair. 1984. *After Virtue: A Study in Moral Theory*. 2d ed. Notre Dame, IN: University of Notre Dame Press.

Macionis, John J. 2011. *Sociology*. 14th ed. Upper Saddle River, NJ: Pearson.

Maduro, Otto. 1993. "Theorizing Tecoatlaxope: For a Reassessment of Latino/a Religious Agency." In *Methodology*, publication of the meeting of the Program for the Analysis of Religion among Latinos, April 15–19, Princeton, NJ.

———. 1995. "Directions for a Reassessment of Latina/o Religion." Pp. 47–68 in *Enigmatic Powers: Syncretism with African and Indigenous Peoples' Religions among Latinos*, edited by Anthony M. Stevens-Arroyo and Andrés I. Pérez y Mena. New York: Bildner Center for Western Hemisphere Studies/PARAL.

———. 1999. *Mapas para La Fiesta: Reflexiones Latinoamericanas Sobre la Crisis y el Conocimiento*. 3d ed. Atlanta: Asociación para la Educación Teológica Hispana.

———. 2004. "'Religion' under Imperial Duress? Post-Colonial Reflections and Proposals." *Review of Religious Research* 45(3): 221–234.

Maine, Henry Sumner. 1861. *Ancient Law: Its Connection with the Early History of Society, and Its Relation to Modern Ideas*. London: John Murray.

Makinde, M. Akim. 1988. "Asuwada Principle: An Analysis of Akiwowo's Contributions to the Sociology of Knowledge." *International Sociology* 3(1): 61–76.

Malinowski, Bronislaw. 1948. *Magic, Science and Religion and Other Essays*. Glencoe, IL: Free Press.

Malloy, Edward A. 1977. "Ethics of Responsibility: A Comparison of the Methodology of H. Richard Niebuhr and Charles Curran." *Iliff Review* 34: 19–33.

Manza, Jeff, Michael Sauder, and Nathan Wright. 2010. "Producing Textbook Sociology." *European Journal of Sociology* 50(2): 271–304.

Markle, Gerald E., and Frances B. McCrea. 1994. "Medjugorje and the Crisis in Yugoslavia." Pp. 197–207 in *Politics and Religion in Central and Eastern Europe: Tradition and Transitions*, edited by W. Swatos. Westport, CT: Praeger.

Marler, Penny Long. 2008. "Religious Change in the West: Watch the Women." Pp. 23–56 in *Women and Religion in the West: Challenging Secularization*, edited by K. Aune, S. Sharma, and G. Vincett. Aldershot: Ashgate.

Marti, Gerardo, and Gladys Ganiel. 2014. *The Deconstructed Church: Understanding Emerging Christianity*. New York: Oxford University Press.

Martikainen, Tuomas, and François Gauthier, eds. 2012. *Religion and Neo-Liberalism: Political Economy and Governance*. London: Ashgate.

Martin, John. 1993. *Venice's Hidden Enemies: Italian Heretics in a Renaissance City*. Berkeley: University of California Press.

Marty, Martin E., and R. Scott Appleby, eds. 1991. *Fundamentalisms Observed*. The Fundamentalism Project, vol. 1. Chicago: University of Chicago Press.

———. 1992. *The Glory and the Power: The Fundamentalist Challenge to the Modern World*. Boston: Beacon Press.

———, eds. 1994. *Accounting for Fundamentalisms*. The Fundamentalism Project, vol. 4. Chicago: University of Chicago Press.

———, eds. 1995. *Fundamentalisms Comprehended*. The Fundamentalism Project, vol. 5. Chicago: University of Chicago Press.

———, eds. 1997. *Religion, Ethnicity, and Self-Identity: Nations in Turmoil*. Hanover, NH: Salzburg Seminar.

Masuzawa, Tomoko. 2005. *The Invention of World Religions: Or, How European Universalism Was Preserved in the Language of Pluralism*. Chicago: University of Chicago Press.

Mayr, Walter. 2009. "The Prophet's Fifth Column: Islamists Gain Ground in Sarajevo." *Der Spiegel Online*, Feb. 25. www.spiegel.de. Retrieved 10/7/2009.

McGuire, Meredith B. 1988. *Ritual Healing in Suburban America*. New Brunswick, NJ: Rutgers University Press.

———. 1994. "Linking Theory and Methodology for the Study of Latino Religiosity in the United States Context." Pp. 191–203 in *An Enduring Flame: Studies on Latino Popular Religiosity*, edited by Anthony M. Stevens-Arroyo and Ana María Díaz-Stevens. New York: Bildner Center for Western Hemisphere Studies/ PARAL.

———. 2002. *Religion: The Social Context*. 5th ed. Belmont, CA: Wadsworth.

———. 2003. "Contested Meanings and Definitional Boundaries: Historicizing the Sociology of Religion." Pp. 127–138 in *Defining Religion: Investigating the Boundaries between Sacred and Secular*, edited by Arthur L. Greil and David G. Bromley. Religion and the Social Order, vol. 10. Bingley: Emerald Group.

———. 2008. *Lived Religion: Faith and Practice in Everyday Life*. New York: Oxford University Press.

McGuire, Meredith B., and James V. Spickard. 2003. "Narratives of Commitment: Social Activism and Radical Catholic Identity." *Temenos: Studies in Comparative Religion* 37–38: 131–149.

McIntosh, Donald. 1977. "The Objective Bases of Max Weber's Ideal Types." *History and Theory* 16(3): 265–279.

Memmi, Albert. *The Colonizer and the Colonized*. 1965. Translated by Howard Greenfield. Boston: Beacon Press, 1967.

Mestrovic, Stjepan G. 1991. *The Coming Fin de Siécle*. London: Routledge.

Miller, Donald E. 1999. *Reinventing American Protestantism: Christianity in the New Millennium*. Berkeley: University of California Press.

Miller, Donald E., and Tetsunao Yamamori. 2007. *Global Pentecostalism: The New Face of Christian Social Engagement*. Berkeley: University of California Press.

Milne, Derek, and Wilson Howard. 2000. "Rethinking the Role of Diagnosis in Navajo Religious Healing." *Medical Anthropology Quarterly*, n.s., 14(4): 543–570.

Morris, James Winston. 2009. "An Arab Machiavelli? Rhetoric, Philosophy and Politics in Ibn Khaldun's Critique of Sufism." *Harvard Middle Eastern and Islamic Review* 8: 242–291.

Muir, Edward. 1997. *Ritual in Early Modern Europe*. Cambridge, UK: Cambridge University Press.

Murray, Harry. 1990. *Do Not Neglect Hospitality: The Catholic Worker and the Homeless*. Philadelphia: Temple University Press.

Nandy, Ashis. 2004. *Bonfire of Creeds: The Essential Ashis Nandy*. New Delhi: Oxford University Press.

National Bureau of Statistics of China. 2013. "China Statistical Yearbook, 2013." www.stats.gov.cn. Retrieved 1/1/2015.

Navajo Rug Repair. n.d. "Fake." www.navajorugrepair.com. Retrieved 11/23/2014.

Neitz, Mary Jo. 1987. *Charisma and Community: A Study of Religious Commit-ment within the Catholic Charismatic Renewal*. New Brunswick, NJ: Transaction Publishers.

———. 2000. "Queering the Dragonfest: Changing Sexualities in a Post-Patriarchal Religion." *Sociology of Religion* 61(4): 369–391.

———. 2002. "Walking between the Worlds: Permeable Boundaries, Ambiguous Identi-ties." Pp. 33–46 n *Personal Knowledge and Beyond: Reshaping the Ethnography of Religion*, edited by James V. Spickard, J. Shawn Landres, and Meredith B. McGuire. New York: NYU Press.

———. 2004. "Gender and Culture: Challenges to the Sociology of Religion." *Sociology of Religion* 65(4): 391–402.

———. 2011. "Feminist Methodologies." Pp. 54–67 in *Handbook of Research Methods in the Study of Religion*, edited by Michael Stausberg and Steven Engler. London and New York: Routledge.

Neitz, Mary Jo, and James V. Spickard. 1990. "Steps toward a Sociology of Religious Experience: The Theories of Mihaly Czikszentmihalyi and Alfred Schutz." *Sociologi-cal Analysis* 51(1): 15–33.

Niebuhr, H. Richard. 1963. *The Responsible Self: An Essay in Christian Moral Philoso-phy*. New York: Harper & Row.

Nielsen, François. 1985. "Toward a Theory of Ethnic Solidarity in Modern Societies." *American Sociological Review* 506(2, April): 133–149.

Nisbet, Robert A. 1967. *The Sociological Tradition*. London: Heinemann.

———. 1978. "Conservatism." Pp. 80–117 in *A History of Sociological Analysis*, edited by Thomas B. Bottomore and Robert A. Nisbet. New York: Basic Books.

Noddings, Nel. 1984. *Caring: A Feminine Approach to Ethics and Moral Education*. Berkeley: University of California Press.

Nuyen, A.T. 2013. "The "Mandate of Heaven": Mencius and the Divine Command Theory of Political Legitimacy." *Philosophy East and West* 63(2): 113–126.

O'Brien, Nancy Frazier. 2012. "Researcher's Advice to Pastors: Spend More Time on Church Suppers." *Catholic News Service*, Mar. 2. www.catholicnews.com. Retrieved 1/1/2015.

O'Dea, Thomas. 1961. "Five Dilemmas in the Institutionalization of Religion." *Journal for the Scientific Study of Religion* 1: 30–39.

Omi, Michael, and Howard Winant. 1994. *Racial Formation in the United States from the 1960s to the 1990s*. New York: Routledge.

Orr, James. 1910. "Science and Christian Faith." Ch. 18 in *The Fundamentals: A Tes-timony to the Truth*, edited by R. A. Torrey and A. C. Dixon. Los Angeles: Bible Institute of Los Angeles.

Orsi, Robert A. 2005. *Between Heaven and Earth: The Religious Worlds People Make and the Scholars Who Study Them*. Princeton, NJ: Princeton University Press.

Owen, Roger. 2012. "Edward Said and the Two Critiques of Orientalism." *Middle East-ern Institute*, Apr. 20. www.mei.edu. Retrieved 3/1/2016.

Overmyer, Daniel L. 1986. *Religions of China: The World as a Living System*. San Francisco: Harper & Row.

Packer, George. 2015. "The Other France: Are the Suburbs of Paris Incubators of Terrorism?" *New Yorker*, Aug. 31. www.newyorker.com. Retrieved 11/15/2015.

Pan Jianxiong. 1990. "The Dual Structure of Chinese Culture and Its Influence on Modern Chinese Society." *International Sociology* 5(1, March): 75–88.

Park, Peter. 1988. "Toward an Emancipatory Sociology: Abandoning Universalism for True Indigenisation." *International Sociology* 3(2): 161–170.

———. 2006. "Knowledge and Participatory Research." Pp. 83–93 in *Handbook of Action Research*, edited by Peter Reason and Hilary Bradbury. London and New York: Sage Publications.

Parsons, Talcott. 1960a. "Some Comments on the Pattern of Religious Organization in the United States." Pp. 295–321 in *Structure and Process in Modern Societies*, edited by Talcott Parsons. Glencoe, IL: Free Press.

———. 1960b. "Pattern Variables Revisited: A Response to Robert Dubin." *American Sociological Review* 25(4): 467–483.

———. 1967. "Christianity and Modern Industrial Society." Pp. 33–70 in *Sociological Theory, Values, and Sociocultural Change: Essays in Honor of Pitirm A. Sorokin*, edited by Edward A. Tiryakian. New York: Harper Torchbooks.

———. 1969. "On the Concept of Value Commitments." Pp. 439–472 in *Politics and Social Structure*, edited by Talcott Parsons. New York: Free Press, 1969.

Parsons, Talcott, and Edward Shils. 1951. "Values, Motives, and Systems of Action." Pp. 53–109 in *Towards a General Theory of Action*, edited by Talcott Parsons and Edward Shils. Cambridge, MA: Harvard University Press.

Payne, M. W. 1992. "Akiwowo, Orature and Divination: Approaches to the Construction of an Emic Sociological Paradigm of Society." *Sociological Analysis* 53(2): 175–187.

Pearce, Barnett, and Stephen W. Littlejohn. 1997. *Moral Conflict: When Social Worlds Collide*. Thousand Oaks, CA: Sage Publications.

Pew Research Center. 2013. "A Portrait of Jewish Americans." *PewForum.org*. www. pewforum.org. Retrieved 9/15/2015.

Piehl, Mel. 1982. *Breaking Bread: The Catholic Worker and the Origin of Catholic Radicalism*. Philadelphia: Temple University Press.

Pipes, Daniel. 1981. *Slave Soldiers and Islam: The Genesis of a Military System*. New Haven, CT: Yale University Press.

Prebisch, Raúl. 1981. *Capitalismo Periférico: Crisis y Transformación*. Mexico, DF: Fondo de Cultura Económica.

Proudfoot, Wayne. 1985. *Religious Experience*. Berkeley: University of California Press.

Putnam, Robert D., and David E. Campbell. 2010. *American Grace: How Religion Divides and Unites Us*. New York: Simon & Schuster.

Reichard, Gladys A. 1944. *Prayer: The Compulsive Word*. New York: J.J. Augustin.

———. 1950. *Navajo Religion: A Study of Symbolism*. Bollingen Series XVIII. New York: Pantheon Books.

Reilly, Ben. 1998. "With No Melting Pot, a Recipe for Failure in Bosnia." *New York Times,* Sept. 12. www.nytimes.com. Retrieved 10/7/2009.

Reitveld, Elise. 2014. "Debating Multiculturalism and National Identity in Britain: Competing Frames." *Ethnicities* 14(1): 50–71.

Repstad, Pål, and Inger Furseth. 2013. *An Introduction to the Sociology of Religion: Classical and Contemporary Perspectives.* 2d ed. London: Ashgate.

Ritzer, George. 2013. *Introduction to Sociology.* 1st ed. Thousand Oaks, CA: Sage Publications.

Roberts, Keith A., and David A. Yamane. 2011. *Religion in Sociological Perspective.* 5th ed. Thousand Oaks, CA: Sage Publications.

Roberts, Nancy L. 1984. *Dorothy Day and the Catholic Worker.* Albany: State University of New York Press.

Robertson, Roland. 1992. "The Economization of Religion? Reflections on the Promise and Limitations of the Economic Approach." *Social Compass* 39(1): 147–158.

Robinson, Kim Stanley. 2002. *Years of Rice and Salt.* New York: Bantam Books.

Rodman, Gilbert. 1996. *Elvis after Elvis: The Posthumous Career of a Living Legend.* New York: Routledge.

Rodriguez, Roberto Cíntli. 2014. *Our Sacred Maíz Is Our Mother: Indigeneity and Belonging in the Americas.* Tucson: University of Arizona Press.

Roof, Wade Clark. 1999. *Spiritual Marketplace: Baby Boomers and the Remaking of American Religion.* Princeton, NJ: Princeton University Press.

Roof, Wade Clark, and William McKinney. 1987. *American Mainline Religion: Its Changing Shape and Future.* New Brunswick, NJ: Rutgers University Press.

Rosemont, Henry, Jr. 1991a. *A Chinese Mirror: Moral Reflections on Political Economy and Society.* La Salle, IL: Open Court.

———. 1991b. "Rights-Bearing Individuals and Role-Bearing Persons." Pp. 71–102 in *Rules, Rituals, and Responsibility: Essays Dedicated to Herbert Fingarette,* edited by M. I. Bockover. La Salle, IL: Open Court.

———. 2015. *Against Individualism: A Confucian Rethinking of the Foundations of Morality, Politics, Family, and Religion.* Lanham, MD: Lexington Books.

Rosenthal, Franz. 1958. "Translator's Introduction." Pp. xxvii–cxv in *The Muqaddimah,* by Ibn Khaldūn, vol. 1. Bollingen Series XLIII. Princeton, NJ: Princeton University Press.

Rostow, Walter W. 1960. *The Stages of Economic Growth: A Non-Communist Manifesto.* Cambridge, UK: Cambridge University Press, 1971.

Roy, Olivier. 2004. *Globalized Islam: The Search for a New Ummah.* New York: Columbia University Press.

Sack, Daniel. 2000. *Whitebread Protestants: Food and Religion in American Culture.* New York: St. Martin's Press.

Said, Edward W. 1978. *Orientalism.* New York: Pantheon Books.

———. 1985. "Orientalism Reconsidered." Pp. 14–27 in *Europe and Its Others, Vol I.,* edited by Francis Barker, Peter Hulme, Margaret Iversen, and Diana Loxley. Colchester: University of Essex.

———. 1993. *Culture and Imperialism*. New York: Alfred A. Knopf.

Sanda, A. Muyiwa. 1988. "In Defence of Indigenisation in Sociological Theories." *International Sociology* 3(2): 189–199.

Schaeffer, Richard T. 2011. *Sociology*. 11th ed. New York: McGraw-Hill.

Schmidt, Bettina E. 2014. "The Problem with Numbers in the Study of Religion." *Diskus: The Open-Access Journal of the British Association for the Study of Religions* 16(2): 1–4.

Scholte, Bob. 1984. "Reason and Culture: The Universal and the Particular Revisited." *American Anthropologist* 86: 960–965.

Schutz, Alfred. 1951. "Making Music Together: A Study in Social Relationship." Pp. 159–178 in *Collected Papers II: Studies in Social Theory*, edited by A. Brodersen. The Hague: Martinus Nijhoff, 1964.

Schwartz, Benjamin I. 1985. *The World of Thought in Ancient China*. Cambridge, MA: Belknap Press.

Scribner, Robert W. 1987. *Popular Culture and Popular Movements in Reformation Germany*. London: Hambledon Press.

———. 1990. "The Reformation Movements in Germany." Pp. 69–93 in *The New Cambridge Modern History*, vol. 2, 2d ed., edited by G. R. Elton. Cambridge, UK: Cambridge University Press.

———. 1993. "The Reformation, Popular Magic, and the 'Disenchantment of the World.'" *Journal of Interdisciplinary History* 23(3): 475–494.

Sekulic, Dusko, Garth Massey, and Randy Hodson. 1994. "Who Were the Yugoslavs? Failed Sources of a Common Identity in the Former Yugoslavia." *American Sociological Review* 59(1): 83–97.

Sells, Michael A. 2003. "Crosses of Blood: Sacred Space, Religion, and Violence in Bosnia-Hercegovina." *Sociology of Religion* 64(3): 3009–3331.

Sen, Amartya. 1990. "More than 100 Million Women Are Missing." *New York Review of Books*, Dec. 20: 61–66.

Sennett, Richard. 2007. "Bureaucracy." Pp. 15–82 in *The Culture of the New Capitalism*. New Haven, CT: Yale University Press.

Shakur, Aaminah. 2014. "Not Your Idea: Cultural Appropriation in the Birthing Community." *The Toast*, Nov. 17. http://the-toast.net. Retrieved 11/22/2014.

Shariatri, Ali. 1979. *On the Sociology of Islam*. Translated by Hamid Algar. Berkeley, CA: Mizan Press.

Sharp, Joanne. 2009. *Geographies of Postcolonialism*. London: Sage Publications.

Sheeran, Michael J., SJ. 1983. *Beyond Majority Rule: Voteless Decisions in the Religious Society of Friends*. Philadelphia: Philadelphia Yearly Meeting.

Shils, Edward A. 1981. *Tradition*. Chicago: University of Chicago Press.

Silber, Laura, and Allan Little. 1994. *The Death of Yugoslavia*. London: Penguin Books.

Simic, Charles. 2009. "He Understood Evil." *New York Review of Books*, July 2: 11.

Simpson, John H. 1990. "The Stark-Bainbridge Theory of Religion." *Journal for the Scientific Study of Religion* 29(3): 367–371.

————. 1996. "'The Great Reversal': Selves, Communities, and the Global System." *Sociology of Religion* 57(2): 115–126.

Smilde, David A., and Matthew May. 2010. "The Emerging Strong Program in the Sociology of Religion." Social Science Research Council Working Paper. *Social Science Research Council*. http://blogs.ssrc.org/tif. Retrieved 10/28/2013.

Smith, Anthony D. 2001. *Nationalism: Theory, Ideology, History*. Cambridge, UK: Polity Press.

Smith, Christian S. 1998. *American Evangelicalism: Embattled and Thriving*. Chicago: University of Chicago Press.

Smith, Linda Tuhiwai. 2002. *Decolonizing Methodologies: Research and Indigenous Peoples*. London: Zed Press.

Soofi, Abdol. 1995. "Economics of Ibn Khaldun Revisited." *History of Political Economy* 27(2): 386–404.

Soyer, Mehmet, and Paul Gilbert. 2012. "Debating the Origins of Sociology: Ibn Khaldun as a Founding Father of Sociology." *International Journal of Sociological Research* 54(1–2): 13–30.

Spencer, Herbert. 1879–1893. *Principles of Ethics*. 2 vols. Indianapolis: Liberty Classics, 1978.

Spickard, James V. 1992. "For a Sociology of Religious Experience." Pp. 109–128 in *A Future for Religion? New Paradigms for Social Analysis*, edited by William H. Swatos, Jr. Newbury Park, CA: Sage Publications.

————. 1993. "Review of *Ritual Theory, Ritual Practice*, by Catherine Bell." *Sociology of Religion* 54(3): 321–323.

————. 1994. "Texts and Contexts: Recent Trends in the Sociology of Religion as Reflected in American Textbooks." *Social Compass* 41(3): 313–328.

————. 1998a. "Rethinking Religious Social Action: What Is 'Rational' about Rational-Choice Theory?" *Sociology of Religion* 59(2): 99–115.

————. 1998b. "Ethnocentrism, Social Theory and Non-Western Sociologies of Religion: Toward a Confucian Alternative." *International Sociology* 13(2): 173–194.

————. 1999a. "Human Rights, Religious Conflict, and Globalisation. Ultimate Values in a New World Order." *International Journal on Multicultural Societies* 1(1): 2–19.

————. 1999b. "The Origins of the Universal Declaration of Human Rights." University of Redlands Institutional Scholarly Publication and Information Repository (InSPIRe). http://inspire.redlands.edu.

————. 2001. "Tribes and Cities: Towards an Islamic Sociology of Religion." *Social Compass* 48(1): 97–110.

————. 2002. "Human Rights through a Religious Lens: A Programmatic Argument." *Social Compass* 49(2): 227–238.

————. 2003. "Cultural Context and the Definition of Religion: Seeing with Confucian Eyes." *Religion and the Social Order* 10: 189–199.

————. 2004. "Charting the Inward Journey: Applying Blackmore's Model to Meditative Religions." *Archiv für Religionpsychologie* 26: 157–180.

———. 2005. "Ritual, Symbol, and Experience: Understanding Catholic Worker House Masses." *Sociology of Religion* 66(4): 337–358.

———. 2006a. "What Is Happening to Religion? Six Visions of Religion's Future." *Nordic Journal of Religion and Society* 19(1): 13–28.

———. 2006b. "Narrative versus Theory in the Sociology of Religion: Five Stories of Religion's Place in the Late Modern World." Pp. 163–175 in *Religion and Social Theory: Classical and Contemporary Debates*, edited by James A. Beckford and John Walliss. London: Ashgate.

———. 2007. "Simulating Sects: A Computer Model of the Stark-Finke-Bainbridge-Iannaccone Rules for Sectarian Behavior." Pp. 131–152 in *Religion in Late Modernity: Essays in Honor of Pål Repstad*, edited by Inger Furseth and Paul Lee-Salveson. Trondheim: Tapir Academic Press.

———. 2012a. "Making Religion Irrelevant: The 'Resurgent Religion' Narrative and the Critique of Neo-Liberalism." Pp. 37–52 in *Religion and Neo-Liberalism: Political Economy and Governance*, edited by Tuomas Martikainen and François Gauthier. London: Ashgate.

———. 2012b. "Reflections on the Conference: The Impact of 3rd Wave Marketization." New Forms of Public Religion, AHRC/ESRC Religion and Society Research Programme, September 7, Cambridge, UK.

———. 2016. *Research Basics*. Newbury Park, CA: Sage Publications.

Spickard, James V., and J. Shawn Landres. 2002. "Whither Ethnography? Transforming the Social-Scientific Study of Religion." Pp. 1–14 in *Personal Knowledge and Beyond: Reshaping the Ethnography of Religion*, edited by J. V. Spickard, J. S. Landres, and M. B. McGuire. New York: NYU Press.

Spickard, James V., J. Shawn Landres, and Meredith B. McGuire, eds. 2002. *Personal Knowledge and Beyond: Reshaping the Ethnography of Religion*. New York: NYU Press.

Spickard, Paul R., ed. 2004. *Race and Nation: Ethnic Systems in the Modern World*. New York: Routledge.

———. 2007. *Almost All Aliens: Immigration, Race, and Colonialism in American History and Identity*. New York: Routledge.

———, ed. 2013. *Multiple Identities: Migrants, Ethnicity, and Membership*. Bloomington: Indiana University Press.

Spickard, Paul R., and Rowena Fong. 1995. "Pacific Islander Americans and Multiethnicity: A Vision of America's Future?" *Social Forces* 73(4): 1365–1383.

Spickard, Paul R., James V. Spickard, and Kevin M. Cragg, eds. 1998. *World History by the World's Historians*. Boston: McGraw-Hill.

Spiro, Melford. 1966. "Religion: Problems of Definition and Explanation." Pp. 85–126 in *Anthropological Approaches to the Study of Religion*, edited by M. Banton. London: Tavistock Publications.

Spivak, Gayatri Chakravorty. 1988. "Can the Subaltern Speak?" Pp. 271–316 in *Marxism and the Interpretation of Culture*, edited by Cary Nelson and Lawrence Grossberg. Champaign: University of Illinois Press.

———. 1996. *The Spivak Reader: Selected Works of Gayatri Chakravorty Spivak*. Edited by Donna Landry and Gerald MacLean. New York: Routledge.

———. 1999. *A Critique of Postcolonial Reason: Toward a History of the Vanishing Present*. Cambridge, MA: Harvard University Press.

Spradley, James P. 1970. *You Owe Yourself a Drunk: An Ethnography of Urban Nomads*. Boston, MA: Little, Brown & Company.

St. Clair, William. 1998. *Lord Elgin and the Marbles*. Oxford: Oxford University Press.

Stark, Rodney. 1987. "Correcting Church Membership Rates: 1971 and 1980." *Review of Religious Research* 29(1): 69–77.

———.1999. "Secularization, R.I.P." *Sociology of Religion* 60: 249–273.

Stark, Rodney, and William Sims Bainbridge. 1985. *The Future of Religion: Secularization, Revival and Cult Formation*. Berkeley: University of California Press.

Stark, Rodney, and Roger Finke. 2000. *Acts of Faith: Explaining the Human Side of Religion*. Berkeley: University of California Press.

Stewart, Charles, and Rosalind Shaw. 1994. *Syncretism/Anti-Syncretism: The Politics of Religious Synthesis*. London: Routledge.

Stookey, Laurence Hull. 1996. *Calendar: Christ's Time for the Church*. Nashville: Abingdon Press.

Stout, Jeffrey. 1988. *Ethics after Babel: The Languages of Morals and Their Discontents*. Boston: Beacon Press.

Sun, Anna Xiao Dong. 2013. *Confucianism as a World Religion: Contested Histories and Contemporary Realities*. Princeton, NJ: Princeton University Press.

Survey Data Archive. University of California at Berkeley. http://sda.berkeley.edu/archive.htm. Retrieved 1/27/2015.

Swatos, William H., Jr., and Peter Kivisto. 1991. "Max Weber as 'Christian Sociologist.'" *Journal for the Scientific Study of Religion* 30(4): 347–362.

Swindale, Ian. 1997–2012. *The Parthenon Marbles*. www.parthenon.newmentor.net. Retrieved 3/10/2016.

Tallet, Frank. 1991. *Religion, Society and Politics in France since 1789*. New York: Continuum.

Taliman, Valerie. 2009. "Selling the Sacred." *Indian Country*, Oct. 14. http://indiancountrytodaymedianetwork.com. Retrieved 11/23/2014.

Terrell, Brian. 2012. "Dorothy Day's 'Filthy, Rotten System' Likely Wasn't Hers at All." *National Catholic Reporter*, Apr. 16. http://ncronline.org. Retrieved 5/11/2015.

Tharoor, Ishaan. 2014. "ISIS or ISIL? The Debate over What to Call Iraq's Terror Group." *Washington Post*, June 28. www.washingtonpost.com. Retrieved 11/15/2015.

Thorn, William J., Phillip M. Runkel, and Susan Mountin, eds. 2001. *Dorothy Day and the Catholic Worker Movement: Centenary Essays*. Milwaukee: Marquette University Press.

Thye, Shane R., and Edward J. Lawler. 2002. *Group Cohesion, Trust, and Solidarity*. Greenwich, CT: JAI Press.

Tindemans, Leo, Lloyd Cutler, Bronislaw Geremek, John Roper, Theo Sommer, Simone Veil, David Anderson, and Jacques Rupnik. 1996. *Unfinished Peace: Report of the*

International Commission on the Balkans. Washington, DC: Brookings Institution Press/Carnegie Endowment for International Peace.

Tobin, Joseph, David Wu, and Dana H. Davidson. 1989. *Preschool in Three Cultures: Japan, China, and the United States.* New Haven, CT: Yale University Press.

Tönnies, Ferdinand. 1887. *Community and Society [Gemeinschaft und Gesellschaft].* Translated by Charles P. Loomis. New York: Harper & Row, 1957.

Trinh, T. Minh-ha. 1989. *Woman, Native, Other: Writing Poscoloniality and Feminism.* Bloomington: Indiana University Press.

Troester, Rosalie Riegle, ed. 1993. *Voices from the Catholic Worker.* Philadelphia: Temple University Press.

Tu Wei-ming. 1979. *Humanity and Self-Cultivation: Essays in Confucian Thought.* Berkeley: Berkeley Asian Humanities Press.

———. 1984a. "Core Values in Confucian Thought." Pp. 2–15 in *Confucian Ethics Today: The Singapore Challenge,* edited by Tu Wei-ming. Singapore: Federal Publications.

———. 1984b. "The Modern Significance of Confucian Ethics." Pp. 100–129 in *Confucian Ethics Today: The Singapore Challenge,* edited by Tu Wei-ming. Singapore: Federal Publications.

Tuchman, Barbara. 1978. *A Distant Mirror: The Calamitous 14th Century.* New York: Alfred A. Knopf.

Turner, Victor W. 1967. *The Forest of Symbols.* Ithaca, NY: Cornell University Press.

———. 1968. *Drums of Affliction: A Study of Religious Processes among the Ndembu of Zambia.* Oxford: Oxford University Press.

———. 1969. *The Ritual Process.* Chicago: Aldine.

Utt, Jamie. 2013. "Racism, Appropriation, and The Harlem Shake." *Change from Within,* 21 Feb. 21. http://changefromwithin.org. Retrieved 11/22/2014.

Uwujaren, Jarune. 2013. "The Difference between Cultural Exchange and Cultural Appropriation." *Everyday Feminism Magazine,* Sept. 30. http://everydayfeminism.com. Retrieved 11/23/2014.

Van Metre, Lauren, and Burcu Akan. 1997. "Dayton Implementation: The Train and Equip Program." Special Report no. 25. *United States Institute of Peace.* www.usip. org. Retrieved 10/7/2009.

Van Norden, Bryan W. 2003. "Virtue Ethics and Confucianism." Pp. 99–121 in *Comparative Approaches to Chinese Philosophy,* edited by B. Mou. Aldershot: Ashgate.

van Wyhe, John. 2007. "Mind the Gap: Did Darwin Avoid Publishing His Theory for Many Years?" *Notes and Records of the Royal Society* 61(2): 177–205.

Vásquez, Manuel A. 2013. "Grappling with the Legacy of Modernity: Implications for the Sociology of Religion." Pp. 23–42 in *Religion on the Edge: De-Centering and Re-Centering the Sociology of Religion,* edited by Courtney Bender et al.. New York: Oxford University Press.

Villaseñor, David. 1966. *Tapestries in Sand: The Spirit of Indian Sandpainting.* Healdsburg, CA: Naturegraph.

Voas, David, and Steve Bruce. 2007. "The Spiritual Revolution: Another False Dawn for the Sacred." Pp. 43–61 in *A Sociology of Spirituality*, edited by K. Flanagan and P. Jupp. Aldershot: Ashgate.

Walker, Thomas, and Christine Wade. 2011. *Nicaragua: Living in the Shadow of the Eagle*. 5th ed. Boulder, CO: Westview Press.

Wallace, Peter G. 2004. *The Long European Reformation: Religion, Political Conflict and the Search for Conformity, 1350–1750*. Basingstoke: Palgrave-Macmillan.

Walzer, Richard. 1962. *Greek into Arabic*. Oxford: Oxford University Press.

Warner, R. Stephen. 1993. "Work in Progress toward a New Paradigm for the Sociological Study of Religion in the United States." *American Journal of Sociology* 98: 1044–1093.

Warner, R. Stephen, and Judith G. Wittner, eds. 1998. *Gatherings in Diaspora: Religious Communities and the New Immigration*. Philadelphia: Temple University Press.

Weber, Max. 1917–1919. *Ancient Judaism*. Translated by Hans H. Gerth and Don Martindale. Glencoe, IL: Free Press, 1952.

———. 1920a. *The Protestant Ethic and the Spirit of Capitalism*. Translated by Talcott Parsons. New York: Charles Scribner's Sons, 1958.

———. 1920b. *The Religion of China: Confucianism and Taoism*. Translated by Hans H. Gerth. New York: Free Press, 1951.

———. 1922a. *Economy and Society: An Outline of Interpretive Sociology*. Edited by Guenther Roth and Claus Wittich. Berkeley: University of California Press, 1978.

———. 1922b. *The Sociology of Religion*. Translated by E. Fischoff. Boston: Beacon Press, 1963.

———. 1922c. *The Methodology of the Social Sciences*. Edited and translated by Edward Shils and Henry A. Finch. Glencoe, IL: Free Press, 1949.

———. 1925. *The Theory of Social and Economic Organization*. Translated by A.M. Henderson and Talcott Parsons. New York: Free Press, 1947.

———. 1946. *From Max Weber: Essays in Sociology*. Edited and translated by Hans H Gerth and C. Wright Mills. New York: Oxford University Press.

———. 1958. *The Rational and Social Foundations of Music*. Edited and translated by Don Martindale, Johannes Riedel, and Gertrude Neuwirth. Carbondale: Southern Illinois University Press.

Weingart Center, Institute for the Study of Homelessness and Poverty. 2004. *Homelessness in Los Angeles: A Summary of Recent Research*. Los Angeles: Weingart Foundation.

West, Richard. 1996. *Tito and the Rise and Fall of Yugoslavia*. New York: Basic Books.

Williams, Melvin D. 1974. *Community in a Black Pentecostal Church*. Pittsburgh: University of Pittsburgh Press.

Willis, Mariaemma, and Victoria Kindle Hodson. 2013. *Discover Your Child's Learning Style*. West Conshohocken, PA: Infinity Publishing.

Wilson, Bryan R. 1966. *Religion in Secular Society: A Sociological Comment*. London: C.A. Watts & Co.

———. 1982. *Religion in Sociological Perspective*. Oxford: Oxford University Press.

Wilson, Lydia. 2015. "What I Discovered from Interviewing Imprisoned ISIS Fighters." *Nation*, Oct. 21. www.thenation.com/article. Retrieved 11/15/2015.

Winter, Miriam Therese, Adair Lummis, and Allison Stokes. 1994. *Defecting in Place: Women Claiming Responsibility for Their Own Spiritual Lives*. New York: Crossroads.

Witherspoon, Gary. 1977. *Language and Art in the Navajo Universe*. Ann Arbor: University of Michigan Press.

———. 1983. "Language and Reality in Navajo World View." Pp. 570–591 in *Southwest*, vol. 10, edited by A. Ortiz. Handbook of American Indians. Washington, DC: Smithsonian Institution Press.

Wolf, Eric R. 1982. *Europe and the People Without History*. Berkeley: University of California Press.

———. 1998. *Envisioning Power: Ideologies of Dominance and Crisis*. Berkeley: University of California Press.

Woodbridge, Roy. 2004. *The Next World War: Tribes, Cities, Nations, and Ecological Decline*. 2d ed. Toronto: University of Toronto Press.

Woodhead, Linda. 2008a. "Gendering Secularization Theory." *Social Compass* 55(2, June): 187–193.

———. 2008b. "'Because I'm Worth It': Religion and Women's Changing Lives in the West." Pp. 147–164 in *Women and Religion in the West: Challenging Secularization*, edited by K. Aune, S. Sharma, and G. Vincett. Aldershot: Ashgate.

———. 2009. "Old, New and Emerging Paradigms in the Sociological Study of Religion." *Nordic Journal of Religion and Society* 22(2): 103–121.

———. 2010. "Real Religion, Fuzzy Spirituality?: Taking Sides in the Sociology of Religion." Pp. 31–48 in *Religions of Modernity : Relocating the Sacred to the Self and the Digital*, edited by S. Aupers and D. Houtman. Leiden: Brill.

———. 2011a. "Five Concepts of Religion." *International Review of Sociology* 21(1): 121–143.

———. 2011b. "Spirituality and Christianity: The Unfolding of a Tangled Relationship." Pp. 3–21 in *Religion, Spirituality and Everyday Practice*, edited by G. Giordan and W. Swatos. Dordrecht: Springer.

World Values Survey. World Values Survey Association. www.worldvaluessurvey.org. Retrieved 1/27/2015.

Wright, George Frederick. 1913. "The Passing of Evolution." Ch. 69 in *The Fundamentals: A Testimony to the Truth*, edited by R. A. Torrey, and A. C. Dixon. Los Angeles: Bible Institute of Los Angeles.

Wrong, Dennis. 1961. "The Over-Socialized Conception of Man in Modern Sociology." *American Sociological Review* 26: 183–193.

Wuthnow, Robert. 2006. *American Mythos: Why Our Best Efforts to Be a Better Nation Fall Short*. Princeton, NJ: Princeton University Press.

Wyman, Leland C. 1950. "The Religion of the Navaho Indians." Pp. 341–361 in *Forgotten Religions*, edited by Vergilius Ferm. New York: Philosophical Library.

————. 1970. *Blessingway: With Three Versions of the Myth Recorded and Translated from the Navajo by Father Berard Haile, O.F.M.* Tucson: University of Arizona Press.

————. 1983. "Navajo Ceremonial System." Pp. 536–557 in *Southwest*, vol. 10, edited by A. Ortiz. Handbook of American Indians. Washington, DC: Smithsonian Institution Press.

Yang, C. K. 1964. "Introduction." Pp. xiii–xliii in *The Religion of China*, by Max Weber. New York: Free Press.

Yang, Fenggang. 2012. *Religion in China: Survival and Revival under Communist Rule.* New York: Oxford University Press.

Yang, Fenggang, Victor Yuan, Anna Sun, Stark Lu Yngfang, Rodney, Byron Johnson, Eric Liu, Mencken, and Chiu Heu-yuan. 2007. *Spiritual Life Study of Chinese Residents.* University Park, PA: Association of Religion Data Archives.

Yao, Xinzhong. 2000. *An Introduction to Confucianism.* Cambridge, UK: Cambridge University Press.

Young, Robert J. C. 2001. *Postcolonialism: An Historical Introduction.* Oxford: Blackwell.

Zuckerman, Phil. 2004. *The Social Theory of W.E.B. Du Bois.* Thousand Oaks, CA: Sage Publications.

Zwick, Mark, and Louise Zwick. 2005. *The Catholic Worker Movement: Intellectual and Spiritual Origins.* New York: Paulist Press.

INDEX

Adkins, Russell, 81–82, 263n1 ch.3, 263n3 ch.3
Adogame, Afe, xi, 35
African American congregations, 117–119, 122–123
Akiwowo, Akinsola, 225, 277n31 ch.9
al 'aṣabiyyah, 16, 141–142, 170, 172; decline of, 148, 149; ethnicity and, 148, 153, 165–166; Islam and, 148–149, 165–167; kinship and, 141, 149; religion and, 146–149, 153, 167–169; sources of, 149, 153. *See also* Khaldūnian sociology of religion
Alatas, Syed Farid, xi, 267n2 ch.5
Ames, Roger, 98, 99–101, 102
Ammerman, Nancy, 14, 38, 41, 42
anti-universalism, 237–241
Aron, Raymond, 63
Arunta totemism, 66, 68–70
Asad, Talal, 34, 60
Ashcroft, Bill, 238, 241
attention, 193, 200–202, 214–216
Augustine (Saint), 75–76, 77, 84, 262n68 ch.2

Barber, Benjamin, 141, 268n10 ch.5
Bax, Mart, 167, 170
Bell, Catherine, 195–197, 201, 273n38 ch.7
Bellah, Robert, 127, 265n62 ch.3; and co-authors (*Habits of the Heart*), 14, 33, 126–128
Bender, Courtney, 35; and co-authors (*Religion on the Edge*) 35–37, 41, 42
Berger, Peter, 32
Beyer, Peter, xi, 34, 97–98
Blackmore, Susan, 200–201, 214–215

Blessingway. *See* Navajo ritual
book's central argument, 15–18, 107, 235–236, 241, 245, 251–252; consequences for scholars, 252–255
Bourdieu, Pierre, 59, 196–197, 242–243

Catholic Church, 5, 54, 120; activists' attitudes toward, 10–12, 205, 210, 211; and France, 50–52, 261n16 ch.2; medieval & reformation, 28, 33, 47, 69; as model for sociology, 58, 69; ritual, 10, 197–198, 200, 210, 211–216, 215, 216, 218, 219; theology, 32–33, 67, 213, 217, 222; Ultramontane, 51–52, 172, 244; Yugoslav (Croatian, Bosnian), *see* Medjugorje
Catholic Worker, 17, 204–223, 274n4 ch.8; activities of, 206–207; Los Angeles, xi, 205–206, 223. *See also* Day, Dorothy; Dietrich, Jeff
Catholic Worker house Masses, 205, 207–223; create community, 220–221, 222, 275n12 ch.8; compared with Navajo ritual, 217, 219–220; double-ritual, 212–213, 221, 222; experiences in, 214–216, 219–221; restore hope, 207, 217, 218–219, 222
Catholics, 3, 12, 45–46, 115, 155, 216; activists, 10–12, 205–223; Latino/a, 37, 119–122; popular Catholicism, 9–11, 13, 37, 45–46, 115, 120–122, 167
centripetal theory of solidarity, 143, 145–146, 153, 166, 169, 172. *See also* edge-focused theory of solidarity; Khaldūnian sociology of religion

ABOUT THE AUTHOR

James V. Spickard is Professor of Sociology at the University of Redlands, where he teaches courses on social theory, the sociology of religion, research design, and social inequality. He is also President of the International Sociological Association's Research Committee on the Sociology of Religion. He has published widely on religion's role in contemporary society, on non-Western social theories, on social research, and on human rights. He is working on a book on religion's future.